W9-BRH-079

ALSO BY DEBORA L. SPAR

The Baby Business: How Money, Science, and Politics Drive the Commerce of Conception

Ruling the Waves: Cycles of Discovery, Chaos, and Wealth from the Compass to the Internet

The Cooperative Edge: The Internal Politics of International Cartels

WONDER WOMEN

SEX, POWER, AND THE QUEST FOR PERFECTION

Sarah Crichton Books Farrar, Straus and Giroux New York

Sarah Crichton Books
Farrar, Straus and Giroux
18 West 18th Street, New York 10011

Copyright © 2013 by Debora L. Spar
All rights reserved
Printed in the United States of America
First edition, 2013

Owing to limitations of space, acknowledgments for permission to reprint previously
published material and illustration credits can be found on page 307.

Library of Congress Control Number: 2013941741
ISBN: 978-0-374-29875-3

Designed by Abby Kagan

Farrar, Straus and Giroux books may be purchased for educational, business, or
promotional use. For information on bulk purchases, please contact the Macmillan
Corporate and Premium Sales Department at 1-800-221-7945, extension 5442, or
write to specialmarkets@macmillan.com.

www.fsgbooks.com
www.twitter.com/fsgbooks • www.facebook.com/fsgbooks

10 9 8 7 6 5 4 3 2 1

Some names and identifying details have been changed to protect the privacy of individuals.

To my parents,

Judith and Martin Spar

contents

WONDER WOMEN

I'm pretty sure I remember the moment I knew I was having it all. It was December 1992, in the women's bathroom at LaGuardia Airport. I had just an hour between flights and so I had rushed straight for the stalls, cramming my bags against the door and pulling off my blouse. Then I perched on the less-than-inviting seat, took out the little Medela "Pump in Style" and began feverishly to pump. From the stall next to me, I heard a gasp of surprise and a hasty flush. "C'mon," I scolded silently, "this is New York. A lady in the bathroom with a breast pump is nothing." After several long minutes of whirring and pressing, fumbling and swearing, I collected my paltry three ounces, pulled the pump and myself back together, and dragged the whole lot out to the sink area. There, before two confused Asian travelers and the girl from Cinnabon, I tossed the milk I'd never use down the drain and tried again to reconfigure my five-weeks-postpartum belly into something that vaguely resembled a business suit. And that's when I realized— wryly, ironically, totally deprived of sleep—that I really was having it all.

It wasn't supposed to be so hard. Like many women of my so-called postfeminist generation, I was raised to believe that women were finally poised to be equal with men. That women, after centuries of oppression, exploitation, and other unnamed bad things, could now behave more or less like men. We could have sex whenever we wanted, children whenever we chose, and career options that stretched to infinity. The first woman astronaut? Of course. The first woman president? Why not? This had been the era, after all, when Barbie ditched the closeted Ken for careers in medicine and firefighting, effortlessly acquiring little Skipper along the way. Women of my generation, growing up in the 1970s and 1980s, no longer felt we had to burn our bras in protest. Instead, with a curt nod to the bra burners who had gone before us, we could saunter directly to Victoria's Secret, buying the satin pushups that would take us seamlessly from boardroom to bedroom and beyond.

But somewhere, somehow, the reality shifted, and instead of lacy strings I was struggling with a nursing bra that defied all notions of femininity and a blouse that refused to close fully over it. I had a five-week-old baby at home, a three-year-old who still hadn't realized quite what had befallen him, and a plane to catch to Michigan. Whatever happened to Barbie's breast pump? And why wasn't it working for me?

I am one of those women who was sure I would never consider my-self a feminist. In fact, I've spent most of my life—professional and personal—steering explicitly clear of any feminist agenda. I didn't take a single women's studies class in college or graduate school and never joined any kind of women's group. Based on what I saw on the television news, I always presumed that the feminists were too shrill and aggressive for me. They seemed to hate men, which I didn't. They had hairy legs, which I didn't. And they always looked so *angry*. I never felt that their Birkenstock-infused lifestyle had anything in common with mine. Oh, sure, we were all women, bound together by the dubious joys of our shared biology. We bled, we bred, we got a bit grumpier every four weeks or so. But a common cause? I didn't see it.

Instead, throughout high school, college, and graduate school, I devoutly believed that I could be a successful woman in a man's world, that I could remain feminine without being *feminist*. So I studied hard in high school—but worked even harder at my cheerleading skills. I read military history and nuclear strategy in college—and devoted at least part of my newfound knowledge to impressing the ROTC guys I dated. Even when I became one of the few girls in most of my classes, I saw this state of affairs as entirely positive: professors tended to notice my hand whenever it went up, and I never lacked for male companions. When I graduated from college in 1984, one of my favorite professors wrote a letter of recommendation that I took, at the time, as wonder-fully positive. "Debora," he wrote, "is the best woman I've ever taught."

When I started graduate school at Harvard University the follow-ing year, the women before me had suddenly disappeared. Accusations of sexual harassment had ripped through the department, forcing two male faculty members to be ushered quietly into newfound research projects abroad. In their wake, six female graduate students—most of the female contingent—had departed as well, apparently reluctant to study in what had become a quietly stressful environment. I should have worried. Instead, I jumped into this new life of the ostensible mind and came to believe that being a woman at Harvard was a very good thing. The university needed female graduate students; it wanted to show off its female graduate students; and the undergraduates whom we taught seemed delighted to have female instructors. The only obvious sign of gender tension was the doors. Every time I entered a faculty office, the professor would swing the door wide open, announcing to his assistant and the world, it seemed, that nothing untoward could possibly occur inside.

I fell in love my first day of graduate school and, three years later, married the boy from the dorm room next door. He took a job in Boston so that I could continue my studies and we soon had our first child. I went into labor moments after the final page of my dissertation rolled out of the printer. One year later, when my son was one and my dissertation polished, I became an assistant professor at the University of Toronto and skipped off into the working world, fully confident of my ability to juggle baby, husband, job, and self.

Throughout this time, I assiduously avoided any contact with feminists. Although I was vaguely aware of the literature that had roiled through my own field of political science, I didn't like the little I knew of it. Radical feminists like Andrea Dworkin, for instance, who catalyzed an entire field of feminist inquiry, asserted that all sex was rape, a position I found both offensive and absurd. I had no interest in reading that stuff.

So life moved on. I left the University of Toronto for Harvard Business School and eventually had two more children. I stayed cheerfully nonfeminist, swearing to the young women in my classes and office hours, in presentations and during interviews, that yes, of course, they could have it all.

Somewhere along the way, though, the resentments started to accumulate, spurred by a seemingly endless march of annoying little events. Like the department chair who responded to news of my second pregnancy with undisguised shock. "Pregnant!" he exclaimed. "How the hell did you find time to do that?" Or the colleague who suggested that I conclude my MBA course by jumping out of a cake. There were the student evaluations that focused on my legs, and the executives who pulled me aside to whisper what they had really been thinking about during my class. After a while, it started to get to me. And eventually it drove me wild.

It wasn't a dramatic transformation. I didn't toss my wardrobe or stop shaving my legs. Most of my male colleagues remained in my address book, and most of my makeup stayed in my drawer. But I started sharing stories more frequently with my few female colleagues and started to think more explicitly about what connected my own experiences—things I'd kept pretty much to myself—with those of the women, and men, around me. I began peeking into areas of research I had avoided until this point and found myself counseling other women in ways I had never expected. Eventually, and somewhat to my dismay, I was asked to help solve the "women's problem" at Harvard—a problem, I hasten to add, that is almost certainly no worse than the "women's problem" at Yale or Princeton, IBM or Google, JPMorgan or Bank of America. I didn't solve the problem. But I did realize that there was one. Or, more precisely, that women across even the top tiers of American society were struggling, continuously and consistently, to make it in a world that remained predominantly male, a world that, despite decades of scrutiny and attention, was still stacked against them.

Many of the women who operated in this world were phenomenally successful. They ran universities and hedge funds, hospitals and museums, investment banking divisions and legal practices. Very few of them complained of gender bias or described themselves as feminists. But outside the boardroom, in bathrooms and book clubs across the country, even the most successful of these women were railing quietly against the "women's problem." They were acknowledging that even if they "had it all," they still had lives that were fundamentally different from and more difficult than men's. They were still, almost always, in the minority. They were still dodging comments and innuendoes that took them aback. They were juggling playdates and dental appointments and flute recitals, all of which were somehow absent from the to-do lists of their male partners. And they were still worrying about how they looked.

These were the issues that feminism sought to slay. By fighting to give women equal access to higher education and workforce opportunities, the feminist movement tried to push women over the barricades that separated them from power and privilege. By fighting for equal rights, it aimed to make them equal citizens: indistinguishable before the law, among their colleagues, and within their homes. And by fighting for reproductive choice, feminism attempted to liberate women from the demands that having sex and making babies had eternally put upon them. Or, as the authors of *Our Bodies, Ourselves* explained in 1973, knowledge about birth control and abortion "freed" women "from playing the role of mother," giving them instead "a sense of a larger life space to work in, an invigorating and challenging sense of time and room to discover the energies and talents" that lay within them all.[1]

It was a lofty agenda and, in many ways, a remarkably successful one. Between 1920, when women won the right to vote, and 1963, when Congress passed the Equal Pay Act, women's participation in the labor force grew steadily, and a handful of women rose to the top tiers of their professions. Between 1973, when *Roe v. Wade* was decided by the U.S. Supreme Court, and 1980, when I graduated from high school, American girls surged into the bastions of higher education, postponed or disdained marriage, and started having a lot more sex. Indeed, the transformation was so profound that many girls of my generation—girls who were born and raised in the immediate aftermath of the tumultuous 1960s—simply presumed that it was over and won. We thought, often without actually thinking, that we could just glide into the new era of equality, with babies, board seats, and husbands in tow. We were wrong.

Here are a few dirty secrets:

- Female job applicants with children are 44 percent less likely to be hired for a job than are childless women with similar qualifications. Fathers, by contrast, are 19 percent *more* likely to be hired than are comparably qualified men without children.[2]

- A recent Harvard Business School study found that only 38 percent of the school's female graduates remain in the workforce. Harvard Business School women also have fewer children than their male counterparts (1.8 to 2.2) and are less likely to be married.
- During the economic downturn of 2008–09, 19 percent of senior-level women lost their jobs, compared with only 6 percent of senior-level men. Below the executive level, job losses were equal.[3]

None of these stories suggest that anything particularly egregious is going on. It's not as if evil men are sitting in the corner offices plotting ways to keep women from gaining more ground. On the contrary, most major corporations now—along with hospitals, law firms, universities, and banks—have entire units devoted to helping women (and minorities) succeed. There are Diversity Officers and Work/Family Offices and gender sensitivity training courses sprinkled across all tiers of American society. Before its demise in 2008, Lehman Brothers had thirty executives devoted solely to running inclusion and diversity programs inside the firm.[4]

The problem with these efforts, however, is that they just don't work.[5] Or, more precisely, that even the most well-intentioned programs to attract women, or mentor women, or retain women still don't address the basic issues that most of these women face. And that's because the challenges that confront women now are more subtle than those of the past, harder to recognize and thus to remove. They are challenges that stem from breast pumps and Manolo pumps, from men whose eyes linger on a woman's rear end and those who rush that same rear end too quickly out the door. They are problems that come from the nearly impossible standards of perfection that women have somehow rushed to embrace, problems that come—inherently and inevitably—simply from being female. Yet they are falling on generations of women who grew up believing that none of these things were supposed to matter anymore.

I began working on this book in the summer of 2009, one year after I left my job as professor at Harvard Business School to become president of Barnard College. It was a radical change. I left teaching for administration, MBA students for undergraduates, and a very large endowment for a perilously small one. I left my garden, and my kids' schools, and even my husband, who was stuck commuting loyally up and down the eastern seaboard. The biggest change, however, was hormonal. At Harvard, I had been surrounded for over twenty years by alpha men of the academic sort—men with big egos, and big attitudes, and an awful lot of testosterone. At Barnard, suddenly, I wasn't. At Harvard, I was almost always the only woman in the room. At Barnard, an all-women's college, there was barely a male in sight. I found the change fascinating—not better or worse, necessarily, and not a cause for either celebration or alarm. Just plain fascinating.

Gradually, I started thinking more and more about how women in the workforce differ from men, and about why women's work lives remain still so complicated. I started thinking about my own career path, and about why I had chosen—unconsciously, perhaps, but stubbornly—to steer far clear of any explicitly feminist agenda. And when, as the newly minted head of an all-women's college, I began to interact with hundreds and hundreds of extremely diverse women, I began to suspect that there were certain patterns at play, patterns determined not only by social structures and embedded norms, but by biology and preferences and the sheer random chance of being born in a particular time and place. I also became increasingly convinced that the goals of the early feminists remain relevant for women today, even for those like me who had either ignored the struggle or disagreed with its tactics.

Consider the facts: even today, women in the United States still earn only 78 cents on average for every dollar earned by men. They occupy only 15.2 percent of seats on Fortune 500 corporate boards and serve as CEO for only 3 percent of the country's largest corporations.[6] Fifty-one percent of families living below the poverty line are headed by women, as are 83 percent of single parent families.[7] More than a quarter of a million women are sexually assaulted each year in the United States alone and, in 2008, nearly twelve thousand reported suffering from sexual harassment.[8] Studies confirm that when a female professor enters the classroom, students presume her to be less competent than an equally certified male and pay more attention to whether she smiles.[9] Despite what feminism promised, therefore, and what my generation believed, women in the United States still face distinctive challenges that cannot be explained solely by reference to class or race or socio-economic status. Instead, women live their lives differently simply on account of their sex.

Wonder Women, therefore, is a tale of just that. It is partly my own story and partly a cultural survey, examining how women's lives have—and have not—changed over the past four decades. It is an exploration of how women born after the tumult of the 1960s grew up, and why the dreams of our childhood proved so elusive. It is a study of how we thought we could have it all and why, in the end, we cannot.

The goal of the book is to take a new look at feminism, reconsidering it, ironically perhaps, from the perspective of women who have disdained its entreaties in the past. Tracing through the ages and stages of contemporary women, *Wonder Women* espouses a revised and somewhat reluctant feminism, one that desperately wishes we no longer needed a women's movement but acknowledges that we still do. It argues that women of my generation got feminism wrong, seeing it as a route to personal perfection and a promise of all that we were now expected to be. Instead of seizing upon the liberation that had been handed to us, we twisted it somehow into a charge: because we *could* do anything, we felt as if we *had* to do everything. And by following unwittingly along this path, we have condemned ourselves, if not to failure, then at least to the constantly nagging sense that something is wrong. That we are imposters. That we have failed.

Meanwhile, in exploring the nooks and crannies of a woman's life, *Wonder Women* also advocates for a feminism based at least in part on difference. Put simply, it acknowledges (along with many earlier versions of feminism) that women are physiologically different from men and that biology is, if not quite destiny, nevertheless one of those details in life that should not be overlooked. Only women can bear children. In the state of nature, only women can feed those children through the most critical months of their lives. From these two unavoidable facts—wombs and breasts—come a vast series of perhaps unfortunate events. We can rue these events, or the gods who apparently predestined them, or we can come to terms with our differences and focus on ways of making them work.

Wonder Women takes this latter tack. Rather than examining the power hierarchies that undeniably still separate men from women, I focus on the practical issues that confound even the most powerful women. Rather than demanding that women be treated always as equivalent to men, I assume that women are actually quite different from men and explore the various ways—from body image to Barbie dolls, baby making and sex—in which these differences manifest themselves. And rather than trying to add to the canon of feminist theory, I concentrate instead on what these theories suggest, where they've been helpful, and where, on occasion, they've steered us wrong. Because the book stems from my own personal journey, it is organized roughly along the cycle of life, starting with girls and girlhood and ending where I stand today—in middle age, reflecting on teenagers and husbands, life choices and careers.

Let me be clear about the biases I bring to this work. I am a working mother of three children, so my view of women is very much taken from this particular perspective. I therefore focus, perhaps overly, on the fates and fortunes of women juggling kids and jobs, the women who so infamously try to have it all. I have been very happily married for twenty-five years, so I write also as a contented wife and a woman who remains extremely fond of men. I believe that most men today want women to succeed; they want them in their firms and in their legislatures and even, generally, on their golf courses. They just don't know quite how to make it work. And how can they, if women don't help to figure it out?

Intellectually, I am an interloper in the area of feminist theory. I didn't study it until recently; I didn't grow up with it; and my interest has developed only later in life. Even worse, I am interloping as a critic, someone who agrees with the goals of feminism but not necessarily with its tactics and assumptions. I also approach this area, as we all do, I suspect, with my own socioeconomic status wrapped tight around me. I am a product of white, upper-middle-class American society; I have never been poor, never had to worry about the provenance of my next meal. I have studied and written about poverty, particularly in the developing world, but I have never personally experienced it. So, insofar as this book draws heavily on my own experiences, it is a book mostly about American women who have been blessed, as I have, with both economic and educational opportunities.

I wish I could be farther-reaching in examining women's lives, stretching to explore the vast number of women who every day face struggles that dwarf my own. Women who worry, not about breast pumps, but about breasts too malnourished to feed their infants. Women denied education on the basis of their sex. Women shunned or even killed for daring to look at a man—let alone another woman. Theirs are the real stories of women's struggle and the real motivation for an action-oriented feminism. But I haven't lived their stories and I don't have the means to tell them here. Instead, I am writing from what I know, and hoping that it will find some broader relevance.

The morning after my epiphany in the bathroom of LaGuardia, I was driving across a bleak Midwestern landscape with my young research assistant. It was her first job out of college, and she was trying masterfully to keep her eyes on the highway as I struggled, again, with the damn breast pump. It wasn't a pretty sight. And so, as I buttoned back my blouse, I tried to ease the awkwardness. "You know," I suggested, "You'll probably be doing the same thing one day." She smiled, but didn't seem too impressed. "Really," I continued. "You'll get married, have a great job, want babies, and then find yourself dealing with your own breast pump and embarrassed assistant!" She smiled for real this time and we drove on.

It's twenty years later now, and we're still in touch. Most of my predictions have come true. Sue, as I'll call her, married a lovely, brilliant man and had two children in short order. While her eldest was a toddler, she finished graduate school, pumping steadily along the way. She ably ran several start-up companies and then, when her husband took a big job in a distant city, left those companies to follow him there. When he got an even bigger job in a different town, she followed again, each time packing up the kids, the cats, the house, and the finances, along with her own career plans. Then one day, during the week of her fortieth birthday, she came across an expensive plane ticket to Milan, stuck amid a pile of papers on her husband's desk. He was already in Milan. The ticket was for one of his young graduate students.

Sue was the third of my close friends to have almost this same experience, the third to try for years to have it all and then despair at some point about losing everything. She was the third—or the three millionth—woman to realize abruptly that the "all" that men take for granted—a partner, a job, some kids—comes much more painfully, or not at all, to the vast majority of women.

So we do what women do. We start dinner for the kids, allow them another round of Guitar Hero, and steal outside for a glass of Chardonnay. I have known Sue long enough by now to know that she will survive, probably even come out of this mess stronger. But as the sun goes down and the faux guitars wail, I can't help wondering: Just how far have we really come? And what will it take to get there for good?

1

GROWING UP CHARLIE

When I was growing up in the early 1970s, there was a commercial for Charlie perfume that appeared on all the network stations. I remember it vividly, as do many women of my generation. It showed a beautiful blond woman prancing elegantly down an urban street. She had long bouncy hair, a formfitting blue suit, and a perfect pair of stiletto heels. From one hand dangled a briefcase; from the other, a small, equally beautiful child, who gazed adoringly at her mom as they skipped along. The commercial never made clear, of course, just where Mama was going to leave her child on the way to work, or how they both managed to look so good that early in the morning. Instead it simply crooned seductively, in the way of most ads, promising something that was "kinda fresh, kinda now. Kinda new, kinda *wow*."

The perfume, if I recall correctly, was not particularly nice. But the commercial was terrific.[1]

So was another of the same vintage for Enjoli, a similarly unremarkable fragrance. This one's heroine was even bolder, strutting home in a tight skirt after an apparently successful day and proceeding directly to the kitchen. As she cheerfully whipped up some kind of dinner delight, she sang a provocative little anthem, which most women of my age, I've discovered, still recall. "I can bring home the bacon," she cooed. "Fry it up in a pan. And never let you forget you're a man. 'Cause I'm a woman. Enjoli." Never mind the perfume. The lifestyle was enchanting.

Both of these commercials aired in the early 1970s, right at the edge of Watergate and the free love of Woodstock. They aired only briefly, selling products that slipped eventually from the public eye. But they stuck somehow in the public consciousness, or at least in the minds of schoolgirls like me, who simply presumed that life in the grown-up world would be just like the ad for Charlie. We'd have careers to skip to, kids to adore us, and men waiting to douse us with perfume the moment we waltzed through the door. Money and great shoes only sweetened the package.

This wasn't, of course, the life that our mothers were living. In 1970, only 43 percent of women worked outside the home.[2] In upper-middle-class white families like my own, the number was slightly higher, hovering by 1974 at around 46 percent.[3] Most of these women worked in "traditional" fields such as teaching or nursing, and they rarely wore stilettos to the job. Yet somehow, girls growing up in that era believed— thought, presumed, *knew*—that they would be different. That instead of replicating their mothers' suburban idylls of parent-teacher conferences and three-tiered Jell-O molds, they—we—would go the way of Charlie, enjoying children *and* jobs, our husbands' money and our own. And through it all, we would be smiling and singing, gracefully enjoying the combined pleasures of life. In 1968, 62 percent of young women had expected to become housewives by the time they were thirty-five. By 1979, just eleven short years later, that percentage had plummeted to 20.[4] The rest of us presumed that we'd leave the world of housewifing far, far behind.[5] In 1979, fully 43 percent of American girls predicted that they would hold professional positions by the time they were thirty-five.[6]

Where did we possibly get such ideas?

I offer three suspects: our mothers, the media, and the feminists.

Let's start with the mothers, since they are always the easiest to attack. Women born between 1960 and 1975 have mothers who were born generally between 1935 and 1950 and came of age, generally again, between the late 1940s and early 1960s.[7] This was a period, in retrospect, of unprecedented prosperity and stability in the United States. Real incomes were growing steadily, and millions of Americans decamped for the suburban towns cropping up across the country. Freed from the rigors of economic depression and war, women of this generation rarely worked outside the home unless it was absolutely necessary. As late as 1955, for example, only 28.5 percent of married American women had paying jobs.[8] The remainder basked in the comforts that their generation could now afford and raised their own daughters—my generation's mothers—to strive for the *Good Housekeeping* version of the American dream: a house, a husband, 2.5 children, and a yard. Or as the poor shopgirl, Audrey, fantasizes in the musical *Little Shop of Horrors*, "A washer and a dryer. And an ironing machine. In the tract house that we share. Somewhere that's green." She ain't exactly Charlie.[9]

But when these girls of the 1940s and 1950s grew up to be mothers, they wanted their daughters to have something else. Something more than the washer and the dryer and the ironing machine.[10] They wanted them, in short, to have careers, and to participate more actively in the social progress that was starting to seep through the seams of American life. So the good girls of the Eisenhower era became the pushy mothers of the Nixon era, dragging their offspring to pottery classes and poetry readings, convincing them that girls really could do whatever they wanted.

My own mother was adamant on this point. After marrying at twenty and having me at twenty-two, she was fully convinced that girls of my generation would face a fundamentally different set of options—even though she had grown up in very comfortable circumstances, graduated from college, and returned to teaching kindergarten when I turned ten. "I never had the opportunities that you do," she would say. "I would have loved to go to law school, but there was no way my parents would ever have let me go." And statistically, she was right. In 1961, when she graduated from Hunter College, only 3 percent of law students in the United States were women. When I graduated from college twenty-three years later, that number had risen to 37 percent. The same thing happened in medical schools, where the percentage of female students rose from 5 to 28 percent over this period, and in business schools, where it rose from 3 to 30 percent.[11] So the women of my generation did indeed have all kinds of opportunities stretching beyond the green lawns of suburbia. And our mothers were chanting from the sidelines, urging us to grab them all.

Meanwhile, of course, the media were driving this fairly radical change as well, luxuriating in and promoting a new brand of American dreaminess. When I started watching television in the late 1960s, the choices were few, far between, and unabashedly wholesome: *Bewitched*,

I Dream of Jeannie, and my all-time favorite, *The Brady Bunch*. While these shows were socially more progressive than the older *Leave It to Beaver* fare that I caught on rare days home from school, they still portrayed a feminine ideal centered largely on the happy suburban mom. The leading women were typically full-time mothers, devoted to their school-age children and their affable if bumbling husbands. They were pretty in a well-coiffed and sensible way, and invariably cheerful. When Carol Brady and her three daughters go on a camping trip with her new husband and his three sons, for instance, Mrs. Brady smilingly prods her grumpy girls into action. "We have three new brothers and a new father," she reminds them, "and if they like camping, we like camping!"[12] Similarly, when the young witch Samantha hears from her husband the rules of suburban wifedom—"You'll have to learn to cook, and keep house, and go to my mother's house for dinner every Friday night"—she is eagerly compliant. "Darling," she gushes, "it sounds wonderful!"[13]

Within only four or five years, however, new figures started slipping across the TV screen, very different kinds of women who hinted provocatively at a whole new sort of post-Brady experience.[14] *Maude* debuted in 1972, portraying an outspoken and strong-willed woman who married four different men (one died; she divorced two), ran for Congress, and decided, when she became pregnant at forty-seven, to have television's first abortion. She was followed by *Rhoda* (1974), a boisterous single woman who manages to date, marry, divorce, and start her own window dressing business all in the show's 110 episodes. Then came *Alice* (1976), a single working-class mom. 1976 also famously saw the launch of *Charlie's Angels*, in which gorgeous, scantily clad women pull firearms from their bikini tops to rid the world of evil. Not surprisingly, the Charlie commercial that captured my imagination debuted around this same time (1974), as did the Enjoli ad. In fact, Shelley Hack, the beautiful woman from the Charlie ad (referred to, of course, as "the Charlie girl") actually became one of Charlie's angels in 1979. It was a good time for Charlie.

Even more dramatic changes were underway in the world of print media. Up until this point, women's magazines had been a staid and comforting lot, led by long-standing publications such as *Ladies' Home Journal* and *Good Housekeeping*. These were, to be sure, fairly serious magazines. They provided a rare outlet for female authors and dealt, at least in passing, with topics like divorce, infertility, and contraception. Their daily fodder, however, was simpler fare, consisting largely of advice on how to clean a perfect kitchen, make a perfect pot roast, or deal with a toddler's sore throat: THE DINING ROOM IS LIKE AN INDOOR GARDEN announced one 1960 headline from *Ladies' Home Journal*. FUN WITH YARNS! promised another. And then Helen Gurley Brown and Gloria Steinem smashed onto the stage, refurbishing *Cosmo* (in 1966), launching *Ms.* (in 1972), and turning the world of women's magazines completely upside down. Because now, instead of reading about pot roast and runny noses, women could read about sexual prowess and adultery.[15] They could learn about homosexuality (LESBIAN LOVE AND SEXUALITY), masturbation (GETTING TO KNOW ME: A PRIMER ON MASTURBATION), and more sex (THE LIBERATED ORGASM).[16] Suddenly, playing with yarn didn't sound like much fun.

By the time we girls of the 1970s entered high school, therefore, the world began to echo—even shout—the words our mothers had been telling us for years. In no uncertain terms, women of my generation were being told, for the first time in history, really, that girls were just as good and as capable as boys, and that women could be, should be, whatever they wanted to be.

And what lay behind this sudden bout of boosterism? Precisely the same thing that had catapulted Helen Gurley Brown and Gloria Steinem to power, the thing that had tossed Carol Brady off the screen and replaced her with Charlie's angels. It was the feminist revolution, hatched in the late 1960s and apparently now here to stay.

To be sure, feminism itself was hardly a new phenomenon. Indeed, as Estelle B. Freedman describes in *No Turning Back*, a history of feminism, the global movement for women's rights had a long and complicated past, including the liberal struggle for women's suffrage launched in the mid-nineteenth century, socialist-inspired campaigns to protect working girls and women in the early twentieth century, and the decades-long battle, led by crusaders such as Margaret Sanger and Emma Goldman, to provide women with access to contraception.[17] But the feminism of the 1960s was distinct. This was a feminism that promoted not the political rights of women, or the legal status of women, but rather the very identity of women. It was a feminism that tore at the very roots of an American ideal and prescribed a whole new model in its place. As presented (and distorted) by the mainstream media, it was a feminism that was greedy to its core, proclaiming that women could have money and children and sex and power, along with fabulous shoes. Like men, in other words, women could have it all. And boy, did I want it.

The Feminine Mystique

Unlike most social phenomena, the feminism that surrounded women of my generation can largely be traced to a single event—a book, in this case, that revolutionized how society saw women and, more important, how they saw and imagined themselves.

In 1963, Betty Friedan, a seemingly ordinary housewife with a husband and three children, published *The Feminine Mystique*, a searing investigation of what she termed "the problem that has no name."[18] According to Friedan, millions of women living in the postwar American idyll were suffering from a dissatisfaction that was both pervasive and profound. Although they had children and husbands they claimed to adore, young mothers reported feeling empty or unsatisfied, searching for a sense of fulfillment that didn't come from being "a server of food and a putter-on of pants."[19] Women, Friedan insisted, wanted more. They wanted lives of their own, and careers of their own, and ideas that belonged to them. But rather than pursuing their dreams, women across postwar America were routinely entrapped by the "feminine mystique," convinced that ecstasy came in a cleaning powder and fulfillment lay in serving others.

In shaping her complaint, Friedan drew heavily on the feminists who had preceded her. Her focus on power and economic conditions, for example, echoed the critiques of Simone de Beauvoir's *The Second Sex*; her demand for women's emancipation followed a line of argumentation that stretched back to Marx and Engels.[20] But something was different about this book. It wasn't making an academic argument, or an abstract one. It wasn't about principles or even politics. Rather, it was written—or at least appeared to be written—by a housewife, for a housewife. It was the literary equivalent of a kaffeeklatsch, something that women could share, quietly and among themselves, in the privacy of their kitchens. Or, as Anna Quindlen recalls in the introduction to the 2001 reissue of the book: "My mother had become so engrossed that she found herself reading in the place usually reserved for cooking."[21]

What was it that Friedan managed to capture? It wasn't really politics, since the political battles of feminism had been raging long before Friedan took up the cause. Indeed, fights over the Equal Rights Amendment (ERA), mandating legal equality for men and women, had been under way for decades.[22] Her book wasn't about economic power, really, or about giving women access to things like birth control or college degrees that had motivated feminists of the past. Instead, she was railing about what could easily have been dismissed as social subtleties—daily routines faced by millions of middle-class moms and the forces that had consigned them to this fate. Or, as Friedan writes in the book's opening passage: "It was a strange stirring, a sense of dissatisfaction, a yearning that women suffered in the middle of the twentieth century in the United States. Each suburban wife struggled with it alone. As she made the beds, shopped for groceries, matched slipcover material, ate peanut butter sandwiches with her children, chauffeured Cub Scouts and Brownies, lay beside her husband at night—she was afraid to ask even of herself the silent question—'Is this all?' "[23]

It's easy to imagine how such a question might well have gone unanswered. Friedan was an unknown author at the time of her book's publication, after all, and the previous two decades had already witnessed a slow but steady retreat from earlier feminist agendas. In 1947, for example, two prominent psychologists published *Modern Woman: The Lost Sex*, a bestselling treatise that described feminism as a "deep illness" and warned that any woman who fell prey to its temptations was "neurotically disturbed" and likely afflicted with a nasty case of penis envy.[24] And in 1955, even Adlai Stevenson, a leading politician esteemed for his liberal leanings and sheer intellect, centered his 1955 commencement address at Smith College on the need for educated women to defeat totalitarianism by teaching their husbands and children the meaning of love. Oh, sure, Stevenson acknowledged, Smith graduates had read Baudelaire and written their own poetry; they had "discussed art and philosophy until late in the night." But now, faced with the Communist menace, their overriding obligation was to focus on the home front, instilling in their children a "balanced tension of mind and spirit" and keeping their husbands "Western, purposeful, and whole."[25] Which wasn't, one might argue, a particularly exciting prospect.

Between 1945 and 1960, roughly 1.7 million women graduated from college, many from elite all-women's schools.[26] Only a fraction ventured on to graduate work or professional employment. The rest slipped silently into the vision of marital middle-class bliss. One of these women, my friend Helene Kaplan, tells a story that I'm sure could be repeated thousands of times over. In 1955, two years after graduating with honors from Barnard, she was married to a man she loved deeply. She had one infant daughter sleeping in the pram and a second, only slightly older, toddling beside. Suddenly, walking with her daughters and husband in Central Park, she sat down on a bench and began to weep. "I was only twenty-four," she recalls, "and my whole life was ruined. I cried to my husband that, as much as I loved my girls, I had always wanted to be a lawyer."

This was the demographic that Friedan so publicly exposed. By the time of *The Feminine Mystique*'s publication, Helene had already taken matters into her own hands, entering New York University Law School with her husband's staunch support when their daughters were eight and nine, and eventually becoming a partner at Skadden, Arps. But most women—demographically speaking—needed a bigger boost. Maybe that boost could have come in another form, or from another author. Maybe the surge that Friedan ostensibly unleashed was really let loose by Kennedy's assassination, or the U.S. civil rights movement, or the coming of age of a generation eager to depart from its parents' ways. Yet there was something about Friedan's pugnacious writing that seemed to strike a chord.[27] Within months of the book's publication, *The Feminine Mystique* had sold tens of thousands of copies and been excerpted in both *Ladies' Home Journal* and *McCall's*.[28] Readers across the United States wrote to Friedan and to the magazines, expressing what one historian later described as an "overwhelming sense of relief." In 1966, Friedan and three hundred supporters launched the National Organization for Women, pledging to "bring women into full participation in the mainstream of American society."[29]

Not everyone, of course, was inspired. Many of the housewives that

Friedan condemned were perfectly happy with their lot and saw *The Feminine Mystique* as an affront to their femininity and selflessness. Others attacked from the left, condemning Friedan for accepting the traditional structures of family and gender rather than pushing more radically against them.[30] And many were only mildly moved, insisting, as my own mother did, that "women's lib" wasn't really for them. But even women who scorned Friedan's agenda seized quietly upon one of its central premises. Even if these women didn't themselves rush back to law school, even if they didn't abandon their kitchens to work for equal rights, *they wanted their daughters to have something else.* They wanted them—me, us—to have different kinds of options, maybe even different kinds of lives. What these options looked like was never really clear. But this was the torch that Friedan passed to a generation of women, and that they then passed to the next. "Is this all?" Friedan had queried. "No," answered our mothers. "There's a lot more out there. You go figure it out."

Betty and Me

I was born in June 1963—eight months after the Cuban Missile Crisis, four months before Kennedy's death. It was a time of vast affluence and imminent change, a time when the cultural norms of postwar America were being shattered by wave after wave of rebellion and reform. I was too young to stay up for any of it. By the time I was even vaguely conscious, the Kennedys, Dr. Martin Luther King, Jr., and Kent State had already disappeared into the past—the stuff of history books but not real life. So, too, with the civil rights movement, with Vietnam and Woodstock. Although I and my demographic peers lived through these tumultuous events, we experienced them as children and therefore somewhat vicariously. I was ten, for example, at the height of the antiwar movement. So while I remember discussing the war with my fifth-grade classmates and even writing an earnest note of protest to Richard Nixon, I was too young to be actively involved in the movement, or to fear losing friends or brothers to the draft. Likewise, while I vaguely recall hearing about busloads of women burning their bras outside the Miss America pageant in 1968 (which in fact never quite happened as described), my more immediate concern at the time was growing into my own. And the closest I came to free love, alas, was seeing *Hair* on Broadway.

What I did get an awful lot of, though, was feminism. Not feminism of the fervent, hard-won sort, but a kind of trickle-down feminism, the feminism wrought by Friedan and transmitted through the cultural ether of the early 1970s. Right about the time that my own mother returned to work as a teacher, the television networks were starting to bombard American girls with that new constellation of female stars, all of whom were strong and funny, sexy and beautiful. Right about the time that I tentatively put aside *Highlights for Children* in favor of *Time* and *Newsweek*, these magazines were trumpeting THE WAR ON SEXISM and THE NEW FEMINISTS."[31] In 1972, Helen Reddy's anthem to the women's movement, "I Am Woman (Hear Me Roar)," shot to the top of the pop music charts. In 1973, Billie Jean King defeated Bobby Riggs in the "Battle of the Sexes" tennis match, adding sports to the apparently now endless list of things at which women could excel. By 1977, therefore, the year I started high school, no one in higher education would have dared to voice sentiments along the lines of Stevenson's 1955 address at Smith. Instead, pedagogy was increasingly about equality, about educating boys and girls, blacks and whites, to tackle society's problems together. At my own school, the commitment to free-flowing learning went so far as to entail removing all the walls between class-rooms. Literally.

But if you had asked me then—in my biology class or at softball practice—if I was a feminist, I would almost certainly have answered no. Because just as my mother had denied any interest in "women's lib," I didn't see any personal connection to the feminist struggle, probably because I presumed it was already over. Women had the right to vote, after all, and the pending Equal Rights Amendment.* Women had Title IX in sports, granting them equal access to college-level athletics, and could attend nearly all of the formerly male Ivy League schools.[32] If you had pressed me harder on these points back then, reminding my

---

*The ERA passed both houses of Congress in 1972, and then went to the state legisla-tures for ratification. Because a sufficient number of states failed to ratify it, however, the amendment expired in 1982 and never became law.

miniskirted teenaged self that these rights came courtesy of the women's movement, I might have been moved to mumble a few words of thanks. But since I had grown up in a world where women—at least on television and in the movies—had always seemed equal to men, it was hard for me to conceive that the struggle had been that tough. *Ms.* magazine, recall, had been around since I was nine. *Roe v. Wade* was decided before I got my period. And Charlie, of course, defined the modern woman.

If you had really decided to go after me with facts at that stage, I might have acknowledged that my mother was one of the very few working mothers around. And that I didn't actually know anyone whose life even vaguely resembled Charlie's.

But I had curly hair to iron nightly.

I had boys to worry about.

I was seventeen.

And I didn't need the feminists.

The Feminist Critique

Regardless of my hair and boyfriend travails, though, the mood inside the feminist community during this era was understandably jubilant. In the twelve months of 1970 alone, *The New York Times Magazine* published a major article entitled SISTERHOOD IS POWERFUL; Kate Millett, author of the bestselling *Sexual Politics*, appeared on the cover of *Time*; Bella Abzug, the feisty New York lawyer and advocate, was elected to Congress; thousands of women went to the streets to join a one-day Women's Strike for Equality; and women working at both *Time* and *Newsweek* charged their employers with sex discrimination.[33] After decades of fighting from the margins, feminists had burst loudly on to the main stage of American life, seizing headlines, gaining adherents, and dominating a substantial swath of political discourse. "Today women's liberation has become a serious national movement," announced *Life*. "The groups vary in every community, but all raise common themes: women are denied opportunity to fulfill their talents; traditional sex roles and family structure must be changed; women must relate in new ways to one another and to men."[34]

Under the surface, however, dissent was beginning to emerge. Some of the burgeoning feminist groups arrayed themselves around Friedan-like goals, lobbying for the Equal Rights Amendment and for reproductive rights such as contraception and abortion. Other groups, led by writers such as Shulamith Firestone, Robin Morgan, and (somewhat later) Andrea Dworkin, argued more radically that gender itself was a function of power and that women could never be free until they broke the bonds of exploitation that men had historically thrust upon them.[35] Taking this structural stance to its extreme conclusion, the activist Ti-Grace Atkinson announced memorably in 1969 that "marriage means rape," while Firestone similarly argued that women needed to be liberated from the "tyranny of their reproductive biology."[36] There was little room in this worldview for the relative baby steps of Friedan-style feminism, directed as they were toward pay and jobs and child care. Or, as one self-styled radical wrote, "We, in this segment of the movement, do not believe that the oppression of women will be ended by giving them a bigger piece of the pie, as Betty Friedan would have it. We believe that the pie itself is rotten."[37]

In another field, at another time, these scuffles might well have remained invisible. But given how new feminism was, how raw and still provocative, divisions within the feminist camp cast an undue influence on how feminism itself was publicly portrayed. National networks and newsmagazines, for example, doted on the more extreme elements of radical feminism, highlighting Firestone's claim that "pregnancy is barbaric," or Atkinson's assertion that "love has to be destroyed."[38] More mundane stories about women working for the ERA or supporting Planned Parenthood, by contrast, rarely made headlines, creating a massive asymmetry between the sprawling contours of the actual women's movement and popular perceptions of feminism. For women who were already in the movement, this unbalanced portrayal was a source of great contention. For those of us who were just a few years younger, however, what we saw was only the news. We grew up, as a result, with a skewed sense of feminism and a vague belief that all feminists hated men, denounced children, and refused to wash their hair.

What made this asymmetry even more pronounced was that the same media channels were bombarding us throughout the 1970s with portraits of Charlie: Wonder Woman, the Bionic Woman, Major Margaret "Hot Lips" Houlihan, and all those damn angels.

All of which led to the massive schizophrenia of the Charlie complex. Before we had even reached puberty, women of my generation not only wanted it all, but firmly expected we would get it: the education, the sports, the jobs, the men, the sex and shoes and babies. And how could we not, when everything around us was screaming "yes"? Indeed, so strong were these cries that we may have been the first generation of girls who could truly imagine that our lives would unfold more or less like our brothers'. Just decades earlier, a girl who announced her ambition to be a doctor or lawyer would likely have been shushed, or ridiculed, or at least talked out of her dream. By the mid-1970s that same girl would be goaded to greater heights: A doctor? Why not an astronaut? A lawyer? How 'bout a judge? It was heady stuff, and yet it had nothing to do, in my mind at least, with the feminists. Feminists were loud and pushy, strident and unfeminine. Charlie, on the other hand, was gorgeous, ladylike, and successful, a working woman *and* a mom. Who needed feminism if you could have Charlie?

It was of course both ironic and unfair. Because just as millions of young women like me were reaping the benefits of the women's movement, we were racing to distance ourselves from that movement and to ignore or even deny the massive role that feminism had played in our evolving lives.

But we were teenagers at the time and—particularly if we were white and straight and affluent—too busy with our own affairs to worry about what seemed to be another generation's long-finished struggle. So we didn't study feminist theory or yearn to burn our bras. We took our place in the Ivy League and NCAA sports but still cherished cheerleading and beauty pageants, and we thought nothing of it.

Then, of course, we became young women, relishing all the possibilities we blithely accepted as our due. We had sex like men—meaning, at least, without much commitment—and a smorgasbord of entry-level jobs. We backpacked around Europe if we were lucky and subleased apartments of our own, barely recognizing that these were things our mothers hadn't been able to do. We took the pill and had abortions, but we didn't fight for reproductive rights.

And then, before we knew it, we became young wives and not-so-young mothers. We bundled our babies in nurturing Snuglis and gave them to our husbands to tote proudly around. Which worked beautifully until the child became a toddler and we found ourselves struggling with the car seat at the day care center as the sippy cup of apple juice erupted over the laptop. We reveled in the theory of shared-care parenting and then nagged our husbands endlessly to please, please remember the dental appointment. We slipped out of committee meetings to buy shark-shaped party favors and crumpled the fenders of our minivans racing between board meetings and ballet recitals. And when our mothers cooed happily about our amazing ability to have it all, we silently begged them to offer the only thing we really wanted: a week of free babysitting.

It was only when we divorced our husbands or quit our jobs or yelled at our children once too often that we finally realized what we should have known all along.

Charlie was dead.

Even worse, we realized at last that Charlie had never lived—that there was never a woman—a real woman, at least—who balanced her life and her loves and her job and her children with the panache that women of my generation believed would come naturally. Instead, as a generation, we found ourselves in middle life shockingly childless, or jobless, or stretched so thin we were about to break. Our mothers, as it turned out, had been wrong. The media had sold us a fairy tale. And all that feminism we rejected? Well, it turns out that perhaps we should have been paying attention.

Specifically, we should have noticed, not that feminism had all the right answers, necessarily, but that it was asking the right questions. That it was prodding us to think about what it meant to be a girl, and a woman, and a wife, and a mother, and about how we wanted to shape and arrange these roles into a life that worked. If we'd been paying attention, we might have noticed that while our mothers and the media were enchanting us with visions of the modern woman—powerful, capable, sexual, fertile—feminism was quietly urging a sense of caution, a warning that women could not in fact have it all. Or at least not, as Betty Friedan would herself later acknowledge, all at once.

In the end, of course, the myth of Charlie was just that: one silly commercial, capturing a particularly far-flung fantasy. It wasn't true, and never was. But it left an indelible mark nevertheless on millions of women and girls, convincing us, seducing us with a dream of feminine perfection. We really thought we could have it all, and when reality proved otherwise we blamed—not the media, as it turned out, and not our mothers. We blamed ourselves.

Today, women and girls around the world have fallen headlong into this same embrace of blame and failure, into a stubborn pattern of believing that anything less than "all" in their lives is proof only of their own shortcomings. Rather than acknowledging that feminine perfection is a lie, we continue both to believe in the myth and to feel guilty when we—inevitably, inherently—fall short of it.

The irony of this situation is that it is precisely the outcome that feminism fought to avoid. Because feminism, after all, was about removing a fixed set of expectations from women, freeing them to be what they wanted and behave as they desired. And yet, fifty years on, women find themselves laboring under an expanded and in many ways more cumbersome set of expectations: to be good wives and workers, sexy yet monogamous, devoted to their perfect children and their own perfect bodies.

This is the unanticipated double whammy that confronts women today: the unexpected agglomeration of all the roles that society has historically heaped upon them *plus* the new roles and opportunities created by feminism.

So what's a girl to do?

One possibility, of course, is to give it all up, to throw in the towel of feminism and retreat to an older and more traditional array of roles and values and norms. Under such a move (supported, not surprisingly, by a range of conservative groups), women would relinquish their career goals in favor of motherhood. They would be workers but not bosses, sexual inside marriage but nowhere else.[39] They would, in other words, go back in time. At the other end of the spectrum, a second possibility would be to leap more radically ahead, urging women to strive for some of feminism's more audacious goals—things like a wholesale destruction of the male-dominated global power structure, or a communal approach to child care and rearing.

Personally, though, as a creature of compromise, I find myself constantly attracted to the murky path of muddling through. I believe that women are entitled to be whatever they want, but that they can't ever expect, any more than men, that they can have it all. I believe that child care should be a joint endeavor, but I suspect that—so long as women carry the chromosomes for wombs and breasts and guilt—they will tend to bear a disproportionate share of their families' needs. I believe that women, in general, enjoy their sexuality in different ways than men, with a higher premium placed on commitment and procreation. And finally, I believe that the feminism of the 1960s and '70s has a great deal to offer to today's young women—particularly insofar as it urges them to focus at least a portion of their energies on common goals and struggles.

We can't go back, of course, and undo the myth of Charlie. For it is there now, buried deep within the psyches of girls far too young ever to have seen the commercial; it exists in the ambitions of women working in the trenches of Wall Street and in the burgeoning markets of Mumbai, Shanghai, and Moscow. It lies in the tired face of every working mother who feels she has abandoned her children, and in the guilty conscience of every nonworking woman who feels she has abandoned her dreams. What we can do, however, is examine how we got to this place: how the women of my generation managed to transform the collective goals of feminism into an individualized quest for perfection; how we have become confused over time by the dazzling array of choices now available to us; and how—slowly, carefully, and with equal measures of common sense and good humor—we can begin to plot a way forward.

2

GIRLS: A HANDBOOK

> One is not born, but rather becomes, a woman. No biological, psychological, or economic fate determines the figure that the human female presents in society; it is civilization as a whole that produces this creature.
>
> —Simone de Beauvoir, *The Second Sex*

> I wanna be like Barbie. The bitch has everything.
>
> —T-shirt slogan

Astronaut Barbie was a feisty little thing. Released in 1965, she sported a silver spacesuit and an American flag, supported as always by her gravity-defying waist and ready-for-takeoff toes. Her sisters-in-charms in the 1960s and 1970s were an equally ambitious bunch: College Graduate Barbie, Surgeon Barbie, Olympic Gold Medalist Barbie—all coiffed, all poised, all smiling brilliantly into the future that we, their playmates, were supposed to emulate. The Barbie of this era was really Charlie, of course: full-blown and ready to tackle anything in her path.

As a toy, Barbie defies both business and social logics. Born in 1959, she was the brainchild of Mattel's cofounder, Ruth Handler, who modeled her on Lilli, a seductive German doll sold primarily to men. Handler took Lilli—blond, Aryan, with feet clad permanently in stiletto-heeled pumps—and redid her for young girls. Working with Japanese factories and an eccentric engineer who described the doll as looking like a "hooker or an actress between performances," Handler removed Lilli's nipples and her permanent promiscuous pout.[1] She added fingers and toes, a soft vinyl body, and hair sewn directly into the scalp. Then she hired a fashion designer and introduced her wasp-waisted creation as a teenaged fashion model, named after her own daughter.

Within months, Barbie dolls were leaping off toy store shelves, generating legions of long-legged competitors and earning prodigious profits for Mattel. By 1965, the company's sales exceeded $100 million—twice what they had been in 1961.[2] By the early 1990s, the average American girl owned seven Barbie dolls. They weren't all identical, and not even all blond. There was, instead, a black Barbie and a Hispanic Barbie, a "Shani" Barbie (available in "mahogany," "tawny," or "beige"), and Malaysian, Jamaican, Australian, English, and Italian models—a veritable United Nations of Caucasian-featured, forever-sleek creatures. Most little girls, though, apparently didn't care all that much about the ethnic specifics of their doll. For decades, American-styled Barbie dolls have sold as well in Asia as in the United States, as well among African Americans as among whites. And for forty years no other doll—not a more realistic one, or a plumper one, or one that actually does anything—has come close to outselling her.

I don't remember the precise moment when Barbie entered my own life, only that she and her kinfolk were permanently scattered across the shelves of my ruffled yellow bedroom, tossed among the baby dolls and stuffed koalas with legs splayed and heads long gone. I played with her haphazardly, spending more of my time drawing, or putting on plays, or reading endless volumes of Nancy Drew. Yet she and her friends were always there, beaming down on us mere mortals and cheering us on to sveltity.

What is it about that doll?

In 2002, more than forty years after Barbie's birth and thirty since my own encounters with her, my husband and I were walking down the streets of Ekaterinburg, Russia, a Soviet-era metropolis with few links to capitalism. We had just met the little girl who was soon to be our daughter. She was six, and had spent the bulk of her life in a spartan Russian orphanage. She had never seen Western television or visited anything that even vaguely resembled a Toys"R"Us. She spoke no English; we had only a smattering of Russian. After thirty minutes in our presence, though, thirty minutes of mentally digesting the fact that these oddly speaking strangers were about to become her parents,

Kristina timidly took my husband's hand and voiced the question that apparently proved love. "*Kupi mnye Barbi?*" she ventured. "Would you buy me a Barbie?" And so we did.

Dollhouse Days

Nancy lived for a while in one of the fanciest houses in my neighborhood. While most of the town was composed of late-1950s split-level tract houses, hers was a colonial that had somehow escaped, a three-story wonder with a sweeping plush stairway. There was lots to do in her house—play Life, watch TV, bake cupcakes in the EasyBake®—but I always opted for the same thing. We would go up that fancy staircase, open Nancy's closet, and take the dolls from their trunks. They were fancy dolls with glossy hair and eyelashes that moved. But what made Nancy's dolls so special was the house that sat to greet them. It was three stories, like Nancy's own, with Victorian spirals and deep black doors. It had real carpets in the bedrooms and tiny gingham curtains in the windows. It had perfect little closets for the dolls' clothes and perfect little tea cookies for their tea. It was the most insanely beautiful thing I had ever witnessed in my eight-year-old life. And I wanted one desperately.

The following year, my parents complied. But because they were practical people, thinking people, who read the news regularly and kept abreast of child development theories, they got me a very different sort of dollhouse. It arrived, I recall clearly, in clunky lengths of pale gray wood, each with several grooves where the pieces could be fastened together. The owner of the would-be house, my parents proudly explained, was free to assemble the rooms as she desired, creating, say, three bedrooms rather than two, or an extra-large living room. That same owner was then equally free to transform the square cuts in the wood into whatever kind of windows she fancied, and to dress the dolls—horrible, vacant, naked things—in clothes of her own manufacture. To spur the creative process, my parents cheerfully provided me with a large bag of wooden spools (for tables! or cars!) and several old yellow pillowcases (dresses! curtains! rugs!). There were no gingham window treatments in my progressive house, no teacups or stairs. And so I gamely cut out pillowcase aprons for a while and feebly painted spools. But there wasn't enough creativity in the world to transform that thing into Nancy's house, and so it eventually just gathered dust in the basement while I mourned my lost Victorian days.

Not that I can blame my parents for trying. They probably gave me that wretched thing around 1972, the same year that Marlo Thomas released her bestselling album *Free to Be . . . You and Me* and three years after Woodstock. The country was awash in exciting new theories about what it meant to be a parent, and to be a child. Mothers were being urged, for the first time, to question their destiny as wives and homemakers, while fathers were being encouraged to participate more fully in the lives of their children.[3] Kids were suddenly people and childhood a time for play and exploration.

Until this point in time, parents had generally been advised to treat their girl children explicitly as girls. Specifically, they were to raise them to be wives and mothers, equipped with the skills and norms that suited women most. Because girls, as the old nursery rhyme ran, were presumed to be made of "sugar and spice and all things nice," they were to be handled nicely but firmly, as befit a fragile creature who smelled good but wasn't particularly competent. Girls might be taught to sew and clean, to make themselves attractive to men and learn to tend to others. They needed to cherish their femininity and keep their virginity tightly under control. But they certainly did not need to learn a sport or a trade, or indeed to have any formal education at all. Writing in the eighteenth century, the Genevan philosopher Jean-Jacques Rousseau was particularly disappointing on this point. "Woman," he stated definitively, "is made specially to please man." Therefore, "the whole education of women ought to relate to men. To please men, to be useful to them, to make herself loved and honored by them . . . these are the duties of women at all times, and they ought to be taught from childhood."[4] *The Girl's Book About Herself*, published in 1912, was only slightly less adamant, warning girls to "put away the trigonometry and do some needlework."[5]

All of which, of course, made a certain amount of sense. Because for centuries, the difference between boys and girls, men and women, was seen simply as nature's most basic dividing line.[6] Boys were boys and girls were girls, with their identities carved literally from the moment of their birth. As science slowly began to unpack the biology of sex, however, it both complicated and reinforced these beliefs. Sex, biologists came to understand around the 1940s, was a sometimes-subtle blend of physical attributes and hormonal cues. At conception, all embryos were endowed with an unchangeable set of sexually determining chromosomes: XX for females, XY for males. This chromosomal mix, set in the earliest seconds after egg meeting sperm, determined to a large extent who, or at least what, the eventual child would be. Yet sexual development did not begin and end with its chromosomal components. Instead, as the embryo developed into a fetus, it was pummeled by prenatal hormones, including, critically, a storm of testosterone released between the sixteenth and eighteenth weeks of pregnancy. In most Y-chromosome fetuses (that is, fetuses destined to be born male), testosterone worked to shape a penis and scrotal sac and to plant the seeds for what would eventually become male features.[7] Occasionally, though, scientists discovered, a Y-chromosome fetus lacked the genetic receptor for circulating testosterone, a condition now known as androgen insensitivity syndrome (AIS). AIS babies are technically male, but they are born looking female, and they tend to regard themselves as girls. They typically play as girls in childhood, develop breasts in puberty, and go on to marry men—even though they are physically incapable of procreating with them.[8] Their sex, in other words, and presumably the sex of all individuals, is thus a combination of chromosomes and hormones, a carefully regulated process that stretches beyond the moment of conception to include the full nine months of gestation.

Biology, therefore, provided sex with the full mechanics of its creation. Boys were boys because they had Y chromosomes and testosterone receptors. Girls were girls because they lacked both. Freud, riffing on these themes throughout the course of his work, argued in large part that women's problems came from the lack of the penis they never had—a vestigial yearning for what could have been theirs in the womb. But beginning in the 1960s, and exploding along with the sexual revolution, came a series of attacks on Freud and biology, and indeed on the entire ancient enterprise of linking gender with sex. According to a new set of scholars, gender—how an individual identified his or her sexuality—was carved not from genes and hormones, but rather from social norms and individual preferences.[9] Boys were not destined to be boys at birth, critics argued, nor girls girls. Instead, in the now-eternal words of the French philosopher Simone de Beauvoir, "one is not born, but rather becomes, a woman." "No biological, psychological, or economic fate determines the figure that the human female presents in society," she continued. "It is civilization as a whole that produces this creature."[10]

Beauvoir's words—and the torrent of literature, research, and commentary they inspired—would prove revolutionary on many accounts. Written first in 1949, her masterpiece, *The Second Sex*, ignited a storm of controversy and inspired a generation of feminist scholars. It served, in retrospect, to jump-start the field of gender studies and carve a serious space in which millions of people could examine the derivation of their own sexuality. In the 1960s and 1970s, though, one of the most powerful and immediate effects of Beauvoir's work was to throw the whole notion of child rearing, and particularly girl rearing, into an enthusiastic tizzy. Because if girls were indeed made and not born, then they could just as easily be made, and unmade, into all sorts of things that had never been deemed possible before. They could be tomboys or surrogate males; they could be hunters and warriors rather than nurturers and protectors. They could learn to build houses rather than pose dolls in them and could don the pants in their family as easily as the apron. By the late 1970s, a host of less scholarly books (with titles such as *Right from the Start* and *Growing Up Free*) had embraced Beauvoir's explicit theory of gender plasticity, urging parents to break with centuries of tradition and raise their girls in an environment free from gender stereotypes. Rather than pushing children to act "like a boy" or "like a girl," parents were encouraged to defy the "cult of sex differences" and celebrate the individual humanity of each child. Doing so meant scorning traditional sex roles within the home, letting Dad change diapers, for example, and Mom toss the football around. It meant shunning pink and blue toys in favor of neutral hues. And critically, it meant prodding children into mixed-gender play, teaching them how to be friends across the divide of sex.[11] Or, as Penelope Leach wrote in *Baby and Child Care from Birth to Age Five*, "children are human beings who happen to be either male or female. They should clearly have the opportunity of exploring all aspects of human behavior as children . . . If you try to make the child stick to the 'right' sex, you deprive him or her of half the world."[12]

Watered down and popularized, these ideas seeped into the fabric of middle America in the 1970s and 1980s. Beginning with its premiere issue in 1972, *Ms.* magazine highlighted advice on RAISING KIDS WITH-OUT SEX ROLES and published a regular column on "Stories for Free Children."[13] Benjamin Spock, author of the era's bible of child care advice, *Baby and Child Care*, literally changed his pronouns in 1976, "getting the discrimination out" of his 633-page book by consistently replacing "him" and "his" in the text with "they," "them," and "theirs."[14] Urban consciousness-raising groups began singing the praises of gender-neutral toys—"more space, science and adventure toys for girls and more dolls for boys"[15]—and even mainstream magazines ran articles advising parents on how to "let your boy know the challenge of tackling a recipe; let your girl know the challenge of tackling another kid."[16]

It was *Free to Be . . . You and Me*, though, with its dashing pink cover and kid-friendly lyrics, that really got the girls of my generation. Released in 1972, *Free* was a breakthrough album with a revolutionary bent. With pieces by writers such as Shel Silverstein and Judy Blume and voices that included those of Diana Ross, Michael Jackson, and Rosey Grier, it was a pop-perfect presentation of a postfeminist world. Publicly, it was the brainchild of Marlo Thomas, famous already for her fresh-scrubbed looks and starring role as Ann Marie in *That Girl*. Strategically, it provided funds to the Ms. Foundation for Women, using well-known names and faces to sing of what tomorrow might bring. There's Mel Brooks (*The Producers*, *Blazing Saddles*) and Thomas, voicing two newborn babies trying to determine their sexes. And Alan Alda (then of *M*A*S*H* fame) recounting the tale of Atalanta, a princess who could run as fast as the wind and who set off to see the world before marrying the handsome lad who won the right to her hand. As album and philosophy it was totally irresistible. Because what nine-year-old wouldn't love what it promised? *A land where the river runs free. A land in the green country. And a land where you and me. Are free to be. You and me.*[17] In this land, apparently, boys always helped; prissy girls were eaten by tigers, and the only advice that grown-ups gave was "Don't dress your cat in an apron (Just 'cause he's learning to bake)."[18] The fact that it was perky and smart—and that Marlo Thomas, who quickly released a book and backup television special, was perky and smart as well—only burnished its appeal. I don't remember if my brother or any of his friends ever listened to the album. But my girl-friends and I ate it up. I even vaguely recall concocting some kind of home-grown show to the music, dancing around the all-female house of my best friend Anne (single mom, three daughters) and giddily con-ceiving a future in which

> Some mommies are ranchers
> Or poetry makers
> Or doctors or teachers
> Or cleaners or bakers.
> Some mommies drive taxis
> Or sing on TV.
> Yes, mommies can be
> Almost anything they want to be.[19]

Looking back, I suspect that Anne, and Nancy, and I—along with the millions of other girls who came of age smack in the middle of the sexual revolution—were deeply confused. For we were being told, on the one hand, to be whatever we wanted to be. We were building our own dollhouses and wearing little bitty hot pants to school. On the other hand, though, we remained drawn to Barbies and fairy-tale glitz, to all those girly things we were supposed to have been freed from. And equality of any real sort was painfully hard to see. Sure, Barbie was an astronaut, but the folks who walked so memorably upon the moon in 1969 were all men. So were the politicians, and the lawyers, and the sports heroes, and the newscasters. In fact, the only real female role models of the early 1970s were TV and movie stars again—women like Mia Farrow and Jane Fonda, who were hugely successful in their own right, but not in the gender-neutral, level-playing-field way that Marlo Thomas promised. And as for Marlo—well, let's be honest: she was thin, gorgeous, and the daughter of a famous actor. Hard to imagine that she ever crafted her own plywood dollhouse.

And so we girls of the 1970s labored under a subtle set of dual ex-pectations. To be smart *and* pretty. Equal to the boys but not in compe-tition with them. Drop-dead gorgeous in clothes we stitched ourselves.

It was a heady combination, to be sure. How to pull it off, though, was not obvious. Did we wind our hair on rollers, as our mothers did, or leave it wild, as the feminists urged? Strive for a career like Neal Armstrong's, or a body like Barbie's? "Work hard," my teachers urged me, "and try to get straight A's." "But don't," my friends and relatives whispered, "ever let the boys know that you're smart."*

The Problem with Princesses

In retrospect, the age of "free to be" didn't last much longer than my childhood. Indeed, by the time I went to college, notions of gender-neutral parenting had gradually receded, replaced by somewhat more traditional notions of separate but equal paths for boys and girls.[20] Rebelling, perhaps, against too many boy toys and "creative" playthings from their own childhoods, the women who became mothers in the 1980s and 1990s made a screeching U-turn in their parenting preferences, embracing their daughters' inner romanticism with an ardor that would have made their mothers blush.[21] Barbie, who in theory should have died or at least hit middle age a long time ago, was still going strong at the end of the twentieth century, along with a veritable kingdom of willowy, doe-eyed princesses: Snow White, Sleeping Beauty, Cinderella, Ariel, Belle, Jasmine. All were sweet; all were gorgeous. All were bought—and begged for, and cherished—by girls no older than six.

Walk through any toy store today and you will be engulfed by a shimmering, glittery, pale pink sea of girliedom. Truly. Here is what hits you as you enter FAO Schwarz, long the fantasy palace for high-end toys: a Madame Alexander doll factory, where little girls can choose their own heads, hair textures, and outfits; a Barbie foosball table (only $24,999); and a hip "Monster High" display, complete with

---

*I can't really blame them. According to a fascinating study completed in 1970, most girls at this time were receiving similarly contradictory messages: to be smart, accomplished, and independent, but not so "unfeminine" that they could never be married. See Matina Horner, "Femininity and Successful Achievement: A Basic Inconsistency," in J. M. Bardwick et al., *Feminine Personality and Conflict* (Belmont, CA: Brooks/ Cole, 1970). Horner subsequently became president of Radcliffe College.

Clawdeen the Wolf Doll (who "likes nothing more than letting her hair down at the beach") and Draculaura (sporting "cute bright pink high-heeled shoes with a monster detail").[22] Lower down the food chain, at Toys"R"Us, the prices are lower but the pinkness remains. There are Fashion Angels (Design a Heavenly Pet Wardrobe!) and Justin Bieber nail polish, T-shirts that scream CAN'T STOP. MUST SHOP! and an entire two-story boutique devoted wholly to Barbie—Cheerleader Barbie, Ballet Teacher Barbie, Fashionista Barbie, and (rather implausibly, one might think) Elvis Barbie. When I casually asked the salesclerk where little girls tend to go in the store, her answer was immediate. "Oh, they run right to the Barbie section," she said. "And then they go wild." Meanwhile, it is princesses who clearly rule the Disney flagship store in Times Square. There, you'll find princess gowns and princess slippers, Pixie Dust body mist and graceful mermaids with light-up tails. The poor six-year-old I dragged along for research was positively bug-eyed by the time we left, clutching a Mulan doll and vaguely worried that none of the slippers she'd seen were likely to fit. A quick peek into the boys' section, by contrast, revealed most of the usual stuff: cars, blocks, various weapons of mass destruction, and Legos by the ton. Things that a child can actually do something with. Things that don't involve looks. Things, I must confess, that are vaguely like my much-despised dollhouse.

It is easy, of course, to disdain the playthings of someone else's youth. And not surprising that a generation reared with one developmental ideology would choose something entirely different to impose upon its own offspring. It's also easy to see how corporate capitalism, manifest in megafirms like Disney and Mattel, could reap real fortunes from hocking fake jewels to impressionable little girls. As Peggy Orenstein wryly notes in her fabulous *Cinderella Ate My Daughter*, Disney's Princess line is not only the fastest-growing brand the company has ever created, but also, with revenues of $4 billion in 2009, the single largest franchise on the planet for girls aged two to six.[23] Yet there is also something inherently disquieting about the current princess fascination, with its fairy dust and magic wands and girls wrapped up in tulle. What is it about Barbie and Snow White? Why do they sell so well? And why do they make so many women—even those who stroke the dolls, and remember the dolls, and buy them for their daughters—feel so darn uneasy?

Partly, it's because these dolls (and crowns and beads and ball gowns) serve as a visual rebuke to the spoken promise of what girls today are supposed to become. "Be a surgeon!" we say to young women. "But get out of your pumpkin and dress like a queen!" Cinderella tosses back. "Work hard and do well!" we urge girls (in schools and Brownie troops and soccer leagues across the country). "Just remember to find your prince!" the mermaid Ariel (who gave up her *voice* to catch her man) giggles back.[24] It is a cultural contradiction that girls experience before they even hit kindergarten, a dilemma we give them no way to navigate. When I was growing up, my parents at least gave me the tools to exercise my imagination in a potentially useful and engaging way. (*Want to be an architect? Great, design your own house!*) Today, by contrast, little girls are being showered with what they really, really seem to like: bling and shimmer and pouf and pink and fantasies 'round every corner. Yet they don't get much of what they are actually going to need: resourcefulness, competence, and a sense of achievement that extends beyond their looks.

Worse, as countless observers have noticed, the looks that little girls prize and emulate are all about sex. Look at Barbie. Her breasts are huge, her waist tiny, her feet as arched as a fetish. Recall that she was modeled on a porn doll. Look at the Bratz pack, the one brand to give Barbie any real competition. All the dolls have lips that are absurdly full and hips perpetually cocked. Look at popdom's most recent tween stars. Britney Spears burst onto the scene in 1999, dressed like a schoolgirl and begging to be "hit one more time." She was followed by Hannah Montana (née Miley Cyrus) who aw-shucksed it up with her dad until she took a turn at pole dancing. And Vanessa Hudgens, the *High School Musical* sweetheart whose nude photos began showing up on Internet sites. These girls look like our girls—presuming ours were especially attractive and inclined to sell it on the corner.

The generational irony here is more than bittersweet. For centuries, girls were raised to comply with the narrowest of norms: to be good wives, housekeepers, and mothers. Their toys, such as they existed, were essentially training vehicles—dolls, needlework samplers, little pots and pans—and their emergent sexuality was fiercely and firmly controlled. Then came the sexual revolution, and a virtual about-face in thinking about girls. Because if women were equal to men, and a child's sexual identity was as much constructed as inherited, then girls had to be given a completely new set of tools and experiences. They needed trucks and blocks and creative playthings, daddies who diapered and lots of male friends. Not all girls of the 1970s and '80s embraced the unisex identity that was thrust upon them. Some of us (yes, me—it's the darn dollhouse again) clamored occasionally for a return to frill and fashion. But at least we had a sense of both the options and contradictions before us: if the astronaut thing didn't work, we could always go back and play house. Today, by contrast, another U-turn in parenting has brought girls to an odd and precarious state. On the one hand, they, like their mothers, are being constantly urged to excel, to do whatever they want and be whoever they want to be. On the other hand, and at the same time, they are being pummeled by a bizarrely narrow set of gender stereotypes. Girls as princesses; girls as sex objects; girls as pretty things to be dressed up, jeweled up, and carried off by

A toddler beauty pageant winner

men. Moreover, unlike generations before them, girls today get little education in how to be a wife or mother (because how retro is that?) and yet also little preparation in what it takes to succeed in life once the princess glare dies down.

There's nothing wrong with girls dressing up. With hair brushing and nail polishing and extreme accessorizing. Even a tiara or two probably won't kill you. What's wrong is the extent to which childhood for girls—having swung all the way to the unisex world of *Free to Be* and back—now seems to emphasize looks and charm and attractiveness to the neglect of all else. In the nineteenth century, as Joan Jacobs Brumberg discovers in her fascinating study of girls' diaries, young women strove painfully to be better people, to help others and perform good works. Or, as one young woman confided to her journal in 1892, "Resolved, not to talk about myself or feelings. To think before speaking. To work seriously . . . Interest myself more in others."[25] Now, by contrast, girls strive equally painfully to be pretty. "I will try to make myself better in any way I possibly can," pledges a contemporary diarist. "I will lose weight, get new lenses . . . Good makeup, new clothes and accessories."[26] Her words are echoed by a five-year-old contestant on the horrifyingly popular TV series *Toddlers and Tiaras*. "When I grow up," says Jasmine (her real name), "I want to be a Disney princess that waves . . . Every girl needs her fashion accessories."[27] Being pretty, in other words, has come to define success for millions of girls and young women. And by setting their sights simultaneously so high and so low, most of them, simply by definition, will not make it.

The Parable of Perfect Girls

In the spring of 2007, the Sunday *New York Times* ran a story that tweaked the frayed nerves of an era. Released, as these stories usually are, in the mad weeks of April when hordes of frazzled teenagers are worrying about their college acceptances, the article told the tale of Colby and Esther, two of the "best students at one of the best public high schools in the country."[28] Along with their classmates Kat and Lee and Julie, these girls were standouts in their classes in Latin and philosophy. They ran track and managed the student theater, sang in the gospel choir and volunteered to feed the homeless. They were all, the piece noted, "amazing girls . . . Girls who do everything . . . Girls who have grown up learning they can do anything a boy can do, which is anything they want."[29] But because they were competing against so many other amazing girls—all accomplished, all hyperachieving, all told all their lives they could be whatever they wanted—they were having a surprisingly hard time getting accepted to college, and an ever harder time juggling their own competing desires. "You're supposed to have all these extracurriculars, to play sports and do theater," confessed Julie, an aspiring doctor. "You're supposed to do well in your classes and still have time to go out. You're supposed to do all these things and not go insane."[30]

I read the *Times* piece with a black coffee clasped in my hand and my stomach in my throat. Because I knew all the amazing girls in the front-page, 4,600-word story really, really well. They were all in my son's senior class at the time, and I was worried that they would be pilloried as privileged or hypercompetitive kids. Yet the story was gentle and poignant, describing Kat, a feisty girl with perfect SAT scores who confessed that "it is more important to be hot than smart," and Lee, who dropped AP Physics to play Maggie in *Cat on a Hot Tin Roof.* The reporter captured beautifully the amazing girls I knew and loved—girls who represented all the hopes and dreams that society heaps upon its most promising young women. Everyone told them, all their lives, that they were perfect. And then, all of a sudden, when it really seemed to matter, they weren't.

This is what happens when princesses grow up.

I don't know whether any of these particular girls played with Barbies when they were young, or ever succumbed to the seductive wiles of Cinderella. But I do know that masses of girls like them—smart, confident, attractive, and bold—are hitting their teenage years with more expectations piled upon them than any magic wand could ever dispel. To excel at school. At sports. In theater. Be original, but not eccentric. Be a leader, but stay popular. Start an NGO. And a blog. Have sex but don't get pregnant. And never, ever grow beyond those size 4 jeans. All Sleeping Beauty had to do, by contrast, was wake up and look pretty.

The weight of these concerns is well documented. Beginning in

1994, with the publication of Mary Pipher's surprise bestseller *Reviving Ophelia*, commentators have noted and despaired about the problems that plague contemporary girls as they enter their high school years. Early adolescent girls, Pipher warns, "crash and burn in a social and developmental Bermuda Triangle."[31] "Girls' IQ scores drop and their math and science scores plummet. They lose their resiliency and optimism and become less curious and inclined to take risks. They lose their assertive, energetic, and 'tomboyish' personalities and become deferential, self-critical and depressed."[32] Pipher's fears are echoed, perhaps even more bleakly, by JoAnn Deak's *Girls Will Be Girls*, which describes adolescence as a time when one-quarter of American girls are depressed, twice as many girls as boys attempt suicide, and 80 percent of ten-year-olds think they are fat.[33] Rosalind Wiseman, author of *Queen Bees and Wannabes*, depicts adolescence as a time of nasty cliques and high-stakes beauty pageants; Rachel Simmons, in *Odd Girl Out*, points to an underground culture of psychological aggression.[34] It's a long way from that land by the sea where the rivers all run free and you and me are free to be . . . you and me.

Diving through all this depression, it's tough to figure out just what's gone wrong—or, more precisely, what has happened to girls in the forty short years since *Free to Be* and the fifty since Betty Friedan. Today's girls, after all, are Betty's granddaughters. If the women of my generation—feminism's daughters—were supposed to have it all, then the Esthers and Colbys of the world—*our* daughters—were supposed to have even more. Instead, if you believe the literature on girls in crisis, or if you pass by the counseling center on any elite campus, you quickly see how wrong it's gone. Yes, girls outperform boys in high school and outnumber them in college. Yes, they are winning more Rhodes scholarships and a slowly but steadily increasing number of lucrative athletic scholarships.[35] But they are also starving themselves in record numbers, having more dangerous sex, and relying increasingly on binge drinking and prescription stimulants to get them through. According to one recent study, twelfth-grade girls increasingly find themselves under time pressure, less satisfied than they once were with "the amount of fun [they] are having" and the "friends and people [they] spend time with." Boys, by comparison, are happier.[36]

To be sure, part of this phenomenon may not be phenomenal at all.

Girls, as Joan Jacobs Brumberg describes in her fascinating history of anorexia, have been starving themselves at least since medieval times, when fasting was considered an integral part of female holiness.[37] They have always experienced hormonal swings at puberty, along, presumably, with the sexual angst and uncertainty these changes bring. They have been obsessed with their own beauty ever since men began noticing it and have indulged in bouts of jealousy-induced nastiness for, well, probably forever. (Do you remember the stepmother in Snow White? Or the evil stepsisters in Cinderella?) Girls being girls is nothing new.

What is new, however, and terrifying, is the height of expectations that girls have thrust upon them. Think, just for argument's sake, of the (somewhat random) examples given above. In medieval times, as Brumberg evocatively describes, "fasting girls" frequently denied themselves food as a way of showing devotion to others, and to God.[38] But they weren't trying to demonstrate their devotion *and* get perfect SAT scores while winning the divisional soccer title. Likewise, women who experienced puberty and sexual stirrings across the broad sweep of history generally had mothers and grandmothers to walk them through it—plus the limited expectation that all they had to do with their sexuality was to keep it in check until their wedding night and then perform duties as assigned or requested evermore. Not fulfilling, certainly. Not a whisper of choice. But straightforward at least, and clear. Similar constraints also applied to careers, which for nearly all of women's history fell more generally under the simple heading of "life." For thousands and thousands of years, after all, women weren't supposed to be doctors or lawyers or pottery makers, or actors or singers or bakery bakers. They were supposed to be wives and mothers, to marry and have sex, make babies and take care of them. These chores, to be certain, could be onerous or even dangerous. As subsequent chapters will describe in greater detail, women in earlier eras were not infrequently killed by abusive husbands or mothers-in-law; they were abandoned for being infertile and died by the droves in childbirth. They also typically worked just as hard as their husbands, tending crops or storing food or laboring in small shops. But they didn't have to contend with Astronaut Barbie—with a set of expectations both lofty and contradictory, widely aspired to yet nearly impossible to attain.

It's useful to spend just a few moments with this particular doll.

Like all Barbie dolls, of course, she suffers from impossible proportions. Blown up to real size, she would boast an 18-inch waist and a 36-something-sized bust. (One shudders to consider the effects of zero gravity.) If NASA accepted dolls, she would have to have earned, at a minimum, an advanced degree in science or engineering. She would be working roughly ten to twelve hours a day, with occasional stints of sixteen days aboard some exciting mission like the International Space Shuttle. As of 2011, the total number of women who had ever flown for NASA stood at fifty-four.[39] It's not clear how many of them had families or children, but none, presumably, had Barbie's physical attributes in addition to their own intellectual ones. Because they can't. She is a fantasy, and they are real.

Older playthings, by comparison, and older expectations were far more realistic. Girls played with the tea sets they would someday own, and with the babies they would almost inevitably have. They played at being mothers and dreamed of things that weren't that far-fetched (even marriage to a prince, really, if you define "prince" broadly enough). They weren't being set up, from childhood, to aspire to a dual, and often dueling, set of goals: to be smart and beautiful, happy and successful, a sex goddess and a scientist.

Admittedly, it would be foolhardy to build any theory around a doll—or even around the entirety of Barbies and Bratzes and princess accessories that surround girls at the turn of the twenty-first century. Yet the contradictions they embody extend across a much wider realm as well. Parents today profess a deep desire to raise their girls to be smart and successful; they buy them Baby Einstein Adventure Gyms and books about the universe. Yet by the time these girls are in elementary school, their parents are already expecting them to do worse in math and science than their brothers.[40] By the time they hit puberty, their self-confidence is starting to plummet.[41] In school, well-meaning teachers insist that girls are just as smart as boys; well-meaning courses now include the history of women's suffrage and the works of female writers such as Toni Morrison and Zora Neale Hurston. At home, though, on television, and on every magazine stand in the country, they are being pummeled by messages that run in a distinctly different direction. "Be the belle of the ball!" "Get your crush in 30 days!" Look beautiful, dress sexy, in other words, and all will be yours. Not much about the virtues of strong girls, or independent ones, or shy and bookish types.

There are, to be sure, exceptions. Girls like Caroline Moore, who built a backyard observatory with her dad and discovered a supernova at the age of fourteen. And Julie Zeilinger, who started a feminist blog for teenage girls (The FBomb) and spent her first semester at Barnard checking page proofs for her own book.[42] There are young women clustered around websites like Feministing (www.feministing.com) and Jezebel (www.jezebel.com), devoted to revisiting the feminist dreams that their mothers and grandmothers laid out for them. But the majority of girls—even the smart, successful, outwardly confident and sunny ones—are struggling with the expectations that surround them. Born to be princesses and astronauts, to fly to the skies with stiletto heels, they stumble when reality sets in and the gold stars start to fade. Or, as Courtney Martin poignantly asserts: "We are the unintended side effects of feminism . . . the inheritors of an unspoken legacy of body hatred, and the manifest undiagnosed anxiety, depression, and eating disorders of our mothers . . . We are the children of the now-faster eighties and the anything-is-possible nineties, the daughters of visionary superwomen with buried bitterness. We are the perfect girls and the starving daughters."[43]

And so they do what girls so often do. They don't blame the media, or the men in their lives. They don't blame their mothers, who urged them to shine, or the feminists, who gave them their dreams in the first place. They blame themselves.

Of Fairy Tales and Feminism

Once upon a time girls were raised as little women. The saddest and least fortunate of them, like unfortunate women across time and place, were used or abandoned to suit the whims of those with power, left to die as infants if the family couldn't afford another mouth or sold off as child brides before they reached puberty. The luckiest and wealthiest were pampered almost as toys, primped and curled and tended to so that they in turn could grow up to tend to others.

Feminism strove valiantly to change all that. To change not only how women were treated in adulthood, but—and even more ambitiously, in retrospect—to change how girls were raised and educated. To make them believe, from the time they could think, that they really could be whoever and whatever they wanted. Or, as Letty Cottin Pogrebin wrote in the opening note of *Free to Be*, "We want fantasy without illusion; stories of excitement without cruelty or violence . . . a literature of human diversity that celebrates choice and does not exclude any child from its pleasures because of race or sex . . ."[44]

Growing up, I never realized the extent to which I was bathed in feminist waters. My dynamic, full-time-working mother was adamantly not a "women's libber." I wore dresses to school and yearned for the frippery of Nancy's Victorian dollhouse. Yet the strains of *Free to Be* were all around me, shaping and prodding and propelling me in ways I never even considered. I wholly expected to be a "doctor or teacher or poetry maker," if not as a natural right, then simply as a matter of due course. I dreamed of finding my prince—but assumed without even thinking about it that I would have the option, like Atalanta, of eating purple plums on a grassy field with him and then setting off to see the world.

Yet for generations of younger women—Gen X, Gen Y, and whatever we will eventually dub the children of the early twenty-first century—the dream of Atalanta has shifted into something new, something shinier and more ambitious perhaps; something sexier and smarter and harder to attain. Atalanta was bright and clever. She could fix things and run as fast as the wind. She was a feminist girl—aspirational, but attainable. Today's heroines are tougher to pin down. On the one hand, millions of young women around the world grew up under the spell of Hermione, the tough, brainy, and incorruptible star of J. K. Rowling's massively popular Harry Potter series. Hermione, as one young woman recently wrote to me, "is the smart one! Yes!"[45] On the other hand, though, stands Bella Swan, heroine of the almost equally popular *Twilight* books. Unlike Hermione, Bella is insecure and dependent. She pines for Edward, her vampire boyfriend, and begs him to consummate their love, even if the act is likely to turn her into a vampire as well. Bella, as another young woman explained, "appeals to her readership precisely because she *is* flawed"—self-doubting, obsessive, and almost constantly in peril from one calamity or another.[46] She is the heroine as victim, a throwback to the days of Grimm when shivering young beauties waited mutely for their princes to ride by. Except Bella, unlike Snow White or Sleeping Beauty, is constantly at risk of being *killed* by hers.

So what is it for today's girls? Bella or Hermione? Hannah Montana or pole-dancing Miley Cyrus? Smart or hot?

The answer, of course, is yes. Both. All of the above. Color in every little circle on the computer-generated test. Check every possible box on your list of achievements. Take three Advanced Placement courses—no, wait, maybe five. Be all you ever wanted to be. Be more. Oh, and try not to lose yourself in the process.

Feminism gave my generation of girls a dream. It gave us open doors and equal opportunity, a chance to run as fast as the wind and choose the lives we wanted. And yet, as we lived those lives and passed those dreams to our daughters, something changed. Somehow—without meaning to—we became convinced, and then convinced them, that having it all meant doing it all. That beauty lay within *and* without. And that being good meant being perfect. Generationally speaking, we yanked our daughters out of Brownies and Girl Scouts, homespun organizations focused on service and community, and plunked them instead in tap dance and toddler yoga, traveling soccer leagues and after-school Mandarin. We told them to be smart, and then doused them with glittery body mist en route to the makeup party at Claire's. My parents, at least, were consistent: Want to do well? Work hard. Want a nice dollhouse? Build it!

Today, by contrast, we cosset our girls from birth until high school, pampering them as princesses and then somehow expecting them to leap painlessly into adulthood. We expect them to share feminism's goals (equality, opportunity, independence) without the sisterhood it once provided, and simultaneously to possess the feminine attributes (beauty, motherhood, a prince to call their own) that earlier generations prized. The result is confusion, and an awful lot of guilt. Or, as Anna, a beautiful and talented twenty-five-year-old, recently confided, "Girls need to have all their grandmothers wanted them to have, while looking as pretty as their mothers wanted them to look . . . You try so hard to be who everyone wants you to be while attempting to maintain some kind of individuality and in the end you seem to lose everything."

All, of course, is not lost. Pint-sized girls across America are trooping out each weekend to race across soccer fields and hockey rinks. Dreaming of Hermione, they are flocking to science classes and spelling bees, handling computers and smartphones far more ably than dust mops. Every day, I am surrounded by young women who dazzle me with their audacity and intelligence. Kit, who bakes bread, climbs mountains, and writes phenomenal slam poetry. Naomi, who took off the year before college to serve with the Israeli army. Serene, already a mother at fourteen, who got into every Ivy League college in the country and yearns to be an astrophysicist. I see these girls and I beam. But I also see the pressure they're under. To be a mother *and* an astrophysicist. A baker *and* a poet. To be perfect.

Recently, Mattel held a competition to determine what the next Barbie should be: architect, anchorwoman, computer engineer, environmentalist, or surgeon. Overwhelmingly, girls voted for the anchorwoman. But in a surprising move, female computer engineers around the country staged a rebellion, urging women to get out the vote and "help Barbie get her geek on." And so Mattel worked out a compromise: Computer Engineer Barbie has black leggings, pink glasses, and a top decorated in binary code. And they released Anchorwoman Barbie on the side.

3

sex and the social contract

Do you love me? Will you love me forever?
Do you need me? Will you never leave me?
Will you make me so happy for the rest of my life?
Will you take me away? Will you make me your wife?
    —Meat Loaf, "Paradise by the Dashboard Light," 1977

Come here rude boy, boy, can you get it up?
Come here rude boy, boy, is you big enough?
Take it, take it, baby, baby
Take it, take it, love me, love me
                —Rihanna, "Rude Boy," 2010

Thirty years later, I must confess, it still makes me cringe. Not the "Oh my God what was I doing" kind of cringe, but the slow-blush cringe, the one provoked by a memory of how awkward you were, and how young.

I was seventeen. Michael, my newly acquired boyfriend, was a year older, talented, funny, and model-gorgeous. He taught himself Russian, ran a 4:38 mile, and when I totaled my parents' car, he sneaked into our garage in the middle of the night and constructed a full-sized, functioning set of training wheels around our remaining Ford. It was the first serious relationship for both of us, and we did all the things you're supposed to do when you're young, unencumbered, and in love.

One evening, though, while Michael was spending time with his family, I went to a barbecue with another, older group of friends. We blasted Bruce Springsteen and Dire Straits, kicked a ball around half-heartedly, and drank lots of warm Budweiser. After some time, I found myself in the back of a car, kissing a sweet boy who smelled of pecan sandies. As he picked up the pace, though, I pushed back, and then pushed him off me entirely. "I can't," I said. "I have a boyfriend." "So what?" he countered. I mumbled something I no longer recall and started to back out of the car. He pulled me back, more pleading than angry, and told me that he'd go home and put his arm through the window if I didn't stay with him. "I can't," I repeated. "I have a boyfriend."

And thus the cringing. Because this was 1980, after all, more than a decade after the sexual revolution had ostensibly freed girls like me to kiss, fondle, and embrace whomever we chose. I had no real ties—legal or social—to Michael, or to any other man, for that matter. I was fully able to get birth control, if I wanted it, or an abortion, if I needed one. Like all girls of my era, I was free—totally and completely free—to have sex on my own terms, shorn of the risks and obligations that had bound the generations of women born before me. Yet in my mind there was still a vestigial link between sex and something important, between what a girl gave (a kiss? her virginity?) and what she got (a husband? affection? a movie and popcorn?). I stayed with Michael for another two years. Pecan Sandy Boy showed up the next day, with his arm in a sling but otherwise unharmed.

Today, the link I felt in that car is almost entirely gone. Twenty-nine percent of American girls have sex before they reach the tenth grade. Roughly one-third engage in oral sex during their high school years. And dating has been almost entirely replaced by a more relaxed culture of hanging out and hooking up.[1] Young women are now free to have sex like men—without obligation, without fear of consequence, without necessarily even knowing his name. Or, as one young woman recently recounted, "Like, I had been talking to this guy and we were just, like, friends or whatever, but, like, I don't really remember what happened . . . I remember getting back to my room . . . I ended up sleeping with him."[2]

These are the freedoms that the sexual revolution unleashed. Before the 1960s, girls had sex as society said they should: after marriage, monogamously, and in private. They had sex to have babies, sex to please their husbands, sex that kept its passions tightly in check. Or, as an article from *Mademoiselle* reminisced, "If you wanted sex, you got married; society required it—it was not optional. Men pursued women ardently and openly; women pursued men ardently and covertly. The game was clear to all players."[3] After the mid-1960s, though—after Helen Gurley Brown cheerfully advised single girls to keep married men as pets and Erica Jong extolled the virtues of the "zipless fuck," after the pill and *Playboy* and *Roe v. Wade*—young women rapidly embraced a radically changed culture. Suddenly, sex was something to be experienced well before marriage. It was about women's pleasures as well as men's. And it had little to do anymore with producing babies.

All of these changes have occurred in a blindingly short period of time. All of them were supposed to be liberating, allowing women and girls to seize control of their sexuality and use their bodies as *they*—not their husbands or their parents or their pastors—wished. Indeed, one of the great cries of feminism during the 1970s and 1980s was for women to see their bodies as blessings rather than gifts, something to be enjoyed and shared rather than hoarded and bartered away. In *The Joy of Sex*, for example, the überbible of 1970s sexuality, women are urged to abandon their physical inhibitions and indulge in sex without rules. Which isn't exactly what their mothers' marriage manuals had suggested. "Explore," *Joy* purrs. "Experiment." "Give (a kiss, a caress, an orgasm) and ye shall receive."

Not surprisingly, few sex manuals traipse easily between the worlds of lust and lucre. Sex is about sex, after all (mixed at least occasionally with affection); money is about money (which does not partake of love). Yet notions of exchange have long been connected to sexual relations. Often, and particularly in ancient societies, the terms of the contract were explicit: one cow, say, three goats, and a dozen gold bracelets in exchange for a wife. More recent terms were subtler but no less clear: for the price of a movie or dinner, a young man might legitimately hope to hold his date's hand or kiss her chastely on the cheek. For a lifetime of financial support, he got her virginity and ongoing sexual access. These are the terms that run through all cultural references to sex and marriage until the early 1960s; they are the terms whose remnants haunted me still in 1980. And these are the terms that have finally, and fundamentally, been overturned by the sexual revolution.

Today, women no longer see their sexuality as something to be bartered for anything else. Instead, following the path prescribed by Jong and Brown, heeding the advice of the sex education classes they have taken since middle school, and armed with the packets of grape-flavored condoms that their schools and mothers freely bestow upon them, women are eagerly exchanging sex for—well, sex. They give oral sex and receive it. Bring their partners to orgasm and expect the same in return. There is no further commitment in the hookup culture and no contract that extends beyond the act, the bar, the night. This is the sexual freedom that women have won; a freedom that makes sex truly priceless.

The question, however, is whether this freedom has come at a cost. Clearly, women today can engage in acts that would have made their mothers blush. They can enjoy their bodies without shame and have sex largely without fear of pregnancy. They face none of the stigmas that paralyzed women in the past and suffer, accordingly, from far fewer inhibitions. In exchanging simply sex for sex, women are truly playing the same game as men—and often, it appears, with the same relish and abandon. "Just like tasting ice cream flavors," one website promises, "sampling sex with a new guy is what being young and single is all about."[4] Yet unless women actually enjoy casual sex as much as men do, and unless they are equally content with no-name, no-commitment relationships, they still, in retrospect, may have struck a deal that works against their own best interests. Because, crude though it may sound, women arguably had more leverage over men when they had the ability and inclination to deny them sex. Presumably, women had greater resources when dating still involved a little bit of financial foreplay. So what, then, have young women gained in their pursuit of liberty? And was it worth the price?

A Brief History of Lust

Prior to the Renaissance, the very notion of courtship made little sense. In most parts of the world, across time, religion, and political regime, women were viewed essentially as property—commodities for their fathers to barter away and their husbands to use. In ancient Athens, for example, "respectable" women (that is, women of the citizen class) were expected to be virgins before marriage and wholly faithful to the husbands who were joined to them through arranged unions. While Athenian men were free to consort with slaves, concubines, prostitutes, and adolescent *gymnasium* boys, women were largely confined to the home, where, presumably, opportunities for love or lust were rare.[5] The sexual affairs of Roman and early Jewish women were similarly constrained (although wealthy Roman women did apparently indulge more frequently in adultery),[6] as were those of Islamic women, who often lived in *harim*, secluded quarters of the home designed to separate women from nonrelated men.

After the fourth century A.D., the gradual spread of Augustinian Christianity across Western Europe quietly redefined the role women played and the freedoms they might enjoy. Because Christian societies increasingly saw women as wives and mothers rather than property, and because they placed such importance on procreative (that is, marital) sex, the areas of the former Roman Empire slowly began to cede greater rights to women. Across Europe, the Church democratized marriage and praised its "companionate" form, in which the man and woman had at least some feelings for each other. It forbade divorce (which arguably protected women as well as occasionally constraining them) and, by celebrating celibacy, gave women a respectable and previously unavailable option.[7] Lust, however, in all its forms, was forcefully condemned. And women's lust, seen as it was as the vestige of Eve's original sin, was particularly suspect. As a result, women living during the long centuries of the Middle Ages were free to love, but only chastely, following the dictates of their husbands, their Church, and their God.

Such restrictions became somewhat less onerous during the Renaissance (stretching roughly from the fourteenth through seventeenth centuries), when a general embrace of science and the arts served to lessen the overarching power of the Church and its far-flung clergy.[8] As the Industrial Revolution unfolded, however, matters became more ambiguous—and in many ways more interesting. Beginning in the early decades of the nineteenth century, the simultaneous explosion of communication and transportation technologies brought millions of laborers into the growing cities of Europe and North America, disrupting centuries-old patterns of rural life and diminishing the traditional pull of families. For the first time, young people were traveling—by boat or railroad or streetcar—far from their homes and parents, and relying on strangers to provide both jobs and advice.

Much of this change manifested itself in the Victorians' notorious embrace of repression. This was the era, after all, when the students of one women's seminary reportedly clothed the legs of their piano in slender, modesty-enhancing trousers.[9] It was an era when preachers, professors, and other sages regularly exhorted their audiences to control the sin that was sexual lust, and when one popular marriage manual calmly advised couples to wait three years between successful acts of intercourse (success, not surprisingly, being defined as the production of a child).[10] It was a time when sexual contact between unmarried couples was expressly forbidden; when men's foremost responsibility in the sexual realm was to control their own passions; and when women were expected only to suffer quietly and bear children. History records these sentiments most famously in Queen Victoria's wedding night advice to her daughter. "Lie back," she is said to have counseled the young princess, "and think of England."

Even as the Victorians were thinking of the empire, though, it appears that quite a few of them were also thinking about sex. Indeed, numerous recent studies suggest that the men and women of the late nineteenth century were a rather raunchy bunch, at least in comparison with their public selves. Between 1850 and 1900, for instance, the rate of premarital pregnancies in the United States rose from under 10 percent of all firstborn children to nearly 20.[11] Since premarital pregnancies (that is, those of women who get married after they're pregnant but before they give birth) tend to coincide with illegitimate pregnancies (those of women who don't marry after becoming pregnant), it is not unreasonable to estimate that up to a third of all supposedly chaste Victorian women may actually have conceived their first child out of wedlock—and this during a time when overall fertility rates among American women were plummeting.[12] More vividly, in a survey of Victorian-era love letters, the historian Karen Lystra reveals that passions among young couples frequently ran high. One James Hague, for example, finished a letter to his fiancée by imploring, "Darling, darling, *darling*. Oh! how I love you!! I want to *maul* you. Good bye, sweetie.

Yours Forever."[13] Unmarried couples, Lystra is careful to note, were not necessarily engaging in sex. In fact, most of them probably were not. But they were engaging in a considerable amount of sexual activity—kissing, cuddling, and, as one amorous suitor implored, "hold[ing] you in my arms, and press[ing] your tired head down to its throbbing pillow with my great square hand."[14] What defined these relationships, though, was a powerful link between sexual intimacy and romantic love. Or, as Lystra writes, "Sexual expressions were read as symbolic communications of one's real and truest self, part of the hidden essence of the individual . . . Sex could be sacred and sexuality might be spiritual, if affection were blended with desire."[15] The bargain, then, for Victorian women was straightforward and rather sweet: sex in exchange for a lifetime commitment of love.

This connection between love and lust—between sexual intimacy and long-term attachment—became a hallmark of social relations in the twentieth century, shaping most Americans' (and to a lesser degree, most Europeans') basic conception of what it meant to want, and woo, and marry. Over the years, the contours of courtship ebbed and flowed, moving, for instance, from the relative freedoms of Jazz Age dating (he pays, she plays, they dance all night and drink illicit gin) to the conservative norms of the postwar years (he pays, she gets pinned, they start planning the wedding). What remained throughout this period, though, was a deep and uncontested sense of the underlying contract that was "the date." Put bluntly, women gave sexual favors—be they kisses or fondles or actual intercourse—in exchange for *something*. Men paid in cash, women in kind. This isn't to say that women in the 1920s, or 1930s, or 1950s were any less smitten with their beaux than their mothers and grandmothers had been. On the contrary, romantic love remained the ideal throughout this period, highlighted now by movies, magazines, and advice books that trumpeted the wonders of that "one special someone." It's just that the path to bliss was longer now than in the Victorian era, cluttered with more options, more opportunities, and a much more explicit set of financial expectations. In 1930, for example, one high school girl laid out her own criteria. "I don't give many second dates," she proclaimed, "unless they can take me to keen places. Some of the fellows I'd like to go with can't afford it, and I just don't go with them, that's all."[16] As if in retaliation, a 1938 "guidebook" for young men offered advice on winning various types of women. For the "prom queen," potential suitors were counseled to "spend money like water. You don't win prom princesses," the author asserted, "you buy them."[17]

Such was the state of affairs until the mid-1960s, when technological developments and changing social mores conspired to unleash the sexual revolution.

Talkin' 'Bout a Revolution

What, exactly, was this revolution? In retrospect, much of it was actually an evolution, a slowly accumulating roster of social changes that had been seeping across Europe and North America since the 1920s: the greater availability of birth control; the rising divorce rate; a growing explicitness around sex; even the explosions of jazz and rock music. By the late 1960s, these various and disparate trends suddenly seemed to coalesce, though, into something new—a wave of sexual permissiveness that engulfed the Western world and smashed social mores to shards.[18]

Much of this change, of course, hinged on the rapidly evolving politics of reproduction. In 1957, following several years of successful trials in Puerto Rico, the pharmaceutical firm Searle introduced Enovid into the U.S. market. Technically prescribed for "gynecological disorders," the drug was also described as causing "possible contraceptive activity."[19] By 1960, when Searle received formal approval to market Enovid as a contraceptive, an estimated half a million women were already taking "the pill," suffering, apparently, from a rash of formerly undiagnosed gynecological ailments. By 1963, a reported 1.75 million American women were using the pill; by 1973, the number had soared to 10 million, making Enovid one of the most successful (and profitable) products ever brought to market.[20]

Wondrous though it was, however, Searle's little pill was hardly the world's first attempt at controlling pregnancy. Indeed, for centuries before its introduction, men and women had been managing contraception through techniques that ranged from potions made of crocodile dung and unripe acacia (the ancient Egyptians' preferred methods) to coitus interruptus and condoms fashioned from sheep's intestines. But something about the pill was different. It was safe. It was easy. And it put the power to control reproduction entirely in women's hands. It may not have been entirely coincidental that Clairol ran an ad for hair dye during this time that coyly asked, "Does she or doesn't she? Only her hairdresser knows for sure." Because that is precisely the privacy, and thus the freedom, promised by the pill. Does she or doesn't she? There were no longer any public markers of a woman's promiscuity. Only her doctor knew for sure. By 1980, when I started college, any young women who showed up at her local clinic—with or without her mother, with or without her boyfriend, with or without a story—could waltz out anonymously fifteen minutes later, a slim disk of protection stashed demurely in her purse.

Meanwhile, the slow but steady expansion of abortion rights in the United States meant that, in those (now much rarer) cases when contraception failed, women still had the ability to prevent pregnancy. In 1973, the landmark case of *Roe v. Wade* ruled that the state could not interfere with a woman's right to choose abortion during the first two trimesters of pregnancy and thus guaranteed, in theory at least, legal access to abortion to women across the United States. France, West Germany, and Italy followed suit with similarly liberalized laws several years later; Sweden, Denmark, and the states of the Soviet bloc had done so in the 1950s. By the late 1970s, therefore, the link between sex and procreation, between wanting men and wanting babies, had been almost entirely severed across the Western world.[21] Women were free to have sex whenever they wanted, unburdened by the fears and consequences that had bound them in the past. This was the driver of the sexual revolution.

Yet, as with all revolutions, the change that ripped across society was bigger and more complicated than the spark that lay at its core. Because in this case, before the pill was really in widespread use, and way before *Roe* was law, changes also started to erupt around the norms of sexuality and the specific terms under which women chose to have sex. In the 1960s, and for the first time in history, women began to play with the possibility of having sex not to have babies, or please their husbands, or abide by the terms of an underlying contract—but solely because they liked it. Until this point, sexual pleasure for women had

been defined almost entirely in terms of vaginal orgasms and monogamous, submissive marriages. If women enjoyed sex (and there was no
expectation that they would), it was because they were craving motherhood or spiritual union, and because their husbands were well trained
and equipped to pleasure them. Or, as Freud, whose analysis dominated discussions of sex in the early twentieth century, described it:
"very often the experience signifies a disappointment to the woman,
who remains cold and unsatisfied."[22] After Freud, however, a stream of
emerging "sexologists" slowly began to unpack the question of female
libido, using novel techniques—including surveys, video cameras, and
a transparent vaginal probe named Ulysses—to explore the drivers of
desire. In 1954, Alfred Kinsey published his path-breaking work, *Sexual Behavior in the Human Female*, arguing, essentially, that an orgasm was an orgasm, regardless of who created it, who enjoyed it, and
how it came to be.[23] In 1966, William Masters and Virginia Johnson
published the even more radical *Human Sexual Response*, describing
precisely how women reached orgasm (clitorally, they insisted) and
how often they were capable of it.[24] For the first time, women were
hearing about sex, and talking about sex, as something that belonged
to them and gave them pleasure, rather than something to be hoarded
and bartered away.

Once the revolution had sprung forth, word of its arrival spread
swiftly. Women's magazines, for example, shifted rather suddenly in
the mid-1960s from describing sex in reverent and hushed tones to
trumpeting its virtues and offering play-by-play accounts of its techniques; men's magazines, led loudly and most famously by Hugh Hefner's *Playboy*, attacked the legal tenets of pornography in the United
States, arguing that sexual content—even explicit and graphic sexual
content—should be protected as free speech.[25] Television and movies
became increasingly more liberal, moving beyond the separate-bedded
scenarios of the 1950s to showcase not only liberated women like Ann
Marie (Marlo Thomas in *That Girl*) and Mary Richards (Mary Tyler
Moore in *The Mary Tyler Moore Show*), but also frontal nudity (*Blow-
Up*, 1966), nude male actors (*Georgy Girl*, 1966), and even oral sex (*I Am
Curious (Yellow)*, 1969). And sexual education, for girls like me, now
began as early as the fourth grade. We didn't have breasts yet. We
hadn't gotten our periods. Almost all of us (well, okay, me) were still

twice as tall as any boy in the class. But thanks to the helpful film that our gym teacher spun on the projector (*Mr. Sperm! Miss Egg! All those body parts we didn't want to mention!*) we were very well informed about the power of the orgasm.

The sexual revolution of the 1960s and 1970s was so sweeping in scope that no single film, or publication, or protest movement can truly be said to capture its essence. Still, two books emerged during this period that seem to have both bracketed the revolution and fomented it—two books that told women what was now theirs to claim.

The first, Helen Gurley Brown's *Sex and the Single Girl*, was published in 1962, right at the revolution's outset and one year before Betty Friedan's far more serious *The Feminine Mystique*. Unlike Friedan's, Brown's book was breezy and stylistically unimpressive, filled not with footnotes and research but rather with the kind of cheerful advice that had long peppered how-to manuals for girls. Rather than bemoaning the status of women, Brown embraced her readers with a perky self-confidence, offering makeup tips ("You need mascara, eyebrow pencil, fluid eyeliner, blush, shadow in several shades and a regular brushy eye brush . . . *all* of these for eye-citement"), wardrobe advice ("Don't buy anything, not so much as a garter belt, you don't *adore*"), and recipes for crabmeat puffs and pepper steak españa. In between, though, she also urged them to have sex—frequently, on their own terms, and way before they were married. "I think marriage is insurance for the *worst* years of your life," she asserts. "During your best years you don't need a husband. You do need a man of course every step of the way, and they are often cheaper emotionally and a lot more fun by the dozen."[26] Sex, according to Brown, "isn't some random piece of mischief you dreamed up because you're a bad, wicked girl."[27] It was instead a "wonderful, delicious, exquisite thing," a thing to be used by women, and enjoyed by women, and even, if necessary, employed against men.[28] This was sex as women's power for the very first time in print; sex that was truly revolutionary in its impact.

The second monumental voice of the sexual revolution was *Fear of Flying*, a novel that would eventually sell more than 18 million copies and capture the voice, or at least the guilty dreams, of an entire generation.[29] In *Fear*, the fictional Isadora Wing famously describes her fantasy of the "zipless fuck," an encounter that is both explicitly sexual and wholly impersonal. This particular fuck, author Erica Jong wrote, "was more than a fuck. It was a platonic ideal. Zipless because when you came together zippers fell away like rose petals, underwear blew off in one breath like dandelion fluff. Tongues intertwined and turned liquid. Your whole soul flowed out through your tongue and into the mouth of your lover."[30] From the perspective of forty years, it's interesting to note (once you stop focusing on all the "fucks") that Wing is actually describing something not all that different from the yearnings voiced by her Victorian ancestors. Because it's kissing, after all, and romance, and garments blown 'round like flowers. No, what really defined the zipless fuck and made Isadora's fantasy so radical was that the relationship was short and the man essentially anonymous. The unnamed soldier makes love to the young widow in the speeding train and then parts silently from her. The passing stranger ignites a passion that the husband long ago killed. Sex isn't just about sex to Isadora. It's about freedom. About passion. About choice. And it has nothing to do, necessarily, with either romance or commitment.

Fear of Flying struck a powerful chord in 1973, shooting onto bestseller lists around the world and staying there throughout 1974 and 1975. Part of its appeal was probably just the sex. Before *Flying*, no woman had written quite so vividly, and so baldly, about intercourse and orgasm, fantasies and affairs. As a result, as Jong later noted, "it became the book teenagers read to learn about sex, the book women read to liberate themselves, the book men read to learn about women."[31] (I know. It saved me from that gym film, my only prior resource.) The bigger bang of *Flying*, though, came from the vigor with which Jong separated sex from romance, and marriage from sex. Until *Fear of Flying*—or, more precisely, until the shift in social norms that Brown captured and Jong brought to conclusion—women were still bound by the contractual nature of courtship: sex in exchange for a husband or protector, two cows or true love. Afterward, it was just about sex.

As with all revolutions, again, the sexual revolution had brought together an unlikely band of fighters, many of whom struggled for entirely disparate ends. Hugh Hefner, for example, was fighting for free speech and (more important, presumably) the right to make lots of money from showing pictures of naked women to men. The leaders of the abortion rights movement, gathered under the powerful semantic umbrella of "pro-choice," were fighting for bodily integrity and health, for women to be able to end unwanted pregnancies safely, securely, and without shame. The purveyors of the pill were selling drugs to make a profit, and the television networks, record labels, and magazine publishers who rushed to the revolution and fed its flames were generally following social trends rather than consciously leading them. Yet, arguably, the changes that were eventually unleashed by the sexual revolution were both bigger than and different from what any of these revolutionaries had intended. Because by the early 1980s, sex had escaped, in nearly all cases, from the confines of marriage. It didn't come with a prescribed list of commitments anymore. It did not lead inevitably to pregnancy. And it wasn't something to be enjoyed only by men.

In the late 1960s, 14 percent of white girls in the United States and 35 percent of black girls had had sex by the time they were sixteen. By the early 1980s, those figures had shot up, respectively, to 33 and 50 percent.[32]

Of Hanging Out and Hooking Up

Many years ago, during the era of ABBA and the Village People, I spent my summer working at the local YMCA. It was one of the best jobs I've ever had. I got to spend an inordinate amount of time lounging around the pool in a swimsuit and learned vital lessons from my fellow (male) swim instructors, like what "blue balls" felt like and how to bake a good hash brownie. (Actually, it was just how to make a hash brownie, period. I really have no idea how to discern quality here.) I played lots of clumsy softball and narrowly escaped tragedy when I crashed my parents' car while driving home our car pool. It was summer. I was seventeen.

One week, I was stuck with art duty. It was usually a relatively easy post, with endless strings of lanyard and tubes of glitter to deploy. But this week it rained. For five gray and endless days. My fellow counselor was a sweet boy named Jonathan Larson (who, though I had no way of knowing it at the time, would go on to create Rent before dying tragically at the age of thirty-five). For the first two days we cheerfully innovated with our lanyards and glitter. On the third day we patiently took our charges through advanced popsicle stick construction. And on the fourth day we lost it. We were out of glitter, out of glue, and just about out of our minds with boredom. So on a whim, we took the lone remaining glue bottle and taught our campers how to play Spin the Bottle. Never in the history of the American Camping Association has a group of nine-year-olds quieted down so quickly. Never has a rainy-day art program become quite as popular as did ours. By lunchtime, the kids were streaming in from the sodden kickball fields and the nature lodge; by the next day, we were the talk of the YMCA and several parents had called to demand our immediate dismissal.

I am happy to report that the Spin the Bottle saga ended gracefully. The sun returned, Jonathan and I kept our jobs, and the kids (none of whom had ventured more than a timid peck on the cheek) returned to their birdhouses and macramé. To the best of my knowledge it was the first—and last—time that glue bottles were ever so happily deployed at the Westchester YMCA.

Today, of course, it's hard to imagine that Spin the Bottle would impress either nine-year-olds or their parents. Instead, kids as young as twelve and thirteen are regularly reported to be attending "rainbow parties" (at which girls wearing different shades of lipstick take turns performing oral sex on boys), or engaging more directly in sexual behaviors that include oral sex.* The old "base" system—a kiss for first, breasts for second, groping for third, and intercourse for home—has been rendered utterly obsolete, replaced by a shifting game whose rules are not quite clear.

Meanwhile, the dating culture that persisted from around the turn of the twentieth century to its waning years seems almost to have disappeared, replaced—for better or worse—by "hooking up." Young men in high school and college no longer ask young women out on dates. Couples don't "go out" or "go steady." Instead, boy meets girl at a party

---

*It's not entirely clear whether these parties have actually occurred or are just commonly being described (by teenagers) and feared (by their parents). See Tamar Lewin, "Are These Parties for Real?" *New York Times*, June 30, 2005, and Laura Sessions Stepp, "Unsettling New Fad Alarms Parents: Middle School Oral Sex," *Washington Post*, July 8, 1999, p. A1.

or frat house or bar and takes her home for sex. This is courtship at the dawn of the twenty-first century. This is "hooking up."

As a phrase, "hooking up" leaves much to be desired. That's because it's purposefully vague, meaning anything from a kiss on the lips to full-on sex. A report prepared for the conservative-leaning Institute for American Values rather politely describes it as "when a girl and a guy get together for a physical encounter and don't necessarily expect anything further."[33] *The Happy Hook-Up* adds "any form of intimacy from making out to heavy petting to oral sex to actual intercourse."[34] But perhaps most useful is the depiction presented in Andrea Lavinthal and Jessica Rozler's *Hookup Handbook* (seriously). Here goes:

- Girl A sort of knows Boy B (maybe they were in the same Psych 101 class, have mutual friends, or perhaps they've even slept together before).
- Girl A goes out to the bar with her friends, and Boy B goes out to the bar with his friends.
- Girl A stands in one corner of the bar, downs cosmopolitans, screams the words to "Like a Prayer" at the top of her lungs, and pretends to ignore Boy B.
- Boy B stands in another corner of the bar and chugs beer with his friends.
- When Girl A finally gets enough courage (i.e., is drunk enough), she approaches Boy B and says, "Hey, what's going on?"
- When Boy B finally realizes that Girl A is the best he's going to do tonight, he answers, "Nothin'."
- The two proceed to make out at the bar and then go back to his place and "hook up."[35]

If we were to follow A and B (along with the script laid out in the *Handbook*) we'd probably find them back in his dorm room, or car, or perhaps hastily squeezed into a convenient stairwell. They would kiss and grope for sure, and might proceed to engage in either intercourse or oral sex. Most likely, they would both be sufficiently drunk so that their memories of the evening and each other would be forever dim. Girl A might nudge Boy B to text the number she quietly entered into his phone. Boy B probably won't. Girl A might join her sisters in the early-morning ritual dubbed "the walk of shame," with makeup smeared and head held high. Boy B might choose to give her a "booty call," a few weeks later, dialing for sex if there aren't other options.

Now isn't that romantic?

In one recent survey of college students, 75 percent of the male respondents and 84 percent of the females reported having hooked up at least once during their college years. On average, the "experienced participants" had had 10.28 hookups during their college years, with no statistical difference in number between the men and the women. In more than half of these cases, the partners had never before met.[36]

In some ways, the advent of the hooking-up culture is a return to the sexual heyday of the 1970s, to a world of liberated women and self-seeking pleasures and free love. Look closely enough and the entreaties of contemporary hookup guides ("It feels good and . . . it makes you feel good about yourself"[37]) reveal the skeletal remains of radical feminism—Germaine Greer's embrace of full-body sexuality, for instance, or Mary Jane Sherfey's celebration of women's multiorgasmic potential.[38] There are echoes of sexual freedom as political freedom, and of women using their bodies as sources of power.[39]

Whereas radical feminism was about uncovering and then dismantling the patriarchy, though, hooking up seems blissfully divorced from any kind of social, much less political or philosophical, agenda. In the 1970s, feminists like Greer and Sherfey were trumpeting sexual liberation as a way for women to attack male authority and end centuries of oppression. Greer, for example, famously declared that "I have always been principally interested in men for sex";[40] Sherfey likewise argued that "women's inordinate orgasmic capacity did not evolve for monogamous, sedentary cultures."[41] By reclaiming the female body as a source of their own needs and desires, women could break from the age-old pattern of defining their lives in terms of pleasing men. By understanding sexual patterns (the virginal bride, the faithful wife, the missionary position) as political structures, women could challenge them and make them change. Or, as Kate Millett argued in *Sexual Politics*, the "goal of revolution would be a permissive single standard of sexual freedom, and one uncorrupted by the crass and exploitative economic bases of traditional sexual alliances."[42]

The hooking-up culture, by comparison, seems perfectly content to let boys be boys—especially if they're well-muscled and tousle-haired and drive a nice car. Men are "hot" rather than oppressive in hookup-land; desirable rather than despicable. Indeed, hooking up lets women paint men much as men have traditionally, or at least stereotypically, painted women: as objects, and playthings, and tokens of success. At Duke University, home to some of the smartest and most successful young women in the country, "Allison," a junior from New York, con-fessed to a *Rolling Stone* reporter that she had hooked up with an at-tractive fraternity guy for more than a year, prompted by a "constant fear of losing." "When you're in a relationship with somebody, espe-cially with somebody in the frat scene, you're lucky to be with him."[43] In theory, then, the advent of hooking up has meant that men are now commodified as easily and frequently as women. In practice, though, it also means that women are no longer in a position to ask for anything but sex in exchange for sex—not marriage, not a date, not even a phone call the next morning or a ride home. Women are as free as men to have sex simply for pleasure. And men are free to do pretty much what-ever they want. Which isn't exactly what the earlier feminists thought would be in store.

Ironically, though, part of what drives the hookup culture is a de-sire for young women to have it all; a desire for a *Sex and the City* life-style full of clothes, shoes, jobs, and (multiple, revolving, ancillary) men. Because young women today are so ambitious, many will insist, and because they have so many options to pursue during their teens and early twenties, hooking up gives them an efficient way to tend to their physical needs without compromising their careers or education. Or, as Laura Sessions Stepp writes in *Unhooked: How Young Women Pursue Sex, Delay Love, and Lose at Both*, "Hooking up enables a young woman to practice a piece of a relationship, the physical, while devot-ing most of her energy to staying on the honor roll, being accepted into a well-known university and then keeping up her academic scholarship while working ten or fifteen hours a week in the cafeteria, playing la-crosse, working out every day in the gym and applying to graduate programs in engineering."[44] My young friend Celia, freshly returned from two summer internships and a solo trip across South Asia, reports nearly the same sentiment. "I really like the freedom of not having a boyfriend," she says thoughtfully over a glass of iced tea. "I mean, I'm so busy, and there's so much going on in my life, and a boyfriend seems like an awful lot of work." So flings and brief encounters serve her fine for now, and relationships can wait.

The question, though, is whether this freedom has come at a cost. Do young women really enjoy their one-night stands—their foam parties and pickups, booty calls and walks of shame—as much as young men do? Are they comfortable with the fact that men continue to evaluate them (online now, and in increasingly public spaces like Facebook) on their looks, their weight, and their promiscuity? Or has their adoption of male behavior actually just given the sexual advantage back to men?

It's hard for me to render a judgment without sounding, and feeling, hopelessly middle-aged. Older people have been criticizing the sexual behavior of teenagers, after all, from time immemorial. And teenagers have continued to have sex all the same—on their terms, in evolving patterns, and without any noticeable damage to the human race. But still, there's something about hooking up that seems to reflect a diminution of women's choices rather than an expansion, a decrease in women's power rather than a rise.

Ultimately, the crux of the matter is whether women truly enjoy the freedom that comes from uncommitted sex. And it's not clear that they do. Instead, as Stepp reports in *Unhooked*, many of the women who embrace the hookup culture for some period of time (usually their freshman year of college) later come to regret it. Rather than feeling empowered by their conquests, they feel abandoned by the men they thought might be their boyfriends. Rather than whisking blithely from one affair to the next, they are waiting by the phone (now, at least, conveniently in their pocket) for last night's encounter to call them back. Because the hookup is so clearly *not* about commitment, though, he rarely does. And the women are left, longing for something they swore they didn't want.

In a recent survey, a team of psychologists interviewed nearly two hundred college students about their hookup practices.[45] In statistical terms, the men and women were essentially identical: roughly the same percentage of both sexes had participated in hookups, with roughly the same level of frequency. Their answers to qualitative questions, however, revealed some interesting differences. When asked, for example, *How do males/females feel after hooking up?* a typical male answer ran something like this: "Males either hope that another pure hookup with this female can occur or they hope that the female does not expect a relationship to come out of this. Females are usually concerned with being considered a whore so they are usually compelled to seek a meaningful relationship." A typical female response, by contrast, grumbled that "Females the next day may feel cheap or used. The males feel like they have fulfilled sexual needs and have added another girl to the list they like to brag about." Similarly, when asked *How does it end?* women say that "It ends when both have satisfied each other and realize that the hookup is complete." Men, more cynically, perhaps, but quite candidly, report that, "It ends when both partners have been satisfied, usually ending with the male. At this time comes an awkward moment when the two put their clothes back on and realize they have nothing to talk about."[46] Reviewing all their data, the researchers also found that feelings of regret varied sharply between men and women. Women who regretted hooking up felt bad because of the hookup itself; they were embarrassed and blamed themselves for engaging in bad behavior. Men, on the other hand, regretted hooking up if they felt they had chosen an unattractive girl.

My friend Celia, sipping her tea, is quiet when I ask her whether young women enjoy hookups as much as young men do. "I don't think so," she says slowly. "I mean, it's fun, and it's easy, but it feels kind of empty. Maybe for the boys *and* the girls. I like having the choice of what kind of relationship to have, but it doesn't always feel like such a great choice."

Terms of Endearment

It is dangerous, of course, to mingle talk of love and money. For love is love, and money is money, and sex—at least in the hookup world—is really just sex. Yet, as noted earlier, sex has long been connected to some underlying notion of exchange; to some sense, in other words, that each of the parties in a sexual relationship was getting something—be it property or pleasure or a lifetime of protection—out of it. Hooking up challenges this historical relationship. Echoing the anthem of the sexual revolution, it presumes that men and women are free to have sex whenever they want, with whomever they want, and with no commitment implied by the act. Accordingly, all of the ancient terms of exchange, be they a cow for a wife or a movie in exchange for a goodnight kiss, fall entirely away. There is no payment associated with hooking up, and no presumed emotional contact. It is the zipless fuck taken to its logical, inevitable extreme. It is, as Jong wrote, "absolutely pure . . . The man is not 'taking' and the woman is not 'giving.'"[47] In a hookup, one blog advises, "[there] is an agreement between both parties not to expect anything emotionally more than an occasional fling. This way no one gets hurt because they're just 'friends with benefits.'"[48]

The question, though, is whether women truly get equal value from a relationship based on "free" sex. Are they equally content to give—and get—sex for nothing, or have they perhaps given men what they want (easy, cheap sex) without getting much in return?

In purely economic terms, the answer must simply be no. No, women are not better off giving away something they once bartered. No, women do not gain by losing the power they once had to force men to buy their favors. In a fascinating paper published in the *Quarterly Journal of Economics* (admittedly, not well known for its spellbinding prose), a trio of leading economists have put rigorous mathematical models around this depressing hypothesis, showing in particular how the advent of abortion and contraception in the United States may actually have worsened the fate of women, or at least weakened their ability to bargain with men. Specifically, they demonstrate that just as women gained the power to prevent pregnancy so, too, did they *lose* the power to commit men to marriage in the case of an unwanted pregnancy. Or as they explain, "when the cost of abortion is low, or contraceptives are readily available, potential male partners can easily obtain sexual satisfaction without making such promises and will thus be reluctant to commit to marriage." "The consequence," they write, "is that after abortion and contraception become easily available, there is a new equilibrium in which no woman—even if she wants children and marriage—asks for a promise of marriage. In this equilibrium if any woman did ask for such a promise, her partner would leave, and she would lose the relationship."[49]

Now, none of this would matter much if women viewed long-term relationships in the same way as men. In other words, if both men and women at the turn of the twenty-first century prefer casual sex to committed relationships, then both have benefited from the mutual embrace of hanging out and hooking up. In economic terms, a shift in the terms of trade (driven by contraception, access to abortion, and a change in social mores) may have increased the gains of trade for both partners.

Yet the evidence, both anecdotal and biological, seems to suggest a very different view. All of the academic surveys of hooking up reveal a distinct uneasiness among the young women involved, a queasy morning-after sense that what they get out of hooking up isn't quite equivalent to what they give. "I was mad at myself and lied to my friends and said we didn't have sex," one young woman reported. "I felt a little used and gypped," confessed another.[50] These views tend to get stronger as the young women get older, and as they start to focus (earlier, and more vigorously than the men in their lives) on the prospect of kids. Meanwhile, scientists who study the dynamics of sex offer strong reasons why men and women may—at a basic, biological level—approach the relationship in fundamentally different ways. In evolutionary terms, after all, men and women are both programmed to perform one critical function: to reproduce themselves, and thereby the species. *How* they perform this function, however, varies dramatically between the two sexes. Men, whose major reproductive role occurs at the moment of insemination, can best achieve their reproductive potential by inseminating as many women as possible. Women, by contrast, whose reproductive role extends through nine months of pregnancy and then years of caring for a vulnerable child, increase their chances of reproductive success by ensuring that someone will help them through the difficult months and years. Or, as Robert L. Trivers, an anthropologist and sociobiologist at Rutgers University, explains, "In the human species . . . a copulation costing the male virtually nothing may trigger a nine-month investment by the female that is not trivial, followed, if she wishes, by a fifteen-year investment in the offspring that is considerable." Given this imbalance, he writes, "the male may maximize his chances of leaving surviving offspring by copulating and abandoning many females, some of whom, alone or with the aid of others, will raise his offspring."[51] In other words, women thrive by finding someone who will help to raise their children. Men thrive—evolutionarily, at least—by sleeping around. Thirty-two percent of men (but only 8 percent of women) report having imagined sexual encounters with over a thousand partners in their lifetime.[52]

Biology, of course, is not destiny. And just because women may have been programmed to seek the comforts of the cavemen who would provide for their young doesn't mean that modern women, armed with clubs and berries of their own, need necessarily to revert to tradition. Yet it's not clear that preferences are changing all that fast—if, indeed, they are changing at all. In one recent national survey, for instance, 83 percent of college-aged women agreed that "Being married is a very important goal for me."[53] In another, 43 percent of women who engaged in hookups reported that the ideal outcome of such encounters was a traditional romantic relationship.[54] If these reports are accurate, and if young women generally still prefer committed relationships to casual sex, then the widespread embrace of the hooking-up norm has been one of womankind's greatest gifts to men. Or, to quote Robert, a college sophomore: "No real commitment, no real feelings involved, this is like a guy's paradise."[55]

My Baruckus

In February 2012 I received a wholly unexpected phone call. It was a dreary late winter afternoon, and I had been worried all day about my younger son, who had called from college that morning to report that he was ill and on his way to the hospital. When the phone rang, I leaped, positive that it was the emergency room doctor calling to tell me the diagnosis. Instead, it was my office, calling to say that President Obama wanted to give the commencement address at Barnard. What does one say? "Sure," I mumbled. "Whatever. I have to get off the phone now."

Over the next few days, matters evolved in a blur. My husband and I raced to Vermont to check on our son who, thankfully, was soon okay. I ran through the list of people who had to be contacted confidentially about the president's visit, and then worked with my staff to craft a careful strategy for releasing the good news. In an e-mail sent early on a Saturday morning, we solemnly informed our students that the president had chosen Barnard and would soon be addressing the college's graduating seniors. The news hit slowly at first, and then exploded in the blogosphere. "PRESIDENT OBAMA IS GIVING THE BARNARD COMMENCEMENT SPEECH," one student swiftly reported on Facebook. "No words. Just wow," commented another. Sheer bliss. By noon, though, the tone had taken a decidedly different, distinctly horrible turn. Out of the woodwork, unidentified grumblers began attacking the college and its students. Most of the attacks were general in nature and could reasonably be explained away as jealousy. "POTUS is smart and he made an intelligent move," groused one. "Better to speak with people without brains than . . . talk with students who are intellectually superior." "Why is Barnard getting President Obama? . . . Why couldn't they get Michelle?" But some were distinctly and disgustingly misogynistic, demeaning, out of nowhere, the career ambitions and purported sexual practices of Barnard students. "Barnard is full of academically inferior students that . . . are stereotypically easy to get in bed," asserted one anonymous post. "What is there to speak at BC?" queried another. "Just tell them to have babies and take good care of your family. Done. Thank you." A handful were so obscene that I can't bear to repeat them here. Other media, however, had no such reservations, and within days the campus was embroiled in a nasty and high-profile fight, a fight about women and sexuality, about women and success, about the complicated boundaries between profanity and free speech.

As an institution, Barnard stands as a beacon to women's rights. Along with the other original Seven Sisters schools (Radcliffe, Wellesley, Smith, Vassar, Mount Holyoke, and Bryn Mawr), we were founded in the late nineteenth century as part of a progressive experiment to provide women with the education then denied them by the Ivy League schools. Along with four of our peers (Vassar went coed in 1969, and Radcliffe, which had been functionally coeducational with Harvard since World War II, signed a merger agreement in 1977), we have remained proudly all-female ever since, committed to an agenda that explicitly advances women's opportunities and women's education. In 2012, we had everything, literally, that a card-carrying feminist might demand. Free condoms at the clinic; a rape crisis center; a regular Valentine's Day performance of *The Vagina Monologues*. And yet in an instant—an instant that had nothing whatsoever to do with sex—we had been hit by a stomach-turning wave of obscenity and sexism, a throwback to the angry days of the 1960s, when it was okay for men to call women whores and demean their sexuality.

That same week, Sandra Fluke, a thirty-year-old law student at Georgetown University, testified before a congressional hearing on health care. Describing her own experience and those of her class-mates, Fluke stated that the exorbitant cost of contraception—$3,000 a year or more—was causing severe financial hardship for many of the school's female students. It wasn't a particularly vivid testimony or, sadly, a particularly shocking bit of bad news. Yet within a week, Fluke's testimony had made the headlines. Rush Limbaugh, the conservative talk show host, lambasted Fluke on his program, calling her a "slut" and a "prostitute" and claiming, "she wants to be paid to have sex. She's having so much sex she can't afford the contraception. She wants you and me and the taxpayers to pay her to have sex."[56] When liberal and feminist groups rushed to Fluke's defense (President Obama even called Fluke personally to express his support), Limbaugh would only offer what he described as a compromise: "So, Ms. Fluke and the rest of you feminazis," he stated on the air, "here's the deal. If we are going to pay for your contraceptives, and thus pay for you to have sex, we want something for it, and I'll tell you what it is. We want you to post the videos online so we can all watch."[57]

Certainly, much of what drove the sexual politics of 2012 was the electoral politicking of that year, a divisive ideological scramble in which both parties were fighting for the "women's vote"—a vote which, if it ever really existed as a distinct category, was now splayed fully across the political spectrum.[58] More surprising, though, and of much greater long-term importance, was that these fights also unearthed a deep-seated ambivalence about sex in America, and particularly about the sexuality of young unmarried women. Because what was revealed by my Baruckus, by Limbaugh's rantings, and by the outbursts that surrounded them both, was that women in 2012—roughly fifty years after the sexual and feminist revolutions—were still being crucified on the cross of the madonna-whore, damned if they do (have sex, like sex) and if they don't. To older feminists, the public eruption of these ten-sions came as a long-awaited confirmation of their insistence that the battle for women's sexual rights had not yet been won.[59] To younger women, and particularly those who had always eschewed any explicit links to feminism, it came simply as a shock. "It's hurtful," reported one woman. "Since when should I have to defend myself just for going to the school I go to?" "Why," asked one of my best students more plaintively, "are they being so mean?"

There are many answers to these questions and to the many similar queries that were flung, suddenly, into the cultural discourse of sex and gender. Why, for example, was contraception once again under attack? Why were sexually active women still labeled as whores or harlots while sexually active men—even those who cheated on their wives, visited prostitutes, or revealed their private parts on Internet sites—were dismissed as gigolos or Casanovas? Why does the English language contain no equally disparaging male equivalent for the word "slut"?[60]

To me, the underlying answer is simple. It comes from the fact—and I argue here wholly and unabashedly on the basis of anecdote rather than data—that most women, most of the time, still take a different view of sex than men. They may like sex as much as men. They may want it as frequently and in the same infinity of permutations. But the link between sex and relationship is stronger for women, as is the social penalty for promiscuity. The sexual revolution gave women the technical means and cultural mores to control their reproductive selves; it allowed women, for the first time in history, to have sex without consequence. But it didn't change men's underlying views of women's sexuality, or the biological reality that sex, for women, will always be more immediately connected to procreation. As a result, women—and particularly young women—are caught again in a double whammy of expectations: to be sexually adventurous but not promiscuous, skilled in the bedroom but ultimately committed to their children, husbands, and home. In other words, to be simultaneously madonna and whore.

With all due respect to the Catholic Church, I am not entirely sure that these aims—in their modern incarnation at least—are wholly incompatible. Women today can be promiscuous for some portions of their lives and monogamous for others. They can experiment sexually and socially without feeling undue guilt or bearing any long-term consequences. But, at some stage, they have to make up their minds and settle into a sexuality that feels right for them—even if that rightness shifts and evolves across the landscape of their lives. They have to own their sexuality, in whatever form it might take, and control the only bits of property that will ever be wholly theirs; the only property, in the end, that really matters. Their bodies. Their selves.

On a balmy evening in April, a dozen young women troop over to my apartment for pizza and brownies.[61] They are a combination of college sophomores and recent graduates, a mix of friends and acquaintances brought together at my request. With two exceptions among the group, I don't know them personally, and I ask them not to tell me their names. We settle somewhat umcomfortably into my living room couches and I start to ask them about sex. Do they hook up? Do they like it? And just what does it mean?

The group start awkwardly, giggling, revealing little tidbits of their lives. And then, within minutes, the conversation explodes. They all hook up, repeatedly, meeting guys they generally don't like and going back to someone's room for a kiss, a grope, or a round of oral sex. Sometimes there is intercourse, it seems, and occasionally an exchanged phone number. But mostly it's anonymous and affectionless. Usually it's oral sex for the guy (particularly among the college sophomores) and not much for the girl.* Several of the girls are still virgins. The others lost their virginity in nearly identical ways—with a man they barely knew and never saw again. "He was gross," one young woman recalled, "but he was safe." Safe, meaning that there was no emotional attachment. Safe, meaning that there was no chance of ever falling in love. "We are so afraid of losing power," another young woman matter-of-factly explained, "that we have to care less than they do."

As the evening wears on and the pizza crusts harden, I learn more about hooking up than I ever really intended. Beth tells of having sex

---

*According to one recent study, about a quarter of hookups involve oral sex but not intercourse. Of these, roughly half were mutual, 37 percent involved the man alone receiving oral sex, and 14 percent involved the woman alone. See Paula England and Reuben J. Thomas, "The Decline of the Date and the Rise of the College Hook Up," in Arlene Skolnick, ed., *The Family in Transition* (Boston: Allyn and Bacon, 2006), p. 72.

from the age of fifteen. "I would find older men and just sleep with them," she recounts. "Because I was, like, this cute young girl." Charlotte, totally straight and super-smart, makes out with girls at parties if guys want to watch. Abby regularly indulges in what she dubs "prostitute sex"—anything but kissing. Most of these encounters, not surprisingly, involve alcohol. "Why?" I ask. "Because someone's going to see you naked," they laughingly explain, "and you're going to need the courage." Interestingly, when I ask these young women how they expect to see their lives unfold, they cluster toward a common, rather commonplace, ideal. Single and adventurous at twenty-five; married with kids at forty. Not a lot of concern about how to make this leap.

At the very end of the evening, one young woman who had described a particularly active range of sexual adventures dropped a sudden question. "Have any of you had orgasms?" Dead silence, then a scramble of agreement. "Nope." "Not me." "I don't feel anything down there. I just go numb." They wonder for a while about what they realize is a rather glaring gap. They acknowledge the probable importance of certain things—like foreplay and attraction—that hookups tend to lack. They push me for advice, and I demur.

And then, in a whirl of coats and plans and handbags, they leave—beautiful, young, intelligent girls, heading off to a Manhattan night. They are looking for something, heading for something, that's not quite love. Not yet. And maybe, I can't help wondering, as I pick up cups and crumpled napkins, not for a long, long time.

4

BODIES AND OTHER ACCESSORIES

Only when a woman ceases the fretful struggle to be beautiful can she turn her gaze outward, find the beautiful and feed upon it.
—Germaine Greer, 1992[1]

Beauty is a statement. Face the future with firmer skin.
—advertisement for Nivea cream, 2012

When I was fourteen, my mother bought me a white bikini. It was cut low on the bottom, and the top, I remember distinctly, could be flipped into three different configurations: halter, strapless, or some complicated thing where the straps and cups traded places. The first time I put it on, I was five feet seven inches tall and weighed 114 pounds. In other words, I had the kind of body you have only if you are (a) a model, or (b) fourteen. When I wore it to a pool party for one of my friends, I was surprised—and confused, and thrilled, I guess—to see her father and brothers staring surreptitiously every time I jumped from the diving board. The next day I quietly started to starve myself.

At first, like millions of fourteen-year-old girls, I just cut out the Cokes and candy from the vending machines. Then the second helpings. Then any meal that my parents didn't witness. Soon I was subsisting on popcorn and canned zucchini, and walking feverishly for miles whenever I had the chance. As the pounds came off, I scrutinized myself even more closely in the full-length mirror that hung in my room. Still way too flabby across the stomach, I concluded. Hips too broad. At least another five pounds to go. At my peak—and oddly, horribly, I still regard it that way—I was down to eighty-eight pounds. My breasts disappeared entirely, as did my periods. When my frantic parents took me to the family doctor, he was nonplussed. "Well, sure," he agreed, "she's thin. But so are most girls. And she doesn't exactly look like a ballerina yet."

I have no idea, really, why I leaped so suddenly into anorexia, or why the obsession lingered for more than three years. All I know is that it was undeniably an obsession, and one whose effects haunted me for a very long time. During high school, I ate so many carrots that my toes and fingers actually turned orange. In college, I scoured the cafeteria for broccoli and purchased Pepsi Light by what must have been the metric ton. My parents begged me to eat; my guidance counselor insisted that I eat; my friends assured me that I was far too skinny. But none of it made any difference. Every day I parsed out calories—eight for a chunk of iceberg lettuce, two for a Tic Tac—and every night in the mirror I peered and poked. And I still looked too fat. Too round. Too fleshy. When I finally started eating again, my weight ballooned and my breasts returned with a vengeance. Things didn't settle down until the birth of my first child, when some mysterious force—time, or hormones, or the sensible diet of pregnancy—reset my metabolism to roughly normal.

In the meantime, though, my body focus had shifted to my breasts, the now indisputable 36DDD behemoths I lugged around with me. There was no blouse that would fit over these things, no man who could look me in the eye while they towered below. I was black and blue from jogging with them and tired of having to creep by any construction site or convenience store. One day, fresh out of college and reveling in a just-completed job interview, I was walking through National Airport in Washington. I had my sensible college-graduate suit on, my sensible low-heeled shoes, my graduation-present briefcase. I looked up, and there was a man staring at me. A very handsome man, the kind of distinguished, enigmatic, maybe-he's-a-spy man I hoped would start appearing in my life. We passed each other. Our eyes met. "Wow, babe," he whistled. "What a pair of tits!"

That was it. Six months later, I found a plastic surgeon and had them cut off—or "reduced," as they say. The doctor thought he was being kind. "Once we get rid of these," he promised, "you'll look so much slimmer. Maybe not quite like a ballet dancer, but we'll try to get close."

So tell me. If men can't keep their eyes off our breasts, why do they want us to look like ballerinas? And why do I still care?

Our obsession with women's bodies is hardly something new. In ancient Egyptian tomb paintings, for example, important men were generally depicted as being overweight, while their wives, daughters, and sisters were invariably svelte.[2] In ancient Greece, mortal females were regularly depicted as goddesses, blessed with the artists' conception of ideal beauty.[3] But we are living, arguably, through a more virulent phase now, a time in which we tuck our tummies and engorge our lips as easily as women of earlier generations once chose the latest bolt of muslin from the dressmaker. Americans spent over $13 billion on plastic surgery in 2007 and $530 million on diet books.[4] The vast bulk of these purchases were made by and for women.

Even a cursory glance at any magazine rack confirms that we are totally and completely obsessed with women's bodies: with their hair, their hips, their breasts. A recent cover of *Vanity Fair*, for instance, showcased Penélope Cruz, wearing a slinky open-backed dress over a "story" entitled VA-VA-VOOM."[5] Next to it, *Esquire* had Kate Beckinsale, looking similarly gorgeous in a black bikini and patent heels, her body only barely covering the headline THE SEXIEST WOMAN ALIVE.[6] Actress Kristin Bell (young, blond, skinny) squatted on the cover of *Women's Health*, promising to tell readers HOW SHE GOT HER ROCKIN' BOD.[7] Meanwhile, the men who showed up across the rack generally got away with actually doing things, like scaling mountains or grilling ribs.

American movies, of course, display precisely this same sexual schizophrenia, with rugged (albeit generally pretty good-looking) men cavorting, almost always, with lithe, exquisite women half their age. Think, for instance, of *Entrapment,* an art world caper that paired the sixty-nine-year-old Sean Connery with the thirty-year-old Catherine Zeta-Jones. Or the classic *Charade*, in which the fifty-nine-year-old Cary Grant woos the thirty-four-year-old Audrey Hepburn. Or pretty much any Woody Allen film. Recent "slacker" films like Judd Apatow's *Knocked Up* make the mismatch even worse, with distinctly unattractive men—slovenly, overweight, unemployed, beer-guzzling—nevertheless managing to bed and keep the beautiful blond catch. Meanwhile, poor female slobs still find redemption only in makeup and weight loss programs. Like Nia Vardalos, who wins the cute man in *My Big Fat Greek Wedding* only after she ditches her glasses and pretties her hair. Or Sandra Bullock, who nabs the handsome FBI agent in *Miss Congeniality* once she transforms herself into a beauty pageant winner. Of course there are exceptions: Charlize Theron can make herself look terrible for *Monster* and Hilary Swank can powerfully portray a transgendered man in *Boys Don't Cry*. But these are clearly anomalies, brief Oscar-grabbing moments that allow exquisite women to demonstrate, occasionally, that they can act, too. Which really doesn't make the rest of us feel that much better.

Because even when we know that Julia Roberts and Anne Hathaway aren't quite so beautiful without their legion of stylists and makeup crews, without machines that blow their hair and computers that erase their thighs, we somehow still believe that their standard is ours. And so millions of girls in my generation spent countless hours trying to achieve Farrah Fawcett's extraordinary mane (don't get me started; my hair looked like a giant sausage roll for two years), just as millions today strive for Beyoncé's body or JLo's butt. Men don't do stuff like this. Sure, they might want to have a golf swing like Tiger Woods or be as clever as Warren Buffett, but these are *competences* that they aim for, not physical attributes. Women, by contrast, tend to treat physical attributes as if they were competences—things achieved through hard work and money rather than a roll of the genetic dice. So we straighten our hair and shave our legs and cut off the body parts that offend us.

It should all seem futile, and even foolish—what plump white teenager is really going to look like Beyoncé, after all? And yet the very same forces that draw women to these transformations also seduce them with the possibility. Think about it. Have you ever been at a grocery checkout when some headline wasn't trumpeting the triumph of radical weight loss? *Rachel dropped 375 pounds—in just six months! Karen lost her baby fat—and found a new man!* Or flipped through a women's magazine that didn't include pages of advice on flatter abs or buffer arms? Again and again, women are being told—promised, really—that their bodies are mutable, that they can be bent and molded into different, better, shapes. Like accessories, bodies are things we tinker with, things we buy according to fashion and discard when they no longer please us.

Once again, feminism fought to change all this. Indeed, one of the earliest and most powerful rallying cries of the women's movement was that women were enslaved to conceptions of beauty that were defined by men and the media and destined to keep them oppressed. In 1968, for example, in what would soon become a symbol for the entire feminist movement, a group of radical feminists traveled to Atlantic City to protest the Miss America pageant, citing it as a symbol of "male chauvinism, commercialization of beauty, racism and oppression of women."[8] Although the protesters never actually burned a single bra (an urban myth that has by now sunk deep into America's collective memory), they did toss a range of beauty products—girdles, high heels, cosmetics, eyelash curlers, wigs—into a "freedom trash can," asserting the right of all women to be free from what they decried as "instruments of torture."[9] Reflecting on the event, Robin Morgan, one of its organizers, wrote: "To deny that you are oppressed is to collaborate in your oppression. To collaborate in your oppression is a way of denying that you are oppressed."[10] In protest, she, like other radical feminists, stated publicly that they would henceforth refuse to succumb to male-dictated standards of beauty. No more perfume, no more cosmetics, no more plucking and waxing.[11] Over the next few years, some of feminism's most vocal and persuasive voices took this argument even further, arguing that the fight against impossible norms of beauty was in fact central to the fight for women's freedom. "In our culture," wrote Andrea Dworkin, "not one part of a woman's body is left untouched, unaltered. No feature or extremity is spared the art, or pain, of improvement . . . from head to toe, every feature of a woman's face, every section of her body, is subject to mutilation, alteration."[12] The only cure, she continued, was "the radical redefining of the relationship between women and their bodies . . . Women must stop mutilating their bodies and start living in them."[13]

Somehow, though, by the early 1980s, just as women of my generation were setting out into the workplace, the well-publicized quest to liberate women from implausible standards of beauty had boomeranged entirely, replaced by another set of endlessly perfect icons: Farrah Fawcett, Bo Derek, Cheryl Tiegs.[14] Far from discarding their eyelash curlers or high heels, they were pretty obviously embracing them. And millions of girls and women, blithely oblivious to the fights of just a decade ago, blindly followed along.

In theory, all of us are built from bundles of characteristics: we have our looks, our intelligence, our personalities, our musical abilities, our penmanship. Yet women are rarely offered salvation through any channel other than their looks. Oh, sure, we can get advanced degrees or learn to knit, but these are rarely seen as transformative events. (How often do you see a headline reading *Sue started playing trombone—and found a whole new life!*) With our bodies, by contrast, change promises redemption. If we could only lose five pounds, women tend to think, or have larger eyes / rounder breasts / silkier hair, life itself would change. *Better body,* we repeat and pray, *better me.*

What We Do . . .

In 1989, Toyota Motors unveiled a new campaign for its high-end Lexus sedan. In glossy ads that reeked of money and power, the company whispered of its "relentless pursuit of perfection." They were referring, of course, to Japanese engineering, but the same could easily be said of American women, committed as we are to the relentless reengineering of our own chassis—our bodies, ourselves.

In pursuit of perfection, we do all sorts of strange things. We drape our legs in hot wax, smother our faces with avocado-based potions, and blanch our hair from gray to platinum blond. Most of these practices are cosmetic by nature; that is, they touch the outer layer of our bodies and demand almost constant repetition: more wax, more potions, more dye. Several, though, go much deeper, striving not just to improve what lies on the body but to fix the underlying structure, changing its very shape into something better and more perfect.

Diets
The most obvious of these bodily fixes is the diet, that proverbial pastime of most American women (and, to be fair, a good number of

American men as well). In 2006, Americans purchased nearly $2 billion worth of diet books and spent more than $8 billion on specialty diet foods.[15] According to a recent Gallup poll, nearly three-quarters of American women have seriously tried to lose weight, along with roughly half of all American men.[16]

Repeatedly, research shows that dieting doesn't work. Indeed, most serious studies suggest that nine out of ten dieters will eventually regain all the weight they initially lose through dieting.[17] But to those in search of the perfect body—or at least thinner thighs—dieting itself becomes an addiction, a promise of change in each container of low-fat yogurt.[18] In the process, according to one pair of researchers, chronic dieters experience "a virtual collapse of self-esteem and sense of effectiveness."[19]

In many cases, and certainly at the extreme edge of obesity, dieting is about health. It is about reducing the bulk that already threatens 68 percent of Americans with chronic conditions such as diabetes and heart disease; about ensuring that the next generation of children does not grow up to be dangerously overweight.[20] For many women, though, dieting is about appearance much more than health; about firming butts rather than protecting arteries. Or as one journalist wrote, citing her own experience: "It was getting more and more clear to me that becoming a woman—at least an attractive and successful woman— meant being able to lose weight. Nothing else seemed to matter more."[21] And clearly she is not alone: according to the Centers for Disease Control, 32 percent of normal-weight women describe themselves as overweight, compared with only 7 percent of normal-weight men.[22]

This obsession with thinness is relatively new. In the Victorian era, when fat was still associated with wealth, a sexy woman was a heavy woman. Not fat, necessarily, but rounded, with ample breasts and hips accentuated by clothing—bustles and corsets and bodices—that made them look even ampler. Then, around the turn of the century, as Americans grew wealthier and more eager to distinguish themselves from the (generally shorter and stockier) immigrants crowding ashore, fashion morphed to dictate a leaner silhouette, something freer and more modern, capable of carrying a woman out of her home and into higher-class diversions such as tennis or bicycling.[23] This movement culminated, by the 1920s, in the embrace of the "flapper"—a much thinner woman than her Victorian mother, and relieved of her corset and commodious bosom. Yet even at the height of the flapper era, the ideal woman's shape was, well, shapely. Mary Campbell, who was crowned Miss America in 1922 and 1923 stood five feet seven and weighed 140 pounds; Annette Kellerman, a champion swimmer who published *Physical Beauty: How to Keep It* in 1918, was five four and 137 pounds.[24]

It wasn't until the 1970s, then, that American women decided to become really, really thin. Twiggy hit the runways in 1966, tipping the scales at just 97 pounds. She was seventeen, and probably genetically programmed to be thin. But her look became all the rage, prodding millions of women to start losing—or, more accurately, to *try* to start losing—millions and millions of pounds. Within a decade, mass-market

Annette Kellerman, circa 1918

fitness programs like Jane Fonda's *Workout Book* added exercise to the agenda, promising to deliver a lean, hard body in exchange for an awful lot of sweat.

Intriguingly, the shift to superskinnydom coincided almost perfectly with the women's movement. In the 1950s and early 1960s, when a woman's place was in the home, the "perfect" woman was still slightly rounded, with breasts and hips that spoke of her reproductive capacities. As women moved into the workplace, however, with their boxy suits and floppy ties, "perfection" became increasingly more slender and androgynous: no breasts, no hips, no fat. By 1990, the average American model was 23 percent slimmer than the average American woman.[25] Faced with such thinness, one might have expected a "normal" American woman to throw in the towel and reach for the Häagen-Dazs, to settle into a size that would have been considered perfectly acceptable throughout history and get on with her life. Yet, prodded in part by the slogans of feminism, women instead embraced the skinny ideal, turning to diets and yoga, fasting and running, to get as close as possible to thin. As a result, ostensibly liberated women often found themselves struggling with three full-time jobs: working inside the home, working outside the home, and trying to be thin.[26]

It's hard to be scientific about just what "thin" means, or how most women relate to their bathroom scales. But the anecdote here is pretty powerful. Most American women want to weigh considerably less than they actually do. Most are either on a diet at any point in time, or contemplating a diet, or just watching obsessively every morsel they eat. The effects are both poignant and absurd. Recently, I had lunch with a well-known writer and her equally impressive editor. Both women are elegant, accomplished, and attractive. Walking across the star-packed Manhattan café, they turned every head. When it came time to order, however, they both reached into their fashionable handbags and pulled out identical spreadsheets—instructions from their nutritionist detailing precisely what to eat at each meal of each day. Today's lunch was filet of sole with steamed broccoli—no oil, no butter, and please remove the breadbasket immediately from the table. When the maître d' reported calmly that the kitchen was out of sole, the normally unflappable duo went into full-scale fluster. Left to their own devices, they simply didn't know how to eat.

Eating Disorders

Usually, when diets don't work, the dieter either gives in to her body or tries another approach, trading Atkins for grapefruit or Pritikin for prunes. Sometimes, though, diets go bad by succeeding too well, tempting women, like me, to embrace a modified form of physical starvation.

As a phenomenon, anorexia (along with its close cousin, bulimia) remains both commonplace and exotic, well studied and yet frustratingly hard to describe. In the United States alone, approximately 10 million women and girls struggle each year with anorexia and bulimia.[27] Official death rates are hard to ascertain, since anorexia eventually kills its victims through proximate causes such as heart attacks or suicide. Those who study the disease, however, estimate that its annual mortality rate among young women is more than *twelve times higher* than the annual death rate due to all causes of death for females between the ages of fifteen and twenty-four, and more than two hundred times greater than the suicide rate in the general population.[28] Ninety-five percent of anorexia's victims are between the ages of twelve and twenty-five. Five to 10 percent of them die within ten years of contracting the disease.

Technically, anorexia is defined as an irrational fear of gaining weight.[29] Doctors diagnose the condition when a patient has lost roughly 15 percent of her body weight over a short period of time. Associated symptoms include anemia, the cessation of menstrual periods, and the growth of fine, light hair all over the body. In severe cases, it can lead to infertility, osteoporosis, kidney failure, and death.

None of these details, though, relate to the maddening nature of the illness. Because anorexia is one of the very few diseases (along, perhaps, with drug- or alcohol-related illnesses) that the patient brings on herself. Young girls don't fall into anorexia; they embrace it, often quite consciously. Indeed, on websites such as www.pro-thinspo.com and www.dyingtobethin.net, "pro-ana" fans, as they call themselves, exchange an astonishing array of starvation tips.[30] "Only eat yellow foods on Monday, and brown foods on Tuesday," advises one helpful source, "or only eat every other day." "Eat while in front of the mirror naked. You will be completely repulsed, and repelled from food. This is a good thing."[31] Pro-thinspo goes so far as to propose an "Ana Creed," which is worth quoting in its full, terrifying length:

I believe in Control, the only force mighty enough to bring order to the chaos that is my world.

I believe that I am the most vile, worthless and useless person ever to have existed on this planet, and that I am totally unworthy of anyone's time and attention.

I believe that other people who tell me differently must be idiots. If they could see how I really am, then they would hate me almost as much as I do.

I believe in oughts, musts and shoulds as unbreakable laws to determine my daily behavior.

I believe in perfection and strive to attain it.

I believe in salvation through trying just a bit harder than I did yesterday.

I believe in calorie counters as the inspired word of god, and memorize them accordingly.

I believe in bathroom scales as an indicator of my daily successes and failures.

I believe in hell, because I sometimes think that I'm living in it.

I believe in a wholly black and white world, the losing of weight, recrimination for sins, the abnegation of the body and a life ever fasting.[32]

When I was growing up, few members of the medical profession viewed, or treated, anorexia as a disease. Instead, doctors like my own saw skinny girls as just that—skinny girls, with nothing much to worry about. As the condition has become both more prevalent and more public, however, the medical field has moved in, armed now with more specific diagnoses and courses of treatment. At the Mayo Clinic, for example, patients receive a combination of psychotherapy, nutrition counseling, medical care, and medications, along with aggressive "refeeding." At the Renfrew Center, a private clinic, special "residential tracks" address the needs of particular anorexics: older women, substance abusers, Orthodox Jews. Hundreds of hospitals, clinics, and specialists list themselves on websites such as edreferral.com and nationaleatingdisorders.org, each offering anorexics (or, more likely, their families) a complex route back to health. What few specialists can agree upon, though, or even speculate about, is the underlying motive. *Why do teenage girls decide to starve themselves?*[33]

One line of reasoning blames sex—or, more specifically, the incipient sexuality brought forth by puberty. As girls mature physically, as the breasts come in and the hips widen out, they see themselves for the first time as sexual beings, as objects of desire and perhaps scorn. If they see this transition as frightening—and let's be honest, it is—some young women may subconsciously try to ward it off by removing its most physical manifestations: breasts and periods. Or, as Naomi Wolf argues, anorexia protects young women from "street harassment and sexual coercion; construction workers leave walking skeletons alone."[34] Was this my story? Did I stop eating once I spied a seventeen-year-old boy looking at my breasts? Maybe. I honestly don't know.

Another line of reasoning blames anorexia on the media onslaught to which young girls are particularly susceptible, the constant stream of picture-perfect bodies attached to picture-perfect women. When I was growing up, the onslaught came as posters of the curvaceous Bo Derek (five feet three and 102 pounds) and television heroines such as the spandex-clad Bionic Woman (Lindsay Wagner, five nine and 125 pounds). Today, it's even younger and lesser-clad subjects like Britney Spears (five five and 105 pounds) or Paris Hilton (five nine and 110 pounds). The average, nameless models who grace the pages of *Vogue* and *Glamour* stand about five feet ten inches tall and weigh less than 115 pounds. Barbie, by comparison, is almost plump.

Bombarded by these images, fourteen- to sixteen-year-olds may naturally try to emulate them, particularly if other cultural influences are pointing rigidly in the same direction. And if they can't procure the models' hair, or legs, or sulky eyes, they can at least approach their weight. Because that's easy. All you have to do is stop eating.

A third line of reasoning sees this ease itself as the driver of disease. In this view, anorexia is primarily an affliction of "good girls," girls who, like me, I must admit, were raised to be good at school, good at home, good, essentially, at everything. As these girls grow older, they start to chafe at the constraints that have been imposed upon them. They look to rebel, or at least to seize some greater measure of control over their own lives.[35] But because they've been so deeply conditioned to be good—not to talk back to the teacher, not to fail the exam, not to drive around with the boy next door—they instead start to control the one thing they can: calories. And because the results are so tangible—

stop eating ice cream, lose three pounds; stop eating dinner, lose ten—they are constantly encouraged to lose more and weigh less.

What makes this obsession so poignant and ironic, of course, is that the anorexic is actually damaging her body in pursuit, ostensibly, of perfecting it. But, much like the yo-yo dieter who persists in trying yet another weight loss scheme, the anorexic lets passion prevail over reason. And passion in this realm is driven much as in that luxury sedan: by the relentless pursuit of perfection.

Cosmetic Surgery

The Coen brothers, makers of films such as *Fargo* and *The Big Lebowski*, are not known for embracing their feminine side. Usually, their movies involve lots of men, and lots of blood, and a decent amount of indecent behavior. In *Burn After Reading*, however, released in 2008, they tell the tale of Linda Litzke, a fortysomething health club attendant determined to go under the knife. "I have gone just about as far as I can go with this body," she tells her lovelorn boss. "I have very limited breasts, a ginormous ass, and I've got this gut that swings back and forth in front of me like a shopping cart with a bent wheel." Desperate to find the thousands of dollars that resculpting her body will require, Litzke soon finds herself embroiled in a scheme involving Russian spies, purloined recordings, and assorted indiscretions (it is, after all, still the Coen brothers). Somehow, when the men have finished finishing each other off, she is still standing—triumphant, unconcerned, and eager to get the remodeling done.

It's a movie of course, and so it happily sounds absurd. Because no woman in her right mind would actually kill for a boob job, right? No one would *die* for it. But in fact they do. In 2007, Donda West, mother of the hip-hop star Kanye West, went into cardiac arrest and died following a routine liposuction and breast reduction. Olivia Goldsmith, author of the bestselling novel *The First Wives Club*, died in 2004 during a chin-tuck procedure. Like many less famous victims, they literally died for thinner thighs and smoother necks.

As a practice, plastic surgery is relatively new, a creation of modern medicine mixed with ancient dreams. In the past, bodily transformations were reserved for mythical beings. Witches or gods could change a maiden into an ogre, for example, or a frog into a prince, but mere mortals were stuck more or less with the stuff they inherited at birth, the stuff that made them too short, or too tall, or occasionally just right. As surgery grew more sophisticated over the course of the twentieth century, however, and both doctors and patients became more comfortable with elective (that is, nonessential) procedures, the field of cosmetic surgery began to grow.

Initially, the bulk of patients who had their bodies reshaped were men—specifically, young soldiers who had had their jaws blown off or faces mutilated during the carnage of World War I.[36] The work was done by a small legion of specialists—ear, nose, and throat doctors, or occasionally dentists—whose only goal was to restore their patients to looking something like normal. "Not so much that they might delight the eye," as one very early practitioner of facial reconstruction explained, "but that they may buoy up the spirits and help the mind of the afflicted."[37] After a few pioneering surgeons used fat from their (female) patients' bodies to expand or round their breasts, critics quickly decried their efforts as vanity: "[the] hunger for beauty of old coquettes who . . . wish . . . to give their sagging breasts a youthful vigor."[38] Slowly, though, and quietly, this hunger began to trump its objections. In 1923, the actress Fanny Brice had a well-publicized nose job; by the end of the decade, readers of the *New York Mirror* could vote to choose the city's ugliest girl, who was then granted both free public surgery and an opera audition.[39] In 1931, a plastic surgeon accompanied by a pianist performed the world's first (and, one would hope, last) public face-lift in the ballroom of Manhattan's Pennsylvania Hotel.[40]

By this point, the objectives of surgery had subtly shifted from correcting deformities to enhancing looks. And the patients had become overwhelmingly female. Psychology had also entered the field, prompting doctors (and their patients) to view cosmetic surgery as a "cure" for feelings of inferiority. "Why should anyone suffer under the handicap of a conspicuously ugly feature?" *Good Housekeeping* wondered in 1940. "Why not let modern science give him a normal face and an equal chance with other people?"[41] In 1982, the American Society of Plastic and Reconstructive Surgery classified small breasts as a deformity.[42]

Today, nearly 12 million Americans a year choose to undergo either cosmetic surgery (like breast implantation) or nonsurgical cosmetic procedures (like laser skin resurfacing). These numbers have increased by nearly 500 percent since the American Society for Aesthetic Plastic Surgery started collecting its data in 1997.[43] The most popular surgical procedure in 2007 was liposuction (456,828 cases); the favored nonsurgical procedure was Botox (2,775,176 visits). Women accounted for 91 percent of all procedures. Outside the United States, these trends are similar and, if anything, growing at an even faster pace. Brazil was the world's number one provider of liposuction and nose jobs in 2009; China, the third-largest provider of eyelid surgeries.[44] Some countries, like South Africa and Thailand, combine their newfound prowess in plastic surgery with their vacation locales, offering, for example, a combination tummy tuck and safari.[45] Really.

Inspired by this surging interest in cosmetic procedures, physicians have recently discovered whole new regions of the body to tuck, trim, and transfer. Don't like your innie belly button? Then try an umbilicoplasty, or belly button enhancement. Nipples getting you down? How about an enlargement? At the Manhattan offices of Dr. Philip Miller, to name just one celebrity surgeon, you can choose from a staggering buffet of beauty treats, including rhinoplasty (a nose job), otoplasty (ear restructuring), buccal fat excision (to "remove fullness from the lower third of the face"), and blepharoplasty (an eyelid lift to "improve that droopy look"). On a recent day in late October, the doctor was also offering a festive "Bootox event" with 20 percent off Botox treatments *and* a trick-or-treat gift bag. No witches, presumably, allowed.[46]

. . . And Why We Care

As with the specific case of anorexia, theories abound to explain why we care so much about our looks, why women will spend vast sums of money to get the fat suctioned off their thighs and the skin stretched tighter across their brows. The most common explanation focuses on the media. According to observers like Susan Orbach and Susan Bordo, for example, women are bombarded almost from infancy by an onslaught of images of bodily perfection. Surrounded by ads and movies and magazines that trumpet a certain standard of beauty, they rapidly fall prey to "the huge fashion and diet industries that first set up the

ages and then exhort women to meet them."[47] When these ef-
ll short, as they are almost certain to do, women are programmed to try again and again, shedding just five more pounds or
another layer of "tired, winter-worn skin." Those who might want to
rebel against this myth are stuck, since there are essentially no alterna-
tives to it. Can you think of an ugly Disney princess? A single normal-
sized cover girl? *Any* movie where the fat girl gets the guy? (Okay, I can
come up with one: *Hairspray*. But that's it.) In 1996, Freedom Communications launched a magazine called *Mode*, designed specifically for
women size 14 and above. But after its first few issues, it began to feature considerably slimmer women.[48]

Feminist scholars such as Naomi Wolf, meanwhile, take these arguments even further, arguing that it's not just the media who are to
blame, but men and society more generally. In *The Beauty Myth*, for
example, Wolf argues that our century's obsession with female beauty
is a product of both the industrial revolution and, ironically, the feminist movement. When men moved into factories and became their
family's breadwinners, she posits, women were forced into a separate
sphere of domesticity, a world defined by housekeeping and child rearing and tending to the needs of their men. As mass markets and technologies for mass communication evolved, advertisers then built upon
this foundation of domesticity to bombard women with the products
they "needed" to perfect their homes—laundry detergents and floor
polish, table waxes and air fresheners. During the middle decades of
the twentieth century, women bought these products in droves, supporting what became a massively successful (that is, profitable) mythology of female virtue: shine that floor, whispered Mr. Clean, and be
a better woman. Whiten those socks and drive your husband wild. After feminism's rise, however, it became tougher to sell American women
on the personal benefits of a cleaner home. And so, Wolf argues, companies and their advertising agents simply shifted gears, replacing
household products with personal products and women's kitchens with
their bodies. As a result, "the diet and skin care industries became the
new cultural censors of women's intellectual space" and "inexhaustible
but ephemeral beauty work took over from inexhaustible but ephemeral housework."[49] When women stopped waxing their dining room
tables, in other words, they started waxing their legs instead.

More profoundly, Wolf and others who write in this vein suggest that the myth of feminine beauty has been subconsciously designed to undermine the triumphs of feminism, to push women out of the spheres of power and, expensively and compulsively, back into the personal realm. Because when women aspire to an unobtainable and usually ill-fitting standard of beauty, they effectively consign themselves to years of fruitless labor and frustration, ceding power in the process to less-encumbered men. While men in their twenties and thirties, for example, are building their résumés and drinking beer with their bosses, women are racing to the nail salon and working on their abs. While men in their fifties and sixties are grasping the reins of power and losing their hair, women are dyeing and highlighting, tucking their tummies and shooting Botox into their brows. In this calculus, a woman's aspiration to be beautiful ties her to society's margins just as effectively as did her mother's mop and vacuum. Which is, Wolf argues, exactly what men want: to keep women in the bathroom and out of the boardroom.[50]

It is a strong argument and a compelling one. Wolf makes you think about just what is happening every time a woman picks up a tube of lip gloss or puts down a forkful of cake. She pushes us to ponder not just the idiocy of injecting ourselves with Botox, but the forces that compel us to do so. Is it the doctors? The corporations? The *men*? With forceful rhetoric and flawless logic, she projects a grown-up version of what all good mothers are supposed to say to their little girls: "It's not what's on the outside that matters."

I wish I could believe her.

But every time I turn around I slam into evidence that suggests a more complicated picture. Like the fact that the "pro-ana" girls are deeply oblivious to what actually makes them look good. Or that my six-year-old daughter, newly adopted from a Siberian orphanage, made an instant lunge across her first drugstore for glittery pink nail polish. Or that every single woman I know worries about her hair. Are we really all just succumbing to male corporate manipulation? Or are we maybe hostages to something deeper and more primitive within ourselves, something that pushes us, even without the prodding of money and power, to perfect our body selves? Or, to put it more prosaically: maybe, at some level and for some women, beauty *is* power. Maybe we lose weight or erase wrinkles not just because men want us to or because Madison Avenue has forced us into submission, but because we like what we can do when we look a certain way. We like men looking at us. We like women envying us. Recall the line from Colluthus's *Rape of Helen*, in which Aphrodite gloats to Hera and Athena after Paris chooses her: "Yield to me, accustomed as ye be to war, yield me the victory. Beauty I have loved and beauty follows me."[51] Maybe we're simply programmed, like grooming cats or preening peacocks, to polish and strut our stuff.

The problem, though, is that all this polishing and strutting takes an enormous toll on women. On an average day, I spend about five minutes putting on makeup and roughly fifteen minutes beating my naturally curly hair into some kind of submission. I generally get a manicure once every two weeks, on average (twenty minutes), and my legs waxed once a month (one hour and an awful lot of pain). Every six weeks or so I color my hair (one hour). Once every three months, I get it cut (another thirty minutes). I typically work out five days a week, for thirty to forty-five minutes. My handsome husband, by contrast, shaves in the morning and washes his hair in the shower (total elapsed time: four minutes). Once a month, he gets a haircut (thirty minutes). You do the math. By the end of the year, I will have spent 282 hours on what most women would classify as basic maintenance. My husband—like the men I work with, the men I teach, the men against whom I compete for jobs, publications, and research funds—will have spent about thirty hours. That means that I'm running a beauty counter deficit each year of 252 hours. Over the course of a forty-year career, I will spend 10,080 more hours than the average guy sitting next to me—*nearly five working years*—trying to make myself look presentable. And that says nothing about the extra stuff I have to lug on business trips.

Yes. I know. Any decent feminist would tell me exactly what to do. Forget the manicures. Stop waxing. Kill the blow-dryer. Don't give in. And I'm tempted. I'm really, really tempted. But look at any woman serving in Congress. Or working for a major law firm. Or running a foundation. Everyone has their hair done, and their nails done, and their bodies in reasonably fit condition. It can't be just that the men and the media are doing this to us. We're doing it to ourselves.

The irony here is that the all-pervasive search for bodily perfection may come, in part, from the feminist movement. Because insofar as feminism liberated women to enjoy their sexuality, it also and simultaneously highlighted the importance of women's physical and sexual attraction. Insofar as it prompted women to control their own destinies, it also prodded them into controlling their bodies. And insofar as it told women to pursue their dreams, so, too, did it lure them into the perpetual pursuit of perfection. This wasn't, of course, what the feminists meant, or even what they said. But as feminist ideas trickled through the ether of American society, they were translated into a vague credo of beauty as power, or at least an implicit belief that powerful women could, and therefore should, still look great. As Courtney Martin recalls in *Perfect Girls, Starving Daughters*, "We are the daughters of feminists who said 'You can be anything' and we heard 'You have to be everything.'"[52]

And so we're the ones, ultimately, who are choosing liposuction and boob jobs, who are nibbling on carrots and spinning like exhausted hamsters. We are the ones who still equate beauty with success and thinness, in particular, with goodness. Surely Oprah Winfrey doesn't have to lose another ten pounds (again) to prove her worth. Nancy Pelosi could probably handle both the House of Representatives and a few wrinkles. And I would almost certainly be better off if I skipped the gym every once in a while and slept in instead. But I don't.

Maybe beauty, like love or sex, ignites a desire that outruns reason. Maybe, as one author muses, the search for beauty is "an expression of the divine, a symbol we hold up against the inevitable humiliations of mortality."[53] Or maybe the feminists have it right, and our obsession with beauty is entirely constructed, thrust upon women by those who seek only to exploit them.

In the end, though, I'm not sure that it makes much difference. Because even if women like me have been manipulated since childhood—even if we know in our heart of hearts that beauty is both foolish and fleeting—there is something that seems to propel us to want it. To want to be thin. To want to be flawless. To want to be wanted. We can condemn this drive all we want, but it doesn't seem to show any sign of going away. On the contrary. It's been nearly 160 years since the women of Seneca Falls tossed off their corsets in favor of more comfortable bloomers, and almost fifty since protesters at the Miss America pageant threw their "objects of female torture" into the freedom trash can. But consider what happened in the aftermath of both those cases. Women at the turn of the century banished corsets—and then embraced a "flapper fashion" that was all about extremely slender bodies and the adoration of an androgynous rather than a reproductively inclined shape. In other words, they got rid of one arbitrary image of beauty just to exchange it for another. Similarly, the beauty fallout from the feminist movement of the late 1960s and early 1970s only served, as Wolf notes, to redefine the female ideal as thinner, sexier, and blessed with much bigger hair. Again, women changed the definition of beauty, but not the desire to obtain it.

So what do we do? On the one hand, it is easy to deride our obsession with bodily perfection and to urge women of all ages just to say no: to toss their creams, ditch their diets, and ignore the seductive come-ons of the glossy magazines. On the other hand, both history and anecdote suggest that this ditching (a) won't come easy, and (b) won't be fun. Because for whatever reason—be it biological programming, learned behavior, or cultural manipulation—we seem to crave not only beauty, but the power to recreate ourselves, and shape ourselves, as beautiful. And maybe this isn't entirely bad. Or, to be more specific, maybe we need to differentiate between things that are harmful and things that are not; between fashion and fun on the one hand, and utter foolishness on the other.

In my case, for example, the descent into anorexia was totally and completely mad. I took a perfectly normal body and wreaked serious damage to it. I don't know if anyone could have stopped me in my teenaged obsession, but I wish they had. By contrast, my decision to undergo breast reduction surgery still strikes me as a very good idea. I was uncomfortable with the "assets" I was perpetually lugging around, and getting rid of them made me lighter, less awkward, and, I'm pretty sure, more attractive. Selfish? Sure. Indulgent? Probably. But foolish? I don't think so. Nor do I cite as foolish my mother's decision, at age fifty, to have her nose done. She had always hated that rather large thing on her very small face, and whittling it down to a more manageable size made her inordinately happy. Again: indulgent, yes. But foolish, probably not.

Other women, with other issues and resources, might draw the line in different ways. My friend Suzanne, for instance, an esteemed journalist and author, decided that she didn't want either a face marked by wrinkles or one that looked artificially done. So she did her homework, saved her money, and, at age sixty, happily indulged in what she swore would be her one and only face-lift. She is overjoyed and looks wonderful. Maria, a Brazilian émigrée of great beauty and limited means, always wanted the "permanent cosmetics"—essentially, tattoos—that are common within the Brazilian community. So she, too, saved her money and searched around before hiring someone to paint, ever so subtly, lines of color across her eyelids. Like Suzanne, she wasn't looking to find a husband or impress a man. She wasn't trying to change her life or prove her worth. She just wanted to look in the mirror and find a bit more joy.

Perhaps the trick, then, is to distinguish perfection from beauty. Because perfection—the stuff of ads, the driver of obsession—is both impossible to define and excruciating to obtain. Perfection is what the pro-ana girls explicitly "strive to attain." It is the seduction of overpriced creams and serial cosmetic surgery; what ads for gym equipment and protein bars promise; and what no normal, healthy, non-digitally enhanced woman is ever going to achieve. Beauty, by comparison, is ever-present and multifaceted. It comes, as scores of feminist theorists have argued, in all shapes and sizes, in all colors and across all ages. Unlike perfection, beauty is frequently attained, even if—and perhaps precisely because—its definition varies across time and place and preference.

Beauty we can revel in, delight in. We can do silly things in its pursuit, and enjoy whatever powers it might bestow upon us. We can spend way too long defrizzing our hair and worry way too much about the shape of our butts. What we can't do, however, is allow ourselves to be swayed by the illusion of perfection, by the belief that we can ever reshape our bodies, much less ourselves, to be fundamentally different than they actually are.

Thirty years after my own bikini troubles, I found myself emergency-bathing-suit-shopping with a sixteen-year-old friend. She was staying with us, the weather had turned glorious, and she wanted to lie out in the sun. After an inordinate time in the dressing room, she nervously asked me to come in. She had on the world's tiniest, perkiest little bikini and looked so exquisite that I almost gasped. "What do you think?" she asked. "It's gorgeous," I sighed. But that clearly wasn't enough. She tried on a half dozen more, flipping the straps this way and that. She peered at herself from every angle, pondering over a line, a shadow. Suddenly, my head started reeling. Had my own teenaged son said something inappropriate to her? Had she stopped eating? Was she tipping into obsession? Should I call her mother? I wanted in that instant to yank her out of the dressing room, keep her safe somewhere, and make her understand how perfect she was.

But thankfully, reason took over.

"Lia," I said simply, "you look beautiful."

5

TRULY, MADLY, DEEPLY

Love, perhaps even more than child-bearing, is the pivot of women's oppression today.

—Shulamith Firestone, *The Dialectic of Sex*

All my fantasies included marriage. No sooner did I imagine myself running away from one man than I envisioned myself tying up with another. I was like a boat that always had to have a port of call. I simply couldn't imagine myself without a man.

—Erica Jong, *Fear of Flying*

If Tolstoy is right and happy families are all alike, then I suppose the same is true for love. Over and over we walk the same lines, sighing as we go: girl meets boy; girl loses boy; girl wins boy back and lives happily ever after. It happened to Cinderella, to Elizabeth Bennet and Holly Golightly, and could even have worked for Juliet, if only that friar hadn't been so confused.

Most ordinary women have stories along these lines as well, stories that they cherish and burnish and share endlessly with their friends. Mine is pretty straightforward. On my very first day of graduate school, as I was lugging my boxes into the dorm and muttering about the preponderance of geeks, a man whizzed by on a cheap bicycle. He was classic: tall, dark, and handsome, with curly black hair enlivened by a single shot of gray. I knew then and there. Knew the way you know a good melon.* Knew that he would either break my heart or marry me—both of which, in the end, came to pass.

We met for the first time over dinner in the communal kitchen. He was making Tofu Helper; I was heating Campbell's cream of cheddar soup. It wasn't an auspicious start. Even worse was his girlfriend back home, the woman I had glimpsed briefly on the first day of class. But slowly, over really bad meals, we started talking. And laughing. And, on my side at least, falling deeply and perilously in love.

After a while, the talking gave way, as it usually does, to more physical forms of interaction. Friends of my "friend," as I still called him, warned me surreptitiously that he still had a girlfriend back home, and that he was committed to returning to her. Friends of my own told me that I was nuts: he was ten years older than me, born in a different country, and of a different religion. Clearly, it wasn't going to work. Blindly, I didn't care.

We went on this way for some time, until I asked him to accompany me to my best friend's wedding. It was out of town and I was consigned to wear one of those horrible Dolly Parton numbers that brides impose on those they love. I couldn't bear the thought of being alone. But, quietly, sadly, Miltos said that he couldn't, that he was still attached to his girlfriend back in Toronto and that things could never work between the two of us. So I did what women do. I cried to my friends, read bad novels, and started dating as many other men as I could find.

Three months later, he showed up unannounced at my summer sublet in Washington. We never said another word about girlfriends or Toronto or ages or religion. The following summer we got engaged. Girl meets boy; girl loses boy; girl gets boy back and lives happily ever after.

In other people's lives, of course, the lines of this familiar plot get twisted into an infinity of permutations. Boy meets boy. Girl meets girl. Girl meets boy who doesn't fancy her at all. Interestingly, though, the underlying plot remains largely the same, as does our fascination with the romance of love—particularly with love that ends in marriage. Think of the past five happy movies that you've seen. Or indeed, of any of the great movies that end happily (*When Harry Met Sally*, for

---

*From *When Harry Met Sally*, my pick for the all-time best movie about romantic relationships.

example, or *Guys and Dolls*—interestingly, most great movies don't end happily; it's even worse with novels). Nearly all of them end with proposals, or weddings, or any imputed future of living happily and monogamously ever after. Now think of five sad movies—*Love Story*, or *Titanic*, or *West Side Story*. They all involve broken marriages, or widowed marriages, or tragic individuals who never marry at all. This correlation apparently runs straight back to Shakespeare. Virtually all of his comedies end with marriage (*As You Like It*; *Measure for Measure*; *A Midsummer Night's Dream*; *Much Ado About Nothing*; *Twelfth Night*; *The Winter's Tale*); all of his tragedies end with the death of lovers who were foiled either in romance or in marriage (*Romeo and Juliet*; *Antony and Cleopatra*; *Othello*).

In Shakespeare's time, of course, marriage made great sense, particularly for the women involved, because in Elizabethan England (as in ancient Greece, or medieval China, or pretty much anywhere across the world until the twentieth century), a woman without a husband was effectively cut off from society. She couldn't have sex or legitimate children, couldn't inherit property, sign papers, or bear witness. Unmarried women ("spinsters," "crones") were regularly regarded as either freaks or failures, sad souls condemned to spend their lives alone.

Today, by contrast, women no longer need the protection that marriage once provided. Instead, we can have sex without marriage, men without marriage, and babies without either sex *or* marriage. Across large segments of society, women are managing to raise children on their own, free from the stigma that once attended single-motherdom. And yet legions of women—educated and uneducated, wealthy and poor—are still rushing headlong toward the altar, determined to marry this person, this one person, *now*—preferably in a lacy dress and with lots of flowers. On every magazine rack across the country, squeezed between the stories of celebrity affairs and self-esteem tips, are bubbly reports of impending nuptials. Chelsea Clinton's 2010 wedding—an intimate event for four hundred people that cost an estimated $3 to $5 million—paralyzed the U.S. media for roughly two weeks, even garnering extensive and effusive coverage in the normally staid *New York Times*.[1] Kate Middleton's 2011 wedding to England's Prince William became a predictably global frenzy, with two choirs, one orchestra, and a reported 3 billion television viewers.

Admittedly, the marriage of a princess (be she royal or Democratic) is a notable event. But our fascination with marriage, and particularly with the fantasy of a happily-ever-after marriage, goes much deeper, extending well beyond the world's monarchies to include our politicians, our celebrities, our cousins, and ourselves. In one recent study, 88 percent of the young Americans surveyed recognized the benefits of marriage.[2] In another, 80 percent of young women (and 72 percent of young men) responded that "having a good marriage and family life" was extremely important to them.[3] Anecdotally, reports Jaclyn Geller in *Here Comes the Bride*, women remain "obsessed" with getting married, defining heterosexual monogamy, still, as their ultimate achievement.[4] Even *Sex and the City*, arguably television's greatest promoter of the single women's lifestyle, ended, bizarrely, with its heroine falling hard for the horrifyingly named Mr. Big and then marrying him in the series's first follow-up movie.

In the realm of matrimony, feminism sought to break the bonds that had historically tied wives to their husbands and made women legally and financially dependent on men. In the United States, after all, women in the 1960s still needed their husbands' signature to open credit card accounts or buy or rent an apartment. They couldn't hold mortgages on their own, or run an independent business. Legally, an unmarried mother had illegitimate offspring; financially, she had few "respectable" means for securing either child care or a well-paying job. These were the constraints that feminism sought to eradicate. If women were given their explicit rights, activists like Gloria Steinem argued; if they had the opportunity to earn their own wages and prevent the pregnancies that had long forced them into marriages of convenience or shame, then women theoretically would not need the legal protections of matrimony. They would be free. Or as Germaine Greer wrote in 1971: "If women are to effect a significant amelioration in their condition it seems obvious that they must refuse to marry."[5]

And yet here we are, more than forty years later, rushing still to the altar in organza and tulle. Women of my age have overwhelmingly chosen to marry (according to the U.S. census, 87 percent of women in their forties and 91 percent of women in their fifties are or have been married).[6] Women in their twenties and thirties overwhelmingly hope to do so.[7] Why? Maybe it's the media, whipping us over the head again with images of bridal loveliness. Maybe it's business, wooing us with $8,000 custom bridal gowns and $400 chocolate fondue fountains. Or maybe, just maybe, it's love.

Love Among the Apes

Scientists tell us that very few animals mate for life.[8] Most, in fact, are naturally promiscuous, coupling and uncoupling as mood and nature dictate. In the wild, a female chimp mates, on average, with thirteen males for each child she produces.[9] Bonobos are even busier, often mating dozens of times per day with multiple partners.[10]

To reproduce themselves successfully, however, even the most promiscuous of beasts must have some strategy for ensuring the health and longevity of their offspring. Fish and amphibians generally do this by hatching large numbers of nearly independent young. Frogs' eggs, for example, hatch directly as tadpoles, immature frogs that are nevertheless fully able to swim, breathe, and hunt for algae. Salmon hatchlings derive their initial nourishment from their egg sacs, then swiftly begin swimming on their own. Because the males of these species have no role to play beyond conception, evolution has nudged them to excel at that. Male frogs actively compete to mate with available females during breeding season, and then they leave.[11] Male salmon simply deposit their sperm over a batch of already-laid eggs. In both these species, there is no reason, evolutionarily speaking, for males and females to stay together beyond the moment of conception. And so they don't.

Matters are quite different, however, among mammals, particularly among the primates who constitute humans' closest biological relations. It takes six years for a baby chimp to become reasonably self-reliant; eight to thirteen years for a great ape; and approximately eighteen for a baby human (not counting four subsequent years of keg parties and college tuition).[12] As a result, if the child is to survive until maturity, someone must tend to his or her needs for an extended period of time, providing food, protection, and a modicum of education. Across the ape world, mothers take care of the first and last tasks, nursing their offspring and carrying them along on foraging trips.[13] Yet, because most apes live in complex social groups, mothers don't do it all alone.

Instead, they rely on the males of their tribe to protect infants against predators and help socialize them as they mature.[14]

In the human kingdom, infants are born particularly needy and childhood lasts a comparatively long time. Someone, accordingly, needs to bear the young and nurse them during their early years. Someone else needs to protect these young and provide food once the bearer and nurser conceives another child. The very earliest humans, anthropologists believe, lived in hunting and gathering bands, tending reciprocally to their young and communally sharing whatever food was found.[15] As is the case with primates, there were no permanent pairings within these groups, and no evidence of monogamy.[16]

As civilizations began to emerge from these nomadic bands, however, so, too, did married pairs—a man and a woman linked by their children and committed to remaining together. What drove these pairings, it appears, and made marriage so widespread, was the dual need of increasingly civilized people to pass specialized knowledge to their children and ensure that these children were "theirs." In other words, when life was dominated by picking berries and finding nuts, humans—like apes and chimps and bonobos—could afford to share. Once humans began to make tools, however, they had an incentive to specialize in certain tasks and teach them to their children. Because these tasks were difficult, and an expert practitioner could generate far more food than a novice, anyone who took the time to raise and teach a child would want to ensure that the child was "his." For women, identification was easy, since the children they bore were obviously theirs. For men, by contrast, living in a world where survival was tight and food hard-won, the only sure way to claim a child was to claim its mother first. Marriage—linking one man to one woman from the time of her virginity—made this work. Indeed, the basic structure of man-plus-woman-locked-in-monogamy was so pervasive among ancient peoples, and so prevalent, that the marriage historian Stephanie Coontz launches her far-ranging exploration of marriage by proclaiming "we know of only one society in world history that did not make marriage a central way of organizing social and personal life."[17] And with that one exception, she continues, "marriage has been . . . a universal social institution throughout recorded history."[18] One man. One woman. With sex, children, and a contract endorsed by society.[19]

To Have and to Hold: The Utility of Marriage

In historical terms, then, marriage is about children much more than it is about sex, or romance, or love. Specifically, it is about lineage and inheritance, proving this one man is linked to this one woman and that her children are therefore his. Read the Bible through this lens, and you glimpse the extent to which the Old Testament is a document establishing lineage as much as anything else. "This is the book of the generations of Adam," states Genesis. "When Adam had lived a hundred and thirty years, he became the father of a son in his own likeness, after his image, and named him Seth . . . When Seth had lived a hundred and five years, he became the father of Enosh." And so forth until Noah, who "became the father of Shem, Ham, and Japheth."[20] Because Shem, Ham, and Japheth are sons of Noah, moreover, they are also heirs to his property, and to whatever titles or power he might have.[21] In biblical times, as in ancient China and Egypt, men might legally be married to more than one wife (Jacob, for instance, was married to Rachel and Leah, as well as to each of their maidservants), but the bonds between them were still fixed and inviolable.

Over the centuries, of course, marriage evolved. Polygamy fell out of favor across the Western world, and the wife's age at the time of her marriage began gradually to rise. Most critically, marriage also became a political tool for extended families, a way of soldering alliances and expanding networks of trade. The logic here was simple. If the nuclear family served, already, as a means of preserving a family's power and property, then this same family could presumably expand its power and property by joining them to those of another. One ancient Babylonian king, for example, seized a powerful city and then immediately married the daughter of a powerful neighboring king to cement his claim to power.[22] Similarly, Australia's aborigines have traditionally distributed their daughters according to geography, marrying each girl into a different community so that the wandering family might have kin to call upon as they traveled long distances across harsh terrain.[23]

As marriage became more formalized, the state, and then the church, gradually extended their blessings upon it. Beginning in Roman times (and stretching, some might argue, right to today's champions of family values), the state actively supported its citizens' marriages, seeing them as a crucial way of preserving social stability and providing the state with a steady supply of properly reared soldiers.[24] Augustus, Rome's first emperor, even went so far as to embed marriage into the law. In Imperial Rome, all male citizens between the ages of twenty-five and sixty and all female citizens between the ages of twenty and fifty were required to be married. Sex by or with a married woman (by any man other than her husband) was considered a criminal offense.[25]

The function of marriage evolved slowly over the following centuries, bending and changing along with patterns of industrialization and religious norms. Peasants in feudal Europe married to pool their resources and bear children who would work the family fields. Aristocratic families in China plotted to marry their offspring into higher-ranked or wealthier households. Always, though, marriage served a purpose, a social function that sat atop the biology of reproduction. Men needed women to bear the children who would perpetuate their family lines. Women needed men to conceive their children and provide resources during those periods when they were either pregnant or nursing. Communities needed a way to extend their networks of trade, and families needed a way to protect and grow their wealth. Marriage, an efficient bundle of legal, sexual, and economic ties, struck a deal that worked.[26] Sex was an explicit part of this package. Love and romance were not.

It wasn't until the early days of the Renaissance, in fact, that love and marriage even began to be seen as part of this integrated bundle. By this point, growing levels of wealth across the Western world meant that fewer young people were either living with their parents or eking out an existence from tiny feudal plots. Life spans were expanding and religious authorities were increasingly frowning upon once-common practices such as divorce, polygamy, and out-of-wedlock births. As a result, couples found themselves staying married for longer, and spending more time together than had once been the norm. Which meant, of course, that it helped to actually *like* your spouse. By the early sixteenth century, religious leaders such as Martin Luther were extolling the virtues of romantic love, insisting that mutual love between husband and wife was a religious mandate, "created, implanted, and commanded by God."[27] By the early eighteenth century, "love marriages" had become the accepted norm across most of Europe and the United States. Ironically, though, this birth of love did not destroy the long-standing utility of marriage.[28] It did not banish marriage's social function, or the fundamental role that monogamy played in regulating birth and death and property. Instead, romance was simply integrated into the marriage contract, becoming one of those things—like sex and money, fidelity and inheritance—that husbands and wives brought into their bargain.

Today, the strangest part of marriage is just how sticky it remains. Because while sexual norms have been turned upside down over the past few decades and baby making has been revolutionized; while women have stormed into the workforce and laws giving preference to husbands been yanked regularly off the books; marriage at the start of the twenty-first century is not all that different from marriage at the turn of the nineteenth, or even eighteenth, century. There is still the ceremony, the blessed union, the explicit contract. Men and women still need a license, literally, to marry. They need witnesses to officiate and a ring (not legally required, but almost always present) to seal the deal.

Again, *why?*

Why in a world of independent women and sexually active girls does marriage still exist?[29] Why do young women spend years engaging in casual sex with often-anonymous partners and then presume that they will somehow spend the rest of their lives in a joyous and monogamous relationship? Why are weddings not only white, but decked out with enough silk, roses, and hot hors d'oeuvres to flood a small village? Sexually, marriage is obsolete. Reproductively, it is no longer necessary. Economically, its value is small and variable. And yet men and women across the United States continue not only to move to the altar, but to embrace it with a particular fervor. According to one recent study, nearly 60 percent of single Americans still hoped and intended to marry. Seventy-seven percent said that it was easier for married people to raise a family and 37 percent that married people were more likely to have fulfilling sex.[30] Around 1970, Gloria Steinem famously stated that a woman without a man is like a fish without a bicycle.[31] So why, then, more than forty years later, are so many of us not only grabbing that bicycle, but dressing it up, dragging it around town, and vowing to love it forever?

Cycles of the Ring

I got married on an unseasonably cold day in April. It had rained hard for the past three weeks, and so when the sun emerged that morning we took it as a good omen. I wore an ivory dress and carried roses. My husband wore a suit his father had sewn for him and a face green with nerves. We held the ceremony in a chapel, but had cautiously removed any visible signs of Christ. The Unitarian minister was glorious; my mother-in-law sobbed; and the food was fine. At least I think it was fine. I don't actually recall eating any of it.

Like many young and idealistic couples, my husband and I had tried to make our wedding different. Unique. True to ourselves and our values. And like most fuzzy-headed prenuptial couples, we failed miserably. Yes, my dress was cocktail-length and vaguely off-white. Yes, we had a single attendant apiece rather than troops of bridesmaids and groomsmen. Yes, we blended religions with a moving "Athens meets Jerusalem" theme. But, in the end, we got married pretty much like everyone else. In a church. With a ring. Launched by a proposal. Read the wedding announcements in any local paper: though the names change and the dates progress, though the matches are increasingly mixed in terms of race, religion, and even gender, the texts and accessories are apparently eternal. Girl meets boy; girl loses boy; girl gets boy back and starts shopping for her Vera Wang.

Today, the bridal industry in the United States accounts each year for approximately $72 billion in sales.[32] The entire bottled water industry, by comparison, generates about $11 billion a year; bookstores account for only $16 billion. Fourteen percent of the bridal industry's total comes from the sale of engagement rings; roughly another 5 percent from wedding dresses.[33] Each of these components is regarded by Wall Street analysts as essentially "recession-proof," with couples regularly spending an average of $20,000 on their special day.[34]

To critics, our enduring obsession with the white wedding proves the triumph of both capitalism and conservatism. Harking back to marriage's contractual past, for example, Jaclyn Geller argues that weddings are inherently destructive, symbols of nothing more than the ancient rites by which women were traditionally "given"—often sold— to men. "Wedlock," she states, "is tainted by the historical residue of female subordination; an overwhelming, oppressive social history that many modern brides and grooms are simply not aware of."[35] Reviewing the wedding phenomenon from another angle, a second critic suggests that weddings are a "ritual of heterosexual celebration," a subversive means of imposing heterosexual values across a more varied population. "What the white wedding keeps in place," she argues, "is nothing short of a racist, classist, and heterosexist sexual order."[36]

Intellectually, I totally buy their arguments. Weddings *are* anachronistic. They are expensive and overwrought and mundane in their conformity. At the turn of the twenty-first century, there is no rational reason why women should get married at all anymore, much less why they should do so with all the lace and frippery embraced by Queen Victoria. She was Queen *Victoria*, after all, who ruled over a now-much-despised colonial empire and didn't talk much about sex. Just because she chose to marry her prince in a pure white gown and lacy veil, why should I? And all my friends? And pretty much everyone I've ever known? Why, for heaven's sake, should twice-divorced women go through the same ceremony all over again, cooing those "till death do us part" vows that didn't work the first time around? And why, after decades of fighting valiantly against the heterosexual status quo, would gay and lesbian couples choose to embrace the same cakes, the same rings, the same dress-and-tuxedo affairs? Surely, Geller has to be right: "marriage mania in modern American women did not arise sui generis. It is the result of millennia of law and social custom that have valued women solely in terms of their relationship to men, predicating female respectability on male stewardship."[37]

Yet one has to wonder whether legions of women—smart, confident, well-educated, ostensibly independent women—are really being hoodwinked to such a massive degree. Because we know, after all, the rough history of marriage. We know our mothers did it, and our grandmothers, and all those long-forgotten ancestors who were likely roped into marrying boys they didn't like at all. We know that feminism freed us from economic dependence and that the sexual revolution gave us the ability to control both pleasure and reproduction. But there we go again—marching down aisles and blushing beneath virginal veils. Something deeper has to be going on here, something more primal than simply striving to tie a public knot.

One possibility is health. In study after study, research shows that married individuals live longer, healthier lives than their single counterparts. Single women, for example, suffer from mortality rates that are about 50 percent higher than those of married women; for single men, the differential is a shocking 250 percent.[38] Single men and women both report higher rates of depression and anxiety than do married men and women, and young adults experience notable drops in depression and drinking problems after they tie the knot.[39] "Having a partner who is committed for better or for worse, in sickness and in health," one marriage study concludes, "makes people happier and healthier."[40]

A second possibility is economics. Harking back to more ancient drivers of marriage, research also shows that married couples are generally wealthier than their single counterparts. In 2009, for example, the median household income of married couples in the United States was $71,830, compared to $48,084 for "male householders" and $32,597 for "female householders."[41] In 2004, median assets for married couples were roughly five times those of unmarried men and women.[42] Increasingly, it does not make a difference—economically, at least—whether the husband or wife is the primary wage earner, or whether either or both of them work. Statistically, men and women are just better off in the state of marriage.[43]

Sensible though they may sound, however, both the health and wealth explanations of marriage present two kinds of problems. The first relate to causality, the second to credibility. Put simply, the causality problem means that it's hard to determine whether marriage causes people to be healthier and wealthier, or if healthier and wealthier people are more likely to be married. In the United States, this problem is confounded by the bleak fact that our poorest and least educated citizens are also the least likely to be married.[44] Clearly, these populations suffer from a lack of two-income families (and from the poor single-mother-led families that predominate as a result). But this complex situation doesn't reveal whether marriage actually causes people to become either wealthier or healthier. Meanwhile, the idea that people would actively pursue marriage in the hope of becoming wealthier or healthier strains our credulity—at least a bit. Yes, we must contend with the intensely annoying reality of *Who Wants to Marry a Millionaire?* And with tabloid tales of twenty-six-year-old bombshells who breezily wed geriatric oil barons. But even if women (or men) really were regularly marrying for money, it wouldn't explain why they spend so much money doing it. Or why that thrice-wed oilman goes through it all—the tux, the cake, the ring, the waltz—again. Similarly, even if married people are healthier, it doesn't necessarily mean that individuals are pursuing marriage because they want to improve their health. Ever met a guy looking for a wife because he was worried about his cholesterol?

Finally, women choosing to marry today may be driven by precisely the same motives that prodded their mothers and grandmothers to the altar—the same motives, in fact, that pushed the biblical Rachel into Jacob's arms and compels female frogs to respond to the males' croaking: they are doing it for the children. Or, more precisely, to increase the odds that they will be able to bear and raise children in a safe, secure, and prosperous environment. In the past, wedlock was the only way for women to get these guarantees—the only way for them to have acceptable sex, the only way to create legitimate children, the only way to ensure that these children received rights, a name, and property. Today these links are far more tenuous, but the pull still exists. Most women would rather raise their children with a father nearby.[45] Most households benefit by having two working partners, regardless of those partners' genders and the division of labor between them.[46] And many family benefits in the United States—Social Security payments, veterans benefits, immigration and naturalization laws—are defined primarily in terms of a presumed nuclear family, led by a predictably married husband and wife.

Yet even the draw of children and families can not fully explain the continued rush to the altar. Because women can, after all, raise children on their own, or with unmarried partners. They can have babies as teenagers or into their middle age. They simply don't need—economically, socially, or sexually—to be married. But they want it. Or, as Lori Gottlieb writes movingly in *Marry Him*:

> Growing up, my friends and I . . . could pursue professional careers, decide not to get married at all, and have our sexual needs met whenever we felt like it. The fact that we didn't need a man to have a fulfilling life felt empowering . . .

But then, in our late twenties and early thirties, as more of us moved from relationship to relationship, or went long periods with no meaningful relationship at all, we didn't feel quite so empowered. The truth was, every one of my single friends wanted to be married, but none of us would admit how badly we craved it for fear of sounding weak or needy or, God forbid, antifeminist. We were the generation of women who were supposed to be independent and self-sufficient, but we didn't have a clue how to navigate this modern terrain without sacrificing some core desires.

We didn't want yet another Sunday brunch with the girls. We wanted a lifetime with The Guy.[47]

Interestingly, research on the topic of marital choice is decidedly slim.[48] There are volumes on how to get married; even more volumes on how to stay married; and dozens of academic works that probe the history and economics of this strange custom. But there is blessedly little understanding of just why we still do it. Indeed, as one scholar of marriage states, "I think the interesting question is not why so few people are marrying, but rather, why so many people are marrying, or planning to marry, or hoping to marry, when cohabitation and single parenthood are widely acceptable options."[49]

In search of a (grossly nonscientific) answer, one of my research assistants decided to embark on a small undercover mission. "I bought myself an engagement ring," she reported, "$15 worth of cubic zirconium with a cheap silver band. I didn't think much of the ring when I bought it, but then I slipped it on my left index finger, which has remained bare for 23 years (my grandmother once told me that wearing a ring on that finger before getting engaged could jinx one's chances of ever finding a husband. I haven't decided which is sillier—this obviously nonsensical claim, or the fact that I have refused ever to place a ring on that finger). But finally my naked digit was adorned and it felt fabulous.

"True," she acknowledged, "there was no man attached and no wedding plans in my future, but wearing that ring made me feel empowered, special, like I belonged, at least hypothetically, to someone and something. Even more surprising was the response I got from people around me. From the woman behind the Starbucks counter to the young girl who works at the cleaners, I received knowing smiles and unnecessary attention. They oohed and aahed at my newly acquired bling, and I felt, in some weird metaphysical way, that I had finally made it."

A Plaintive Cry for Love (and Lust)

It is blissfully easy to be cynical about marriage, and to revel in the disdain that critics shower upon it. It's easy to laugh at absurd reality shows like *Bridezilla* and *Bridal Bootcamp*, or to deride the poor families who squander their savings on a frivolous, lavish affair. Yet there's something else running through our continued obsession with marriage, something that is obstructed—but not yet entirely obliterated—by the white-wedding, big-diamond culture. And that something is love.

It sounds so corny to say. Such a throwback to the Donna Reed, Hallmark card, prefeminist view of marriage. But most women today—most people today—still seem to get married not because they want the dress or the ring; not because they are consciously looking to bolster their health or their finances or their baby-rearing status. They get married because they fall in love, and because they truly believe, for one mad weekend or a lifetime, that being linked with one other person is all that really matters. "All my fortunes at thy foot I'll lay," Juliet pledges to Romeo, "and follow thee my lord throughout the world."

Arguably, weddings are the silly part of this equation. Weddings are the anachronistic rituals that pay homage to a contract that no longer exists: the virgin bride, the village approval, the exchange of physical goods. But weddings, critically, are not marriages. They symbolize marriage, of course, and signify its start. Yet it is the marriage, hopefully, that endures; and the marriage, hopefully again, that motivates even the frothiest and most foolish wedding. People don't marry just because they want a wedding. They have a wedding to celebrate and inaugurate a marriage. Yes, a disturbingly large percentage of these marriages will fail over time. Yes, many contemporary weddings are absurd in their excess and terrifying in their gender-based conformity. Yet people still embrace marriage, as a recent Pew study shows, because they believe in the power and primacy of monogamous love, of a love that actually endures.

Shulamith Firestone, perhaps the most radical of the second-wave feminists, understood this relationship at its core. Drawing heavily on Marxist theory, she argued that women were oppressed, not just by economic class or political stature, but by their need for male love, and in particular for married, monogamous love. Just as Marx proclaimed that members of the working class were blinded to their plight by a lack of class consciousness, so, too, did Firestone describe women as blinded by an "all-consuming need for male love," a love that serves "actually to validate [their] existence."[50] This kind of love, she explained, was not the product of media madness or postindustrial society; it wasn't embedded in little girls' minds by fairy tales or their mothers' fantasies. It was instead a product of biological differentiation—of the immutable fact that men and women were separated by their reproductive functions. Women, according to Firestone, didn't just want to love their husbands; they needed to. Searching for a solution to this historical problem, she, like Marx, proposed a revolution: a feminist revolution, in this case, in which women would use the emerging technologies of assisted reproduction to break forever the bonds of love and sex and marriage. Only then, she declared, would the tyranny of the biological family be broken and women attain true equality.[51]

It is intriguing to think about how Firestone, like Marx again, may have been right in her analysis and wrong in her prescriptions. Maybe women are condemned by love, just as people in general are motivated by self-interest. Maybe they strive—in general, and during at least some stretch of their lives—to bond with a single mate, to bear children with him, share resources, grow old. Maybe this situation is not ideal, either for individual women or for the species as a whole. But maybe, like gentoo penguins and Canada geese, that's just who we are, pining—despite the history, the inequities, the bad bridesmaids' dresses and three-tier cakes—for someone to love and to cherish, till death do us part. Or, as Robin Morgan, one of the most ardent of the radical feminists, wrote in describing her own complicated marriage: "When they look into one another's eyes in a certain coherent light, two living spirits try to reach each other . . . Something in each will love the other until death, ceremony or no ceremony, ritual or no. If that were not so, the rest would be easy. And the world would be lost."[52]

Certainly, the rise of gay marriage seems to suggest that there is something particularly powerful about committed and monogamous pairs, something that transcends both convention and reproduction. Gay couples, after all, do not need the sanction of marriage to bear or acquire children. (In fact, it's often still easier for a gay person to adopt as a single man or woman than as half of an openly gay couple.) Until very recently, they received no legal benefits from a formal union—either the benefits were simply not available to homosexual partners, or they were awarded equally to domestic partners regardless of their legal status. And yet, starting in 2004, thousands of gay couples began flocking to the few available altars in the United States, fiercely determined to wed. By 2009, nearly 150,000 same-sex couples in the United States reported being married.[53] Part of what drove this development, of course, was the fight for and acknowledgment of equal rights. By entering into marriage—traditionally defined as a union between one man and one woman—gay men and women were claiming a status that had long been denied them. As married couples, moreover, they had access to specific benefits, from tax treatment to visitation rights, that had always been reserved for their heterosexual peers. Yet it wasn't just rights and privileges that drove so many couples down the aisle. It was also, again, about love, and about the public demonstration of a private commitment. Richard Dorr and John Mace, for example, who celebrated sixty-one years together in 2011, chose to get married at the ages of eighty-four and ninety-one, respectively. "To be able to start a new phase of life by being married after sixty-one years would really be a completion of something that's been quite marvelous and wonderful for us both," the couple stated. "We've always thought of ourselves as a couple, as a pair. It would be wonderful to be able to say we are married."[54] Rather than destroying marriage, as so many conservative critics had predicted, gay unions seem only to have strengthened it, reaffirming marriage, not as a sexist construction or reproductive structure, but a choice made out of love.

Clearly, women today don't need to get married. They can have sex without marriage, children without marriage, careers and status and bank accounts on their own. Women can revel in unembarrassed solitude, if they so choose, or enter into a series of anonymous relationships. They can treasure platonic friendships or live for decades with lovers whom they never want to marry.[55] And yet, for better or worse, marriage remains a part of most American women's lives, an aspiration that stubbornly persists and that defies the most reasonable case against it. Even Gloria Steinem, after all, got married at sixty-six, decades after she first decried marriage laws as being designed for a "person and a half." Describing her new husband (who, sadly, died just three years later), the always-eloquent Steinem sounded vaguely, even if only briefly, like a besotted bride: "We love each other," she confessed to Barbara Walters, "and, you know, this is the most important thing, that we really want to be together . . . We both felt that we wanted to be responsible for each other."[56] In other words, they fell in love.

Feminism, except in its most radical incarnations, never demanded that women give up either love or marriage. Yet, for the generations of women born and raised after the 1960s, feminism's gifts of choice and independence seemed to compel young women—particularly young women with education and ambition—to seize all the options they could possibly grab. To date all the men who appealed to them. To experiment with all career paths. To travel and build friendships and indulge their multiple passions. To have it all.

Yet marriage, by its very definition, is not about "all," but about "one." It's explicitly about giving up an infinity of possibilities and selecting a single mate. Forever. In historical terms, the monumental shift for women occurred with the rise of companionate marriage and the belief that women were free to choose their own spouses, rather than having a third party—a father, or pastor, or matchmaker—make that choice for them. What did not change, however, was the monogamy and finiteness of choice itself. In other words, the problem of marriage for women raised with great and boundless expectations is that it means making choices, not just enjoying them. Choosing this man and not that one. Sleeping with this one and never again with the others.

In the past, women were so strictly confined by the structure of marriage that the idea of choice was impossible. Women no more chose their husbands than they chose their parents or place of birth. Today, by contrast, women swim in a sea of marital options: whether to marry, whom to marry, what gender to marry. This choice often confounds and perplexes young women, or urges them to delay marriage until they have the perfect career or the perfect guy or have exhausted their romantic wanderings. What all this choice seems not to have done, however, is to reduce the status or affection that marriage still enjoys. If anything, marriage elicits a nostalgia today that is greater than it was in the prefeminist era, when even the most educated and affluent woman felt compelled to have a ring on her finger and a man at her side by the time she turned twenty.

Ironically, then, turning marriage into a choice has upped the ante on perfection. Once upon a time, women married because someone forced them to, or because marriage was the only route to prosperity, children, and sex. Now, with so many alternative pathways to these other goodies, marriage has become more ambitious, in many ways, and more fragile. It's not just about settling down comfortably with a reasonably inclined spouse; about finding a mate who will simply conceive children and provide for them. Instead, it's about fireworks and coparenting; about lifelong romance, ecstatic sex, and partners who will truly be everything for those lucky enough to snare them.[57] "He's not just my husband, he's my best friend!" coos one happy tabloid bride after another. "First he swept her off her feet," runs another common story line, "and now he's sweeping the twins' cookie crumbs from the expensive Italian tile!" We want our marriages to be about more than sex or children, which is good. We want our husbands to be partners rather than just providers. But by embracing these multiple goals—by aiming and expecting to have it all again—we have also turned marriage into a romantic ideal, a fairy-tale vision in which princes stay charming forever and unions are perpetually blessed. Maybe that's why we throw white weddings with such gusto; why gay couples are scrambling to the altar in such numbers; why my research assistant felt such a zing of satisfaction from her faux engagement bauble. We are primed to be perfect, and the perfect marriage—complete with perfect husband, perfect children, and the perfect three-tiered wedding cake— remains an inherent part of the picture.

In fact, maybe our continued obsession with weddings stems from a deep-seated realization that marriage, no matter how good it is, will never be perfect. The cake will quickly get eaten. The kids will inevitably get sick. The perfect groom won't sweep those Italian tiles for too long, and may even remain a dirty-linoleum guy all his life. Love, if you're lucky, remains. So do contentment, and comfort, and sex. But the passion of the first embrace, by its very definition, dies. So does the adrenaline of the hookup hunt, or the stolen foreign affair. In some subconscious way, maybe we know this. We know, in other words, that the bargain women strike in marriage today is different from what it was for our grandmothers. Because they got things—sex, a family, a lifetime of respectability—that could exist only in marriage. We give some things up. And so rather than mourn the loss of those things, we embrace a tipsy view of the perfect wedding. A glamorous event. A magical event. An event that can be controlled and managed and paid for in a way that actual marriage defies.

Weddings, in the end, are both easy and silly. Love is what's hard.

Several years ago, I was teaching a class about the international diamond cartel. It was largely a class about market control and marketing; about how the diamond industry has brilliantly created an "illusion of scarcity" by stockpiling the bulk of diamonds mined in a given year and then prompting young men to demonstrate their love in the only suitable way—with a diamond engagement ring costing, the industry helpfully suggests, around four months' salary. The class proceeded as one might expect. The male students (and they were predominantly male) unpacked the strategy of the diamond myth. They marveled at the genius of diamond stockpiling, enviously analyzed the price control that the diamond producers exerted. Those who were married or engaged told stories of their own fumbling engagement purchases—and how, in retrospect, they felt somehow duped or pressured into buying that ring. At the end, however, one young woman resolutely put her hand up. Her name was Susannah, and she was both brilliant and beautiful—a tiny southern blonde who was one of the smartest students in the room. "I know I'm not supposed to say this," she drawled, "but I really want to get married someday. And if anyone out there is listening, y'all better know this: I want a really big ring!"

6

MYTHOLOGIES OF BIRTH

"Give me sons," cried Rachel to Jacob. "Give me sons or I shall die."

—Genesis 30:1

Pregnancy is barbaric.

—Shulamith Firestone, *The Dialectic of Sex*

Before she even enrolled in graduate school, Christy Jones had co-founded a technology company, served as president of the spin-off firm that grew from it, and been featured on three separate covers of *Forbes* magazine. She breezed through her MBA program and, in her second year, stumbled upon a frighteningly good idea: freezing eggs for young and ambitious women of means, women who, like herself, had the inclination to have children but not, necessarily, the time or appropriate partner. In 2004, Jones launched Extend Fertility, a start-up company that promised the "best-in-class service to women wanting to preserve their fertility." For roughly $13,000 plus annual storage fees of $450, Extend Fertility offered women what Mother Nature did not: the chance to align their procreative schedules with their professional ones. The chance, in other words, to have it all.

At this point, the science behind egg freezing was uncertain. Scientists had succeeded in producing a small number of pregnancies from frozen eggs, but the numbers were small, the success rate tiny, and the circumstances dire—usually involving women with cancer or some other disease that forced the premature removal of their ovaries. But

Jones was both a diligent learner and a brilliant marketer. She hired the best fertility researchers in the world, partnered with the leading IVF clinics, and announced—at business schools and law schools, urban cocktail parties and women's forums—how egg freezing could free women at last from the constraints of their own biology. By 2006, the company had frozen eggs for roughly two hundred clients and had released news of its first six births. In the meantime, Jones married at age thirty-four and soon had her own first baby. The old-fashioned way.

There's something about babies—and pregnancy and birth—that remains central to most women's lives. Even women with high-powered, high-pressure careers; women without husbands or financial means; women born without wombs or ovaries still want to procreate, to create and nurture children of their own. Today, women looking to become mothers can select from a virtual Chinese menu of options. They can freeze their eggs and buy their sperm, rent a surrogate womb or "adopt" an orphaned embryo. They can select their offspring's genes with a cutting-edge technology known as PGD (preimplantation genetic diagnosis) or pay a premium for eggs "donated" by Ivy League girls. They can have their babies pretty much when they want, how they want, and with whomever they fancy.

What remains wholly unchanged, however, is the underlying desire: the desire to procreate, to reproduce, to have children and to mother them. This yearning transcends all boundaries of race and ethnicity. It transcends class and socioeconomic status. And it even apparently transcends sexual orientation, as witnessed by the recent baby boom among gay and lesbian couples. Although there is evidence that women in some parts of the world (Italy, most spectacularly, and Japan) are choosing to have fewer children, nearly all women, at some point in their lives, become mothers. Indeed, as of 2008, women around the globe had each given birth, on average, to 2.5 live children.[1] What makes this number particularly remarkable is that roughly 10 to 15 percent of any population are believed by demographers to be technically infertile. Essentially, then, virtually every woman who can produce a child does—one way or another, by hook or by crook, with or without that ideal guy.

The strength of this desire is not, on its own, surprising. Women, after all, are biologically programmed to procreate; like men, and indeed like individuals of all species, we are driven by our genes to reproduce some version of ourselves. "Be fruitful and multiply," commands the Bible. "Procreate and abound in numbers," exhorts the Qur'an. These ancient exhortations are simply capturing the reality of life: unless we give birth, we die.

For nearly all of history, this biological necessity was reflected in the societies that sustained it. Women's fertility was treasured and cherished, and women's chastity was ferociously guarded. Women were presumed—or pressured, or forced—to remain virgins until marriage and then faithful ever after to the husbands whose paternity was thereby ensured. With no means of birth control apart from abstention, women had their babies early, often, and at whatever intervals Mother Nature determined. From analyzing ancient birth records and observing still-indigenous cultures, demographers estimate that premodern women gave birth to an average of about four to five children over the course of their lives. Roughly two of these children did not survive infancy, and many of their mothers died in childbirth.[2]

With the advent of the Industrial Revolution, however, these dismal facts began slowly to improve. Chastity belts gave way to corsets, couples embraced crude but moderately effective means of birth control, and growing medical knowledge about the mechanics of puerperal fever (a major cause of death in childbirth) led eventually to steady declines in maternal mortality. By 1880, birth rates in the United States had fallen from 7 children per woman (the rate in 1800) to 4.2. By 1930, they had plummeted to 2.4.[3] Similar trends prevailed in the United Kingdom, where English birth rates fell from 5.5 per woman in the 1870s to 2.4 in the 1920s.[4]

Even greater changes, though, emerged in a tightly compressed period between the 1960s and the 1980s, when a series of scientific breakthroughs suddenly changed everything the world had ever known about the business of making babies. Once the pill became widely available in the mid-1960s, women—for the first time in history—were able to separate sex almost totally from reproduction, seizing control over what had long been Mother Nature's domain. Once abortion was safe and legal (1973 in the United States, by the late 1970s across Europe and in most of Asia), women could decide whether to proceed with a particular pregnancy, weighing—again for the first time in history—the desirability of a child's birth against its costs. And once in vitro fertilization (IVF) became possible (beginning in 1978), women (and men) could have children at times, and in circumstances, that once would have been simply impossible.

For many feminists, the combined effect of these technologies was revolutionary, promising to cut the complicated chains that had long bound women to their baby-making roles. In the early 1980s, for example, a group of lesbians established the Feminist Self Insemination Group, using syringes and turkey basters to inseminate themselves with sperm from homosexual donors and proclaiming, "Doing it ourselves [is] one of the roads to getting in charge of our reproductive capacities."[5] Shulamith Firestone was even more ecstatic, predicting that technological advances would at last liberate women from their reproductive function.[6] In a muted form, these visions seeped into the public realm, inspiring both mindless fantasies such as *Three Men and a Baby* (no woman in sight to help with diapers and bottles and playdates) and dystopian horrors such as *The Handmaid's Tale* (in which breeding is the forced occupation of a select, fertile few). Cutting across the media, though, from feminist critics to Hollywood producers, was a central premise: that technology had loosened women's ties to conception and made motherhood a more varied and elective affair.

As was the case with sex, however, changes in the nature of motherhood have played out differently than either the most enthusiastic feminists or their most conservative critics had expected. Yes, on the one hand, women are acquiring babies through a startling array of newfangled means. They are having children later in life, as single women increasingly, and often in same-sex relationships. They are choosing their children's genes and genders, their hair color and desired athletic prowess. On the other hand, though, women are still succumbing to precisely the same yearning that drove Rachel to despair, the same yearning that drove their mothers to the altar and their foremothers to ancient fertility sites. They are still dying, in a handful of tragic cases, from the pursuit of pregnancy and are still afflicted by all the physical attributes that accompany the ability to breed: menstrual periods, hormonal shifts, breasts. These are not the pretty parts of pregnancy (except, I guess, for the breasts), but they are undeniably part of the whole want-a-baby/have-a-baby package. And because so many women—regardless of social change and technological breakthroughs—continue to want babies and have babies, they are also continuing to face the same baby-related issues that bound and confounded their ancestors. Bleeding. Breast-feeding. Morning sickness and colicky nights and harried trips to the emergency room.

Together, changes in technology and the social mores of motherhood led women of the postfeminist generations to believe that conception and childbirth were experiences they could control. That unlike their mothers and grandmothers, they would be able to time their children's births and luxuriate in the sensual pangs of labor. That they could banish the sheer bloodiness of childbirth and embrace instead the joys of a perfectly birthed, perfectly planned, perfectly endowed child. And to some extent they can. With assisted reproduction, women can now exert a considerable measure of control over the timing and genetic composition of their offspring. Thanks to the decades-long struggle for reproductive rights, they can avoid unwanted pregnancies and choose a mode of childbirth (with or without drugs, surgery, or video recorders) that suits their individual style. They can have babies with or without partners, and with or without men.

Yet despite these advances, pregnancy and childbirth remain mysterious, often messy events, the burden of which falls almost entirely upon women. It is women, after all, who carry the child from the instant of its conception; women whose bodies change with pregnancy; women who bleed and miscarry and are pummeled each month by hormones. No scientific advance has changed these vital differences; no work-life-balance plan can ever hope to eradicate them. Which is fine. For as both the fertility industry and the natural birth movement proclaim, pregnancy is a blessed thing, a profound and mystical moment reserved solely for women. The problem comes when we forget that the majesty is also very messy, and that the blessings of childbirth also give women burdens that men simply don't have and can never fully understand. For obvious biological reasons, women experience babies differently than men. They yearn for babies, in most cases, more strongly, and they parent differently as a result. This is not necessarily a bad state of affairs, or one that condemns women to a lifetime of bed rest and infant care. But it is a core reality that we ignore at our peril.

Women want babies. They bear babies, in a complex and still

occasionally dangerous process. Over the past few decades, science and social movements have given women (and, to a lesser extent, men) a vast and unprecedented range of reproductive options—artificial insemination, egg donation, egg freezing, IVF, ICSI, and PGD. Individually, each of these choices gives a woman a wider berth in which to build her life. Together, they provide women with a million ways to pursue perfection in the fine art of baby making. And a million ways, of course, to somehow get it wrong.

The Quest for Conception

If there's anything that men and women share equally, anything that depends on a specific and special contribution by each member of a heterosexual couple, it would seem to be conception. You need, after all, both a man and a woman to create a child through natural means. You need an equal combination of one egg and one sperm; one penis and one womb. And yet men and women's contribution to conception, and their experience of conception, are totally and fundamentally different.

Consider what happens when you go to the doctor—not to a specialist, even, but just an everyday general practitioner. A dentist, even. Everyone—man, woman, and child—fills out the same basic forms. Insurance coverage, medications, family history. But women are asked an additional series of questions: *Number of children. Number of births. Number of pregnancies.* They seem relatively innocuous, but the underlying math essentially captures the story of a woman's most intimate life. If the number of pregnancies is higher than the number of births, of course, then the woman had an abortion or experienced a miscarriage—both presumed to be searing, even tragic, events. If the number of births is different from the number of children, then she either watched a child die, or acquired one through means other than pregnancy. In these three questions, therefore, lie a woman's reproductive history: the children she had, the children she didn't have, the children she lost or found. These facts define a woman's life much more than a man's. These crude numbers—of births and conceptions, miscarriages and loss—embed themselves in a woman's identity and shape who she becomes.

It is not surprising, therefore, that throughout history, across time and place and culture and race, women have been driven by the quest to conceive—to bear a child and call it their own.[7] In ancient Rome, women lit torches and built fires to honor Diana, the goddess of fertility; in Scandinavia, they paid homage to Freyja, daughter of the sea god who controlled life and death.[8] Again and again, history records the obsession with which societies approached mothers and pregnancy and birth. They built statues and shrines to fertility gods and developed elaborate rituals to both prompt and celebrate conception. Remnants of these rituals are still with us today, from ceremonies such as the traditional Jewish circumcision (*brit milah*) to celebrations like baby showers.

Technically speaking, most ancient cultures realized that both a man and a woman were needed to make a baby appear. In fact, one prominent school of research in Europe assumed for centuries that women provided only the nourishment of the egg, with men delivering a tiny, fully formed human each time they ejaculated.[9]

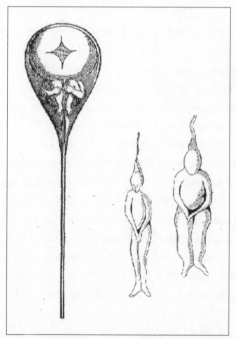

Homunculi in sperm as drawn by N. Hartsoecker in 1694

Yet the responsibility for producing a child still fell, oddly enough, upon women, who were routinely and often harshly punished if children failed to appear. In ancient India, for example, a husband could tie up his childless wife and burn her. In China, the childless wife was not permitted to die at home.[10] Across the world, until well into the nineteenth century, infertility was defined almost entirely as an ailment of women. Men were deemed infertile only if they were incapable of maintaining an erection—which, as it turns out, wasn't even the case.*

Accordingly, women have long devoted themselves to the pursuit of pregnancy. They have begged for babies and prayed for babies and indulged in rituals ranging from the poignant to the bizarre. During the Middle Ages, for example, women drank potions of mule urine and rabbit blood and doused themselves with herbs believed to induce pregnancy. They kissed trees, slid on stones, and bathed in brackish water thought to resemble the blood of childbirth.[11] In eighteenth-century London, wealthy socialites paid 500 guineas a night (roughly $37,500 in today's dollars) to sleep with their husbands on a "celestial bed" said to promote fruitfulness by "powerfully agitating" its occupants in "the delights of love."[12]

It is easy, of course, to blame these excesses on societal pressures. After all, for most of recorded history, childless women have been pushed and prodded to produce that longed-for child: the heir to the throne, the worker in the field, the son who will carry his father's name. Women have been routinely abandoned for failing to conceive, scorned by their families and communities. Think of King Henry, for instance, who annulled his marriage to Catherine of Aragon when she proved unable to produce a surviving male heir and then executed his second wife, Anne Boleyn, for her similar failure. Or of Napoléon Bonaparte, who divorced his beloved Josephine when, after fourteen years of marriage, she had not borne him any children. Because women are defined so sharply by their reproductive prowess, as feminist critics have long argued, *not* reproducing becomes a woman's sin; a sign of failure before her family, society, and God. Or, as Adrienne Rich wrote in 1967, "Woman's status as childbearer has been made into a major

---

*Technically, impotent men are not necessarily infertile. So long as their sperm is viable and can be transported into a woman's womb, they can conceive.

fact of her life. Terms like 'barren' and 'childless' have been used to negate any further identity. The term 'nonfather' does not exist in any realm of social categories."[13]

Yet the quest to conceive seems to run deeper than even society's most rigid constraints, deeper than the demands of husbands and dashed expectations of mothers-in-law. To put it simply and anecdotally: most women, at some point in their lives, want children. Want children so badly, in fact, that they will do nearly anything to get them. Want children who aren't their nephews, or their students, or the toddlers from next door. They want to conceive and bear children that they can call their own.

Consider my friend Dina. She is forty-two and French, a gorgeous and glamorous woman who is regularly described in European media as part of the intellectual jet set. She has produced several documentaries and television shows, each of which has been widely and enthusiastically reviewed. After a decade of dating some of the Continent's most eligible bachelors, she settled down about five years ago with a lovely and wildly successful author. They decided to start a family. But Dina had been suffering for years from a strange malady that no doctor could quite diagnose: massive back pains, severe endometriosis, complicated fibroid tumors. It didn't appear that she could carry a pregnancy, or that she should try. So she and Laurent began investigating surrogacy—illegal in France but available in the United States. They spent tens of thousands of dollars and weeks of time shuttling across the Atlantic, interviewing surrogacy agencies, possible surrogates, and doctors willing to extract Dina's eggs without subjecting her to the massive hormonal injections that might upset her fragile body. They made embryos and froze embryos and implanted them in strangers' wombs. Nothing worked. Dina upped the ante. She delayed the production schedule for her next film, declined several major speaking engagements, and agreed to a much more punishing—and potentially dangerous—regimen of hormonal stimulation. No luck. So now she is back in France, undergoing IVF again and preparing to carry whatever child she might conceive. Dina has been at this now for over three years. She has put a stellar career on hold and is eagerly hoping for a pregnancy that could well compromise her health. "It's so hard," she confessed to me recently. "So sad. But I just want a baby."

Lida, a former student of mine, has a very different tale. Born in Ukraine, she earned a Ph.D. in that country before emigrating to the United States and attending Harvard Business School. She graduated with honors and began a high-powered career as an automotive executive, concentrating on the production of energy-efficient batteries. She is probably around thirty-seven. Recently, Lida sent me a note. "Believe it or not," she wrote, "I am thirty-five weeks pregnant. I kept looking for that special guy, but it just did not happen, unfortunately. So I decided to be a single mom. It is a little girl who is moving a lot and having hiccups often and her name will be Julia." Lida promised to send me pictures of the baby as soon as she arrived, and then continued, "I know of course it would have been ideal for Julia to grow up with a father and a mother. It was not an easy decision and I still feel guilty. I probably always will. But I am very happy and can hardly wait to meet her." By the time you are reading this, Julia will hopefully be a happy, healthy child. And Lida will have joined the roughly six million American women who, despite having wonderful careers and exciting lives and boyfriends aplenty, are going to once unimaginable lengths to get what they still crave: a baby.

My own path to parenthood was decidedly less complicated. I got married at twenty-three and pregnant just over two years later—earlier than expected, to be honest, and before we had actually decided "to try." When my first son was two and a half, and I was about to enter my first semester of teaching, my husband and I realized we had a tiny little window of opportunity: if we conceived in December, the baby would be born in October, giving me about three months before I had to be back in the classroom in January. (Harvard Business School had no official maternity policy at that time.) We seized the moment, and Baby Number Two showed up precisely forty weeks later. By the time we all survived the toddler years, my husband and I presumed we were done. Two boys. Two parents. One badly behaving cat and a phenomenally good nanny. Why go anywhere else? So I got an IUD and that was that.

Until about five years later, when I suddenly and inexplicably started fantasizing about another child. A girl, specifically, with long dark hair. This made no sense. We had no room in our lives or our house for another person. The boys were now happily ensconced in elementary school (no more diapers! no more finger paints!) and the nanny, shuffling now from arthritis, made it clear she couldn't stay with us much longer. Still, I plaintively started to lobby my husband for a third. "Just one more," I said. "A little girl." "No problem," he would always joke back. "You can have as many more as you want. With your next husband."

Then one day, a few months after my thirty-seventh birthday, I went to my favorite deli and ordered chopped liver and sour pickles—just because it kind of felt right. It didn't cross my mind that I could possibly be pregnant—until, all of a sudden, I was. Reading that darn stick in my upstairs bathroom, I flew into a frenzy. Because if I was pregnant, it had happened with an IUD in place—which, I vaguely recalled, was not a good thing for the baby. I ran to my study, started throwing papers around, and finally found the little instruction sheet I had buried long ago. "In the uncommon event you get pregnant while using an IUD," it read, "seek emergency care because pregnancy with an intra-uterine device can be life threatening and may result in loss of pregnancy or fertility." Shit. I called my gynecologist and wasted no words. "I'm pregnant," I said, "and the IUD is still there. You have to take it out. Now." She started talking about blood tests and false positives, but I wasn't hearing. "I'll be there in twenty minutes," I said. Oddly, I never— for a minute, a second—contemplated abortion, or even letting the in-place IUD do its dirty work. Instead, like Dina and Lida, like millions of women with good reason to do otherwise, I simply wanted that baby.

The pregnancy did not go well. I was thirty-seven, after all, and had gotten pregnant against all medical odds. Two days after my doctor removed the IUD, a sonogram showed an alarming but unidentifiable dot. A blood clot, the doctor speculated? Maybe a twin that hadn't survived the procedure? My husband took the news with remarkable aplomb but couldn't wholly embrace it. We didn't tell the boys. Six weeks later, reading on a couch in Vermont, I started bleeding. Very, very badly. Since the rest of my family was skiing at the time, I wound up at the mountainside clinic, miscarrying alongside the teenaged snowboarders with busted ankles. But when I finally reached the local hospital, the stunned nurse found a heartbeat. The baby had somehow survived, and I trundled back home, convinced I was carrying a miracle child.

Four weeks later, though, alone in the radiation suite at Boston's Brigham and Women's Hospital, I watched the technician try, and fail, to find that heartbeat again. It wasn't there. The baby had died. Tests later revealed that it had been a perfectly healthy girl.

Looking back all these years, I still somehow feel that I had no right to take it so hard. Unlike Dina, and the millions of women who wrestle with infertility, I had already had two easy pregnancies and produced two wonderful, healthy children. Unlike Lida, and the growing numbers of women who choose single motherhood, I had a husband and family in place. But even while pushing middle age; even with the kids I had and a job that absorbed all my time, I was seized again by the myth of motherhood. The beautiful myth of having babies, and raising babies, and loving them no matter what.

On the Frontlines of Fertility

In my case, the complications of pregnancy unfolded along a fairly standard path: old-fashioned, heterosexual sex, in the context of marriage. For Dina and Lida, though, and for millions of women like them, technology has now produced at least fifteen additional ways to have a baby, none of which involves sex. All of these new means involve technology, money, and the participation of other people. They aren't very sexy. But they have given growing numbers of women what Rachel craved: a chance to have a baby before they die.

In the United States, large-scale assisted reproduction emerged in the 1950s, a product of both scientific advance and a postwar embrace of babies, motherhood, and happy nuclear families. The first major breakthrough was the discovery of hormones, bodily substances that scientists had suspected for some time as having links to reproduction; substances, they realized, that were produced differently in men's and women's bodies. By the 1930s researchers had finally identified the full range of "female" hormones and had plotted the intricate chemical dance that drives a normal ovulatory cycle. Shortly thereafter, they managed to extract small quantities of the key fertility regulators, estrogen and progesterone, and began quietly experimenting with hormonally based treatments. For all practical purposes, these substances remained both inordinately expensive ($200 for a gram of progesterone in the 1930s) and wildly ineffective in actually "curing" infertility. Yet the sheer fact that they could be procured and provided meant that doctors now had some means of prodding fertility, some way, short of prayers and magic, of helping a woman's body to conceive.

Meanwhile, another cast of researchers was approaching infertility from the male side, peering into cases where an apparently fertile man (that is, one who could produce an erection) was nevertheless unable to produce a child. The first breakthrough occurred in nineteenth-century Philadelphia, when one insightful physician noticed that many of his "infertile" female patients were married to men who had contracted gonorrhea at some earlier point in their lives. Although the men had technically been cured of the disease, the doctor saw a distinctive pattern and began to suspect a cause. To test his theory, he—rather shockingly, even for the nineteenth century—persuaded his young patient to undergo an "operation" that he said might cure her infertility. The operation he performed, however, was an insemination, taking sperm from his best-looking medical student and injecting it into the woman's womb.[14] And thus began two now long-standing practices: using artificial insemination to address male fertility and relying on good-looking medical students to provide the raw material.

Over the decades that followed, artificial insemination evolved along a "friends and family" model. If a couple suspected that the male partner in a relationship might be sterile (that is, wholly infertile), they quietly asked friends or family members to provide the missing sperm, inseminating the wife themselves or with the help of an accommodating physician. As these physicians become increasingly aware of both the demand for artificial insemination (AI), however, and its relatively high rate of success; and as more and more doctors began to see infertility as a curable illness, the medical profession eventually embraced AI as a formal treatment. By the 1950s, a growing array of clinics and infertility specialists offered to quietly find sperm for their patients, drawing largely upon the largesse of medical students or, occasionally, um, their own resources. By the 1980s, sperm banks had gone commercial, paying donors for their contributions and selling specific kinds of sperm (from a promised blond and blue-eyed donor, for example, or a varsity athlete) to a growing range of customers.[15] Today, large-scale banks such as the California Cryobank provide sperm recipients with twenty-four pages of information about "their" donor, including religion, hair texture, occupation, and years of education. Fairfax Cryobank in Virginia offers extended donor profiles for $70, including childhood photos and a silhouette. It also provides a personal shopping service in which clients send photos of the person they would like their child to resemble.[16]

The second major breakthrough in fertility treatment came in 1978, with the surprise birth of Louise Brown, the world's first "test tube baby." Technically, of course, Louise wasn't born in a test tube, or even a petri dish. She was the product of in vitro fertilization, a path-breaking technology that would eventually win its creators a Nobel Prize in Medicine. In theory, IVF is a breathtakingly simple process. To treat women who cannot conceive on their own, doctors retrieve an egg from the woman's ovaries and collect sperm from her desired partner. They then mix the egg and sperm in the laboratory (in "vitro," or glass), collect the embryo that results, and implant it back in the woman's womb. The pregnancy that proceeds from that point is perfectly normal, as are the children born as a result. Practically, though, the procedure took decades to perfect. And politically, it let loose a bombshell.

Most of the excitement that initially surrounded IVF came from its critics—from religious leaders who deplored the disruption of God's presumed laws and philosophers who worried about issues such as degradation and dehumanization.[17] Politicians likewise wavered this way and that, careful not to speak ill of the thousands of would-be parents already clamoring for IVF treatment but wary of endorsing the science behind it. And feminists split into various, often warring, camps, some embracing the new technologies as the tools that would finally liberate women from their reproductive function and others condemning them as yet another male-dominated invasion of women's lives and bodies.[18]

As the feminists were debating, however, the technology of reproduction was galloping ahead. In the early 1990s, researchers began to experiment with egg donation, using the eggs of one woman (typically a healthy young woman) to create embryos for another (typically older and less fertile). On the male side, doctors perfected a delicate technique known as ICSI (intracytoplasmic sperm injection, pronounced "icksy") in which they removed a single, healthy-looking sperm from an infertile man and injected it directly into an egg. Most dramatically, perhaps, researchers began tinkering in the early 1990s with the embryos conceived through IVF, searching for ways of identifying the genetic characteristics that each contained. While early efforts along these lines concentrated on identifying the markers for devastating diseases like Tay-Sachs and cystic fibrosis, doctors swiftly realized that essentially all the genetic markers of a child—gender, eye color, height, hair texture—could be read well before that child's birth, giving parents an unprecedented window into who their child might become.

In many respects, these high-tech interventions merely return to women the power that nature denied: the primal power to produce a child. Using IVF, for example, women born without fallopian tubes can give birth to perfectly normal, perfectly healthy children. Using PGD, women whose genes carry the threat of a devastating illness can consciously decide to avoid this threat, and to implant an embryo likely to grow into a normal, healthy child. In both instances, assisted reproduction is essentially bringing women back to normal, allowing them simply to realize the eternal myth of motherhood.

At the same time, however, high-tech baby making also creates a whole host of new myths, myths that have already become deeply entwined with the very definition of modern motherhood. Because just as assisted reproduction allows women to do things that were never before possible, so, too, does it prompt them in that direction. If you can have a child at fifty-two, for example, why not? If you can choose the contours of your embryos, why not go for twins or triplets? Two blond-haired girls, perhaps, plus a little boy? If you *can* freeze your eggs or select your sperm, then maybe you *should*.

Recall that assisted reproduction has been possible for only about thirty years—fifty, if you count the early availability of sperm donation. Yet in just that time, a mere speck in the span of human reproduction, women have embraced high-tech baby making, not only as an option when nature fails, but as a menu of sorts from which they can nibble over the course of their lives. Consider my friends Dina and Lida. Thirty years ago, neither of them would have had the choices they now confront. Lida would either have married earlier or resigned herself to being single and childless. Dina would probably have adopted.

Now, though, the presence of choice—in all its magical, medical guises—has prodded them both in new, and fairly scary, directions. Lida will be raising a child on her own, in middle age, in a foreign country. Not impossible, of course, but tough. Dina, by the end of her travails, will probably have spent hundreds of thousands of dollars and undergone months of painful and possibly dangerous medical procedures. And she still may not have a child.

The pressure of choice is most pronounced in two of assisted reproduction's newest and most high-tech corners: egg freezing and egg donation. Here, women are facing options that would have shocked and confounded their grandmothers. Here, they are truly grabbing what was once the rallying cry of feminism: the opportunity to control their reproductive lives.

In their natural state, a woman's eggs are difficult to come by, much less manipulate. They lie hidden in the ovaries, released sparingly—once a month, at a precise but mysterious time—over the course of a woman's life. They are finite in number and rapidly lose their vitality as a woman ages.[19] Since time immemorial, then, women's reproductive lives have been dictated by their ovulatory cycles: they have had their babies, literally, when and while their eggs were ripe. Using egg freezing and egg donation, however, women can now turn this dynamic upside down, having babies when they, and not their eggs, are ready. They can freeze their eggs after law school, for instance, and defrost them once they've made partner. They can use their sisters' eggs to make their babies once theirs have grown too old, or trawl the Internet for young and willing egg donors, women who, for anywhere between $6,000 and $25,000, will eagerly, in the parlance of the trade, "give the gift of life and love." At sites like the Egg Donor Program (www.eggdonation.com) and Egg Donation, Inc. (www.eggdonor.com) they can scroll through hundreds of possible donors, choosing them (or more precisely, their genes) according to factors such as hair color, SAT scores, and musical taste.[20] If you live in a major city like New York or Los Angeles, take a quiet peek someday at all those adorable twins peering from their double Maclaren strollers. Look at their mothers. Look closely again. Look often enough and, statistically speaking, you will be staring into the face of egg donation and designer babies. Chosen children, and children of choice.

All of these children, presumably, were desperately wanted. All are, hopefully, living good lives and bringing their parents great joy (until they become teenagers, of course. But that's another chapter). The question, though, is how to define the outer limits of choice. Do we really want sixty-two-year-old women to be mothering infants? Or women of any age giving birth to octuplets? Should young women consciously delay motherhood to pursue their careers, or provide the raw material that makes others' pregnancies possible?

Most important, is all this choice really good for women? Does it give them freedom, or just up the ante? To be sure, the advent of assisted reproduction means that women in the twenty-first century can choose whether to have children, and when to have children, and who, to some extent, these children will be. Yet, for many women, the sheer possibility of such choices can also become oppressive: because they can have it all, they feel that they must. The perfectly timed family. The perfect balance of career and kids. The perfect donor to create a perfect child. It's an awful lot of pressure to place on a woman—and even more to place on that perfect child, that mythical child, whose conception was planned for a decade and cost upwards of $150,000.

In my own case, I eventually gave up on both pregnancy and choice. At thirty-eight, burned by pregnancy but determined to have a third child, I started to do what made no sense: to pore through online listings of "waiting children," searching for a little girl to adopt. For over a year, in my office and behind closed doors, I read and read and read. "Irina is a little angel," I learned, "waiting for her forever family." "Sophia likes to play with dolls and wants to be a doctor." Every so often, after two days or a week of sifting, one little face would suddenly leap off the screen and into my gut, begging me to choose this one and make her mine. Soon their pictures covered the floor of my study: big eyes, floppy bows, too-big dresses, and sad, forced smiles. When it was really bad, I'd take a picture to my husband, nudging him to see what I had found. "Don't her eyes remind you of your mother?" I'd try to say casually. Or, "I swear I had a dress like that when I was her age." Finally it was too much, for him and for me. So one night, Miltos laid out a bargain. We could have another child; travel to the other side of the world and bring a stranger home. But we wouldn't choose her. Instead, we would go to an adoption agency and let someone—a social worker, a bureaucrat, God—make the decision for us.

Almost exactly nine months later, the envelope arrived. I was at work and so my son ripped it open. Breathlessly, he described the photo inside. "Mom," he screamed, "she's here! And she's the most beautiful girl in the world!"

Pregnancy Pornography

These days, adoption gets a pretty bad rap. There are stories of orphans who were really stolen; of overeager social workers pushing false documentation; and—in the most harrowing cases—of exhausted adoptive parents trying to send their children back.[21] If one more person says to me, "We really would have adopted, but we wanted a child of our own," I swear I will hit them. Pregnancy, by contrast, is blessed by the same light of adoration that glimmers off Renaissance madonnas. JLo gleaming in *The Backup Plan*. Katherine Heigl heavenly in *Knocked Up*. Tabloids screening daily for signs of beautiful bumps on Jennifer Aniston or one of the apparently infinite Kardashians. High-risk pregnancies, ironically and unfortunately, seem to attract particularly effusive praise, focusing generally on how healthy and adorable the eventual babies are and how rapidly the new mom has slipped into both her new role and her old jeans. After Thandie Newton's daughters Ripley and Nico were born in a birthing pool, the *Crash* star positively drooled about the wonders of her birth experience, recalling that "every fiber of your being is alive. It's like you are conducting electricity, literally creating something."[22]

Really? "Conducting electricity?" *Really?*

Not that I want to burst any pretty birth bubbles or anything, but I went through this supposedly electric experience twice, and I don't seem to remember it quite that way. No, I remember something akin to torture, something that involved twenty-four hours of excruciating pain and more blood than anyone had warned me about. I remember three shifts of doctors I'd never seen before, threats of forceps and plungers, and at least one child who looked distinctly like Yoda at the moment of his birth. Not an electrical shower in sight.

The adoration of pregnancy is, I suspect, a fairly recent phenomenon, the creation of both modern medicine and modern media. Admittedly, societies across the globe have long worshipped the pregnant figure and depictions of the mother-child bond. But the adoration of pregnancy itself—of the physical circumstances surrounding conception and birth—is a very modern concept and one that, in its own way, imposes a whole new set of myths upon expectant women.

Until the turn of the twentieth century, recall, pregnancy and birth were dangerous, mysterious events. Women had little understanding of how the fetus inside of them was developing and few tools for diminishing the pain that inevitably accompanied childbirth. Stillbirths were common, as were a host of dangerous maternal complications, many of which still haunt women in poor countries today. Obstructed labor. Vaginal fistulas. Puerperal fever. As a result, the actual process of childbirth was for centuries an event more feared than revered, something for women to survive rather than enjoy.

Attitudes began to evolve only around the turn of the twentieth century, when two major medical breakthroughs changed the equation of childbirth. First, after decades of finger pointing and false hypotheses, scientists proved categorically that germs caused certain illnesses, and that puerperal—or "childbed"—fever in particular was caused by a virulent form of streptococcal bacteria passed from doctor to patient during childbirth.[23] The cure was blissfully simple: for doctors and midwives to wash their hands and instruments before touching a woman in labor. Remarkably, tragically, many in the medical profession continued to resist even these most basic precautions, and American women continued to die from puerperal fever until well into the 1930s.[24] Gradually, though, science and common sense prevailed. Between 1935 and 1950, maternal mortality rates in the United Kingdom fell from 34.1 deaths per 10,000 births to only 7.2.[25] In the United States, deaths fell similarly from approximately 60 per 10,000 births in 1930 to 1.3 by 1968.[26]

Meanwhile, just as scientific advance was taking some of the danger out of childbirth, it was also—and at long last—promising to remove the pain. Beginning in Germany, where the treatment was known as *Dämmerschlaf,* or "twilight sleep," doctors began to offer pregnant women a way to dull the pains of labor, or at least to wipe them from their conscious mind. Using a combination of morphine and scopolamine, they essentially drugged women just as they were entering labor, sedating them with a toxic cocktail that eliminated any conscious memory of the hours that followed. Women who underwent the treatment swore they had no recollection of their labors and instead simply awoke feeling "happy and animated . . . their babies all dressed [and] lying upon a pillow in the arms of a nurse."[27] They also rallied around twilight sleep, ironically perhaps, as an achievement of feminism, a way for women to stand up to men and medicine and seize some control over their labors. "The women of America are demanding that the administration of painlessness shall not be left to the decision of the doctor, but of the mother," exhorted one advocate of twilight sleep.[28] "We have to accept painless childbirth for the good and comfort of motherhood," proclaimed another.[29] So what if women were unconscious at the moment of achievement? At least they were literally feeling no pain. Over time, the fervor of twilight sleep diminished, beaten back by a series of bad stories—one of its major advocates died during the birth of her fifth child—and a growing understanding of the drugs' possible effects. Yet the desire for painless childbirth remained, evolving along with the chemical advances of the era: Thorazine, Benzedrine, nitrous oxide, Demerol.[30] As recently as the early 1960s, nearly all women in labor were sedated in one way or another while their husbands were ushered gently into a nearby waiting area.

But then came the revolutions of the late 1960s and 1970s—the sexual revolution, the feminist revolution, and a media revolution that made it much more acceptable to talk about bodies. Suddenly, childbirth became a key part of women's sexual identity, an experience to be prized rather than endured.[31] Suddenly, the pains of labor were something to be treasured and cherished, evidence of a woman's power and her enduring link to the child. In *Our Bodies, Ourselves*, for instance, the authors urge women "[not] to accept routine tampering with our bodies, our strengths, and the safety of our children."[32] In a 1989 article in *Mothering* magazine, one new mother described the "sensation of sexual ecstasy, the voluptuous feeling of penetration" that marked her baby's birth.[33] The central book in this genre, however, the book that has been on the bestseller list for 487 weeks, or essentially forever, is *What to Expect When You're Expecting*. It's a lovely book, a comforting book, a book that every pregnant woman is apparently legally required to purchase. In warm and reassuring tones, it coaches the nervous mother-to-be through the nine months of her confinement with help-ful hints like "all pregnancies, like all babies, are different" and "in more than 95 percent of cases, prenatal diagnosis turns up no apparent abnormalities."[34] It tells young mothers to eat well (asking themselves, with each forkful, "Is this a bite that will benefit my baby?") and to relax as fully as they can.[35] And it prepares them extensively for child-birth, with helpful tips about arranging for a videographer, bringing a laptop to check e-mail during delivery, and remembering to watch a good childbirth video.[36]

I hate this book. Although it provides 553 pages of cautious, careful wisdom, it still manages to say little about the blood of childbirth, or the pain. It soothes women into believing—I suppose because they want to—that if they are strong enough, childbirth is akin to sex. That if they prepare assiduously enough, labor will be manageable and easy to control. That all the decisions of childbirth—the pace, the position, the choice of a cesarean or other intervention—are essentially theirs to make. In other words, the book convinces women that if they don't sail through childbirth, they have somehow erred as mothers—*before they've even begun!* How much pressure is that? I think I'd rather be drugged.[37]

Meanwhile, of course, there are other issues of pregnancy—medical issues, messy issues—that rarely rate more than a passing mention in any of the "expecting" books or celebrity-mom spreads. Like hormones, for example, and breast-feeding. Every woman, regardless of how she became pregnant and gave birth, will have been pelted by the time of her baby's birth by roughly ten months of hormones. These are very powerful substances and they do not depart a woman's body immedi-ately upon delivery. Instead, they are joined by another small chemical armada—oxytocin to stimulate milk production and jump-start ma-ternal bonding; estrogen to kick the oxytocin into overdrive. Some women ride out this onslaught rather peacefully, but others take it hard. They can become despondent, even suicidal, or experience mood swings that, especially in combination with the sleep deprivation in-duced by a new infant, can make it difficult to concentrate. At the same time, they are also experiencing the joys of breast-feeding—joys that aren't necessarily all that joyful for some women, or all that easy to make happen. Indeed, many women report serious difficulties with their first attempts at breast-feeding; difficulties so severe that they risk under-nourishing their babies. Yet this, too, is rarely either acknowledged or accepted. Instead, the noted experts in the breast-feeding arena, the La Leche League, are equally well noted for their near-maniacal dedication to breast-feeding perfection. "Within the first hour or so," they promise, "he will take the breast. You hold him close and he nuzzles your breast. His tiny mouth grasps your nipple. It seems no less than amazing! You and your baby can relax."[38] You can do it, they insist. And you must.

Because I had my first two children young, I became for a period of time the go-to person on pregnancy, the one my friends called when their due dates were looming and they were starting to worry. My advice, I'm afraid, wasn't very encouraging: throw out the books, take the epidural, and pack lots of extra socks for the bleeding. My husband was even blunter. "Just don't look down," he would warn impending dads-to-be. "Hold her hand, pretend you're breathing, and don't for a minute believe you're doing any of the work."

Great Expectations

Several years ago, I spent a lot of time overseeing the recruitment process for new faculty. Our arrangements were straightforward, exactly what you would expect at any university, and not that far, I imagine, from the norm at any large organization. The candidates would give a public presentation of their work, suffer through a faux-informal lunch or dinner, and then meet individually with the senior members of the area. Afterward, the senior members would gather by themselves to compare notes and, ultimately, select the final candidate. Inevitably, different people would have had different kinds of chats. Some focused on mutual friends or interests, others on work styles or pathways to promotion. Always, though, I—and I alone—had been pelted by questions about children, particularly if the candidate was female. Did I have them? Could she? Was this a place where pregnancy was even possible? My male colleagues, by contrast, learned nothing, and they knew better than to ask.

Now, maybe this forthrightness was due to the baby pictures I had prominently displayed on my desk. Maybe it was because I looked younger, or softer, or less inclined to discuss general equilibrium models. But I suspect that it was simply because of my sex. Women talk to women about babies. It is the all-purpose icebreaker, the way women mark territory and establish their identity. I can't recall how many times I have been seated on a dais with other women, preparing to talk about female empowerment or human rights or economic development in Africa. Within five minutes of arrival, though, before the microphones go on and the public conversation begins, we are all talking about kids. "You have children?" "Yeah." "Me, too. How many?" Just like those infernal forms in the doctor's office. Number of children. Number of pregnancies. Number of births.

You might have thought that this would have changed by now, that once women had joined the Senate and piloted fighter planes, their status as mothers would have become less relevant. But it hasn't. Despite what feminists of all stripes had desperately hoped, once women become mothers, they are still largely defined—both by others and themselves—by the children they bear.

What has changed, however, are the expectations that increasingly surround conception, pregnancy, and birth. In the past, it was enough for a woman to have children and see them live through childhood. Now, by contrast, the entire course of what should be an utterly natural process is fraught with myths of possibility and perfection, myths that have actually raised the ante on what it means to mother. Rather than enjoying our babies as they come, we are actively plotting and planning their conceptions, timing births—and marriages, and relationships—to coincide with particular points in our lives and careers. Rather than acknowledging the pangs of labor and the perils of pregnancy, we are acquiescing to the ultimate madonna fantasy, reimagining birth as a safe and sexy sideshow, the kind of celebration you want to share with your neighbors and father-in-law. And, most seriously, rather than cherishing the children of chance, we are actively and increasingly choosing their genetic profiles, selecting eggs, sperm, and wombs as if they were items on a buffet. Quintuplets? Sure. Two sets of fraternal twins? No problem. A tall boy with brown curly hair and artistic potential? Yes. You can.

Not all of these choices are bad, of course. But having so many options can be overwhelming, thrusting all would-be parents, would-be mothers in particular, into a frenzy of both options and guilt. Because once it becomes technically possible for women to control the most intimate details of their reproductive futures, social pressures can rapidly push them to seize these levers of control, even if they are not necessarily in their own interest. Once we have expectations of perfect mothering—beginning literally at the moment of conception—then women feel compelled to be these perfect mothers, delivering babies who are equally perfect and preinsured. What is left, therefore, of the sloppiness of life? Or of the mystery and majesty that rightfully belong to all women, regardless of their childbearing choices?

Clearly, conception is an area where we don't want to go back. Women of the postfeminist generations have been incredibly lucky to have the reproductive options that feminism fought for, and won. The right to control their bodies. To time their children's births. To experience labor and pregnancy on their own terms. Yet we must be very careful not to take our expectations of expecting too far, or to fall into the trap of believing that conception and childbirth can ever be bent fully to our individual will. I want my students to know, regardless of how they feel at eighteen or twenty-two, that they will probably, someday, yearn to have a child. I want them to understand that their own fertility is precious, and that it declines precipitously as they age. I want them to realize that childbirth is a messy, painful process. And that having a child—whether through labor, or adoption, or surrogacy, or IVF, or fostering, or whatever—will almost certainly be the most beautiful event of their lives.

Over the course of my career, I have been lucky to teach thousands of students, including many young women whose lives and careers I have subsequently followed. But one will forever remain in my mind, particularly with regard to babies and choices and the risks of falling prey to myth.

Monica was diagnosed with retinoblastoma at the age of six months. Had she been born twenty, or even ten, years earlier, her diagnosis would have been a death sentence. But doctors in Philadelphia, where she lived, had recently made great strides in treating the disease, and

Monica was lucky to be treated early and well by one of the country's best specialists. The treatment, however, was extreme. Before she was a year old, Monica had undergone a month of radiation to both eyes and was declared legally blind. At twelve, she was diagnosed with osteogenic sarcoma of the right sinus—a delayed side effect of her earlier radiation treatment that caused doctors to remove her right eye and palate. Three years later, when she was fifteen, Monica was diagnosed with cancer again, this time in her heart.

By the time I knew her, Monica was one of those amazing young women you meet from time to time: funny, insightful, and forced by bad luck to become both incredibly determined and resolutely optimistic. We spent a fair amount of time talking about her job options and possible career paths. One day, though, we suddenly started talking about babies.

Earlier that week, Monica had gone for one of her regular medical checkups, participating in a long-term study of retinoblastoma survivors. The good news, she said, was that her doctors had told her that she could become pregnant and that, because scientists were now unraveling the genetic markers for cancers such as hers, she could also screen future embryos for signs of the disease that had so ravaged her. The bad news was that long-term studies were also showing that survivors of retinoblastoma were liable to develop uterine cancer in their twenties and thirties.

Monica, for the first time since I'd known her, seemed paralyzed. "So, what am I supposed to do?" she asked drily. "Have a healthy baby so that I can die? Freeze my eggs now and hope I find a guy willing to take these risks before I lose my uterus?" Her parents, she imagined, would have a tough time endorsing genetic screening; if such screens had been available at the time of her conception, after all, they never would have created the incredible young woman that was now Monica. Her doctors, equally understandably, were outlining her options without providing any guidance through them. Because the choices, of course, were all hers: to become a single mother or not; to choose a "healthy" embryo or not; to pass her complicated genetic code on to her offspring, or to resist. Given her medical history, adoption was probably not going to be an option. Given her complicated prognosis, waiting—until she found a partner, and went to graduate school, and had a measure of financial stability—was not advisable. "It's great," she laughed, "to be given all this information. But how the hell do I decide? And what if I screw it all up?"

No one, of course, would want to turn back time here, or erase the medical miracle that is Monica's life. Twenty years ago, a woman with her genetic profile would not have reached adolescence, much less have had the ability both to reproduce and to screen her offspring against potential disease. Such options, though, have also come at a price. For women like Monica, they mean a million new pressures atop those they already face. They mean expectations—of a once-impossible baby, a baby that can now be perfected—that may never be met. And they add dollops of complexity to what remains a primal impulse for most women: to bear a child before they die.

Monica and I talked in circles for an hour. Then finally, gingerly, I ventured, "Maybe you should just go out and have sex."

7

THE GOOD WIFE'S GUIDE TO LIFE AND LOVE

> Housekeeping is not beautiful; it cheers and raises neither the
> husband, the wife, nor the child . . . it oppresses women.
> —Ralph Waldo Emerson, *Domestic Life*

> I'm a mediocre mother like the vast majority of women, because
> I'm human.
> —Elisabeth Badinter [1]

It is just another day.

My eldest son stayed home from school for a few hours so that he
could finish his college applications with me around to proofread,
write checks, and provide obscure information, like his Social Security
number and the year his dad graduated from university. The high-tech
Internet connection that this same dad furnished last year isn't working (again), so my son needs to use my computer instead. Two hours
later, envelopes in hand, he leaves, reminding me that (a) he needs the
car tonight, and (b) he can't be around to watch his younger siblings.
After he's gone, I dash to the grocery store and purchase dinner fixings.
I come home to the cat and a writhing, half-dead chipmunk. I leave the
chipmunk on the rug, lure the cat away, and try to figure out the best
combination of open doors and closed windows to give the poor rodent
some chance of escape.

Meanwhile, my younger son calls with an enigmatic message. Something critical. Tonight. At seven o'clock. I can't call him back because
he dropped his phone under a moving car two days ago and it doesn't

get incoming calls anymore. I can't figure out how I'm going to get him wherever he needs to go, because Son A already has dibs on the car, and I'm supposed to be at a black-tie dinner that starts at six.

I head back to the computer and deal with the dozens of messages that have accumulated, trying desperately to pretend that I actually have some control over my life, my work, my calendar. I pack up my daughter's clothes for soccer practice and put her Hebrew homework where she has at least a remote chance of actually encountering it. Then I need to start roasting the chickens for dinner—one for my kids, and one for the friends whose son is undergoing chemotherapy.

In between garlic cloves, I check on the chipmunk, which is now expiring sweetly on the downstairs rug. Should I whisper quietly to it? Administer tiny little Heimlich maneuvers? Pick it up with the dust pan or bundle it into a shoebox, as I have in the past, leaving my daughter to administer nuts and thimblefuls of water? The cat drags in injured rodents all the time, probably, as my children keep reminding me, because I named her after my husband's ex-girlfriend.

While the chickens roast, I go to the computer again, this time, finally, to write the speech on stem cell research that I'm due to deliver tomorrow. Because it is, after all, a workday.

Sometime around five, my husband calls. My daughter is off to soccer by now, and my sons (after several rounds of intermediation) have coordinated their evening plans. One serving of dinner is on our table, the other packed up and ready to go in Tupperware. I've thrown together something that will hopefully pass for a speech and thrown something on that will hopefully pass at tonight's black-tie affair. I haven't yet figured out how to handle tomorrow morning, when the three kids need to be at three different schools and my conference begins at 7:30.

"Hello, babe," my husband says sweetly. "Is there anything I can do to help?"

My husband is in Buffalo. It seems to me that he is in Buffalo a lot. It's cold there, I'm pretty sure, and it snows. But I'm in Boston, with the kids, the chickens, the Tupperware, and the dying chipmunk. "No," I say, trying not to sound too bitter. "We're all set."

On my kitchen door, I have tacked up an article from a 1955 issue of *Housekeeping Monthly*. It's called "The Good Wife's Guide," and it doesn't beat around the bush. According to the Guide, it's easy to be good. Step 1: "Have dinner ready. Plan ahead, even the night before, to have a delicious meal ready, on time for his return. This is a way of letting him know that you have been thinking about his needs." Step 2: "Prepare yourself. Take 15 minutes to rest so you'll be refreshed when he arrives. Touch up your makeup, put a ribbon in your hair and be fresh-looking."

Clearly, I am a very bad wife.

The next morning, I get up at 5:45. I stumble into the shower, pull on what will subsequently turn out to be a wholly inappropriate suit, and try to make my hair look a little less ethnic. From the morning news, I hear that there has been a freakishly early blizzard in Buffalo. The entire city is shut down, including the airport. There went my ambitious plan to have husband retrieve children at day's end, on this, the one day of the week when we don't have child care. There is now a track pickup looming at 4:00, a piano lesson at 6:00, and a part-time job that starts at 5:30. My speech is scheduled from 4:30 to 5:30. I'm toast.

I creep into my daughter's room and silently open the lid on her shoebox. The nuts and water are undisturbed, and he's there, eyes closed, curled into what I can only take to be a position of resignation and accusation.

The chipmunk has died.

In economic terms, the traditional nuclear family is an ideal organization, perfect for maximizing economic opportunities and supporting the offspring who will, in turn, advance the family's financial goals. Think about it: two parents are necessary, in biological terms, to create the child. But only one parent is necessary, biologically again, to physically sustain that child in the delicate months and years after birth. It makes perfect sense, then, that the parent equipped for sustenance— the parent with breasts, in other words—should take care of the child, while the parent without breasts leaves to forage for nuts, berries, and stock options. In biblical times, women were expected to care for their children while men worked the land. In ancient China, women were almost entirely restricted to working from home, raising children (ideally, sons) and processing silk. And across much of sub-Saharan Africa, women tended to crops and children while men concentrated on herding, hunting, and clearing the land.[2] Although anthropologists occasionally trumpet an isolated tribe or society in which women apparently exert a disproportionate share of the power, such cases are rare, and often, under closer scrutiny, still display the breast-driven division of labor that prevails elsewhere.

Structurally, therefore, most traditional societies didn't stray too far from the Good Wife's Guide.[3] The women of the community had their foragers' dinner ready for them and, we can well imagine, the children washed, and dressed, and ready for bed. Why? Because biologically and economically it just made sense. In a pairing of two people, the one who comes equipped to feed the children should do so, assuming along the way whatever other chores attach themselves to the home. That leaves the other partner free to focus on different tasks, especially those that involve leaving the home—and the children—for extended periods of time. Friedrich Engels saw this relationship clearly in his 1884 essay "On the Origin of the Family, Private Property and the State," noting that the subjugation of women stemmed inherently from the accumulation of economic surpluses: as families began to acquire lands and crops and property, so, too, did the men of these families need women to mind these lands and to ensure that the children born to farm them were raised appropriately and well.[4] Or, as Engels explained, "The man fights in the wars, goes hunting and fishing, procures the raw materials of food and the tools necessary for doing so. The woman looks after the house and the preparation of food and clothing, cooks, weaves, sews."[5] More recently, Gary Becker, an economist at the University of Chicago, has been even blunter, arguing that a sexually based division of labor remains economically efficient. "If all members of a household have different comparative advantages," he asserts, "no more than one member would allocate time to both the market and household sectors."[6] So in other words, once you have the womb and the breasts, you get everything that the marital division of labor eventually pushes your way: the children, the day care, the doctor's visits, the pot roast, the school plays, the clarinet lessons, and the chipmunk.

Feminism was supposed to have changed all this. Indeed, one of Betty Friedan's major arguments—and, one might argue, the central tenet of the movement she helped popularize—was that women could be, *had to be*, liberated from the chores that bound them to the home. That they had to throw off the tyranny of the Good Wife's Guide and unlink the chains that bound them, not to their children or husbands necessarily, but at least to all the accessories they seemed to imply. Friedan is both eloquent and adamant on this point. "The first step," she insists, "is to see housework for what it is—not a career, but something that must be done as quickly and efficiently as possible."[7] Yet as the feminist revolution has unfurled over the past four decades, sending millions of women traipsing blithely into the workforce, patterns of household labor allocation have barely budged. Instead women, regardless of their jobs or income, still tend to do the bulk of both household and child-rearing tasks. According to the most recent data, married women with children do seventeen hours of housework a week, while their husbands do only seven. Around the world it appears, wives—doctors and lawyers, bus drivers and waitresses—still buy the socks and fold the socks. Mend the clothing and the fences. And there still doesn't seem to be a dad on the planet who knows how to book his kids' dental appointments. Or at least not in my neck of the woods. Between them, my kids have had seven dentists and orthodontists. I swear that my husband never knew a single one of their names, much less their office addresses.

Once again, therefore, the goals of feminism seem to have gone unfulfilled. The good news is that women of my generation got the fast-paced job opportunities we craved; the forty- (or sixty-, or eighty-) hour workweeks that once belonged solely to men; the chance to hunt and provide for our own families. The bad news is that we did not lose any responsibilities in the process. And so women are now routinely juggling hunting and foraging and tending the hearth, caring for the children while providing for them. Or as one working mother recently confessed to a sympathetic reporter, "We got equality at work. We really didn't get equality at home."[8]

Indeed, the problem of balancing work and family remains, for many women, more a problem on the home front than in the workplace. At the office, men are gamely trying to support female colleagues and promote more women through their ranks. But at home, even the most well-intentioned spouses tend, it appears, to slink back into more traditionally gendered patterns, playing with the children but not driving them to ballet lessons; preparing for the fancy dinner party, maybe, but not the seven-day-a-week drudgery of meat loaf and potatoes. What accounts for this persistence of social patterns? Part of it, as usual, may be that men are simply less primed for the messier parts of family management, less tied (through genes or hormones or social conditioning) to the mundane responsibilities of a complex household. Part of it may be that the male side of the feminist revolution is just taking longer to catch up—and indeed, couples of the Gen X and Gen Y decades do subscribe, at least in theory, to a more even distribution of work and family responsibilities.[9] Yet part is also driven, I would argue, by the deep-seated expectations many women still have of their housekeeping selves—visions, ironically, that have only expanded since our grandmothers' days. In the original Good Wife's Guide, after all, women were just expected to "clear away the clutter" and "run a dustcloth over the tables" before their husbands came home."[10] Now, if we heed the advice of seductively glossy publications like *Real Simple* and *Martha Stewart Living*, we are supposed to be creating temples of gastronomy in our kitchens and oases of tranquillity in our bedrooms. If we read popular marriage manuals such as *A Woman's Guide to Loving and Understanding Her Man*, we are supposed to be learning to "regulate our husbands' emotions," "feel our mens' hearts and secrets," and be always refreshed, like a "breath of fresh air."[11] And that's before you even get to the parenting side of the equation.

For hundreds and hundreds of years, women spent the bulk of their lives struggling to be good wives and mothers, to raise their children, tend to their homes, and care for their husbands. One might have thought that these expectations would be tempered by women's entry into the workforce, and by the sexual rebalancing of power that feminism unleashed. One might have thought, in other words, that as women assumed more and more of the responsibilities that were once traditionally men's, they would have handed over, or at least abandoned, some of the responsibilities that were long traditionally theirs—some of the child care, for example, or some of the washing and cleaning and bed making. Yet—ironically, sadly—this doesn't seem to have happened. Instead, rather than cutting back on the home front, many women appear to be upping the ante, racing to create the perfect holiday costume, the perfect gluten-free bake-sale brownie, the perfectly pillowed home.

It is no longer enough to be good wives, it seems. Now, in housework, as in so many other areas of life and love, we are aiming for perfection.

Shifting into Second

Like the "mommy track" or the "beauty myth," Arlie Hochschild's well-crafted phrase "the second shift" has become a commonplace of social conversation, an evocative distillation of a complex set of facts. Writing first in 1989, Hochschild laid out the parameters of a problem. Women, she noted, were finally streaming into all ranks of the American workforce. They were working long hours, making good money and, in many cases at least, advancing in their jobs and careers. Yet these same women—statistically and demographically—were also still getting married, having children, and managing to put food on the table. How, Hochschild—herself a young mother in a dual-career family—wondered, were these women doing it? How much help were they receiving from their equally working husbands?

What she found didn't surprise her. (It probably shouldn't have, since she begins the book by describing how she brought her infant son to her office during his first months of life.) Nor will it surprise any woman who has ever rushed through the door with a toddler clutched in one arm, a bag of groceries in the other, and a cell phone jangling madly in her purse. Put simply, Hochschild found that across educational levels and racial lines, in both happy marriages and frustrated ones, working mothers were coping with their dual set of responsibilities by, well, doing them both. Coming home from the office to attack the kitchen, and then the kids' bath and bedtimes, and then finally, exhaustedly, the pile of half-dry clothes languishing on the couch. According to one study that Hochschild cites, working women in the United States spent an average of three hours a day on housework in 1965–66, while men averaged only seventeen minutes. Women spent fifty minutes a day exclusively with their children; men spent twelve.[12] In the aggregate, she calculated, and using broader studies conducted throughout the 1960s and 1970s, women worked roughly fifteen hours more each week than men. Over the course of a year, they worked *an extra month of twenty-four-hour days.*[13] This was the second shift.

In the two decades since the publication of *The Second Shift*, numerous authors have plumbed Hochschild's analysis and recalculated her sums. And it all seems pretty much the same: regardless of their working status, regardless of their children, regardless of their educational level, women consistently did more housework than the men to whom they were married.[14] According to one particularly gloomy analysis, 43 percent of high-achieving women actually felt that their husbands created more housework than they contributed.[15] According to another, working mothers were still placing limits on their responsibilities in the workplace and subscribing to traditional gender-role identities at home.[16] Overall, then, as one 2009 study succinctly concluded: "Although egalitarian attitudes are often found to lead to greater equality, the relevant empirical evidence is not consistent, and women continue to do most of the housework, despite contemporary egalitarian ideology."[17]

Admittedly, men have changed their working patterns—fairly dramatically, in some cases—to accord with the reality of seriously working wives. Married fathers more than doubled their housework hours between 1965 and 1985, from four to ten hours per week. They tripled their time spent on primary child care between 1965 and 2000, from two and a half hours per week to nearly eight.[18] Three percent of families with young children were "manned" in 2007 by stay-at-home dads—many of whom gave up their own careers to be their children's primary caregiver.[19] These patterns are even more dramatic among working-class families, in which 42 percent of fathers care for their children at least part of the day while their wives work.[20] Ironically, therefore, in statistical terms at least, New Age dads are much more prevalent among the truck driving and steelworking men of this country than among their briefcase-toting, Ivy League–educated peers.

Unlike statistics on women's wages and professional advancement, though, where the devil can really be in the details of the data, statistics on the second shift seem somehow less interesting than the anecdotes and responses they generate. Ask a working man, a working dad, how he is and you'll generally get a standard answer like "Fine," or "Great," or "Doin' okay!" Probe a little further, and you'll likely hear about a new deal at work, or a big project, or, sadly, these days, about a slow-down driven by the economy. If you ask specifically about the man's family, you'll probably get happy generalities again. "Oh, Sam's doing great! Really loving his judo lessons / frisbee team / investment bank-ing internship this year!" Ask a woman, by comparison—either a work-ing woman or a stay-at-home mom—and the first words out of her mouth generally have to do with some form of exhaustion. "Oh, I'm all right," you often hear. "I just can't get a break. I'm racing to get Ashley ready for chess camp and Gideon's got his third round of the water polo competition coming up. John's been insanely busy at work, and of course this was the week when the boiler had to go." If there's another woman present at the conversation, things quickly escalate into com-petitive collapsing. "You're so lucky it was only the boiler! My dish-washer crashed this week, right before I was due to host the entire Girl Scout troop. Rachel had four ballet rehearsals in three days, Connor's water cycle project was due on Thursday, and I barely managed to drag myself to the staff meeting yesterday." Think about it. When's the last time you heard a woman brag—or even report—about how relaxed she was, or how well things were going at work? Instead, we're worn out, overworked, and insanely tired of picking socks up from the floor. And we are rarely—very, very rarely, it seems—simply "doin' okay!"

As countless studies have now demonstrated, women's second shift has been driven by men's general unwillingness to embrace the household chores their wives (or mothers, or maids) once performed.[21] Because while husbands at the turn of the twenty-first century are far more likely to be involved in their children's lives and activities than their own fathers were, they are still not particularly inclined to forage for socks, or make dental appointments, or drive the van to gymnas-tics. (Try it. Poll your friends and colleagues and see how many men actually phone the dentist. I've found two, plus one ex-boyfriend who felt so guilty when I pointed this out that he quickly took over all dental planning activities in his household.) And so women who work outside the home are forced into active double duty, doing the "men's work" of the office, shop, or factory, along with the traditional "women's work" of the home.

Yet it doesn't seem quite fair to put all of the blame on men. Because even if much of the asymmetry of the second shift is being driven by their deep-seated reluctance to do the laundry or make the sandwiches, part, too, is being driven by women's equally deep-seated reluctance to cut back on these tasks; to let the laundry go unfolded, maybe, or have the kids buy lunch at school. Women could cut corners at home, in other words, much as they already cut back their hours at work. Yet increasingly, remarkably, we resist.

At the turn of the twentieth century, doing the laundry for a family of five or six (for families were considerably larger then) involved making ley or soda to ensure soft water, owning and storing more than fifteen washing-related articles, and manufacturing starch, a process that took several days. It meant soaking and sorting the clothes the night before, and then resoaking, boiling, and rinsing them by hand—a process that generally occupied an entire day.[22] Cooking, say, a roast chicken meant walking to the market, plucking and cleaning the chicken (presuming someone else was kind enough to kill it for you), and then tending to it for hours in a slow-heating oven. My late mother-in-law, who grew up in rural Greece, had to take all her baked items (chicken, bread, eggplant, potatoes) to a communal oven several times a week, carrying the pans back and forth for hours. Now, by contrast, we simply pop our clothes in the washers and dryers that sit in more than 90 percent of American homes. Chickens come plucked and cleaned, or even conveniently preroasted (not to mention frozen, stir-fried, or disfigured into nuggets). We should be saving hours and hours of household time each week. Yet, as Betty Friedan realized as early as 1963, American women have not translated the gains of housekeeping innovation into any real gains of time.[23] Instead, we are building bigger and bigger houses, buying more and more clothes, and spending more and more time tending to them. Between 1965 and 2000, the number of working mothers in the United States rose from 45 to 78 percent of all mothers, and the average time that an American woman spent in the paid labor force increased from nine to twenty-five hours a week. Yet the amount of time that women devoted to family care (housework, childcare, and shopping) remained stubbornly pegged at around forty hours a week.[24]

How can this be? It's because, rather than grabbing the time gains of the Maytag spin cycle, we are shoving the clothes into the dryer and then racing to get the neatly starched shirts from the cleaner down the street. Rather than enjoying some decent Chinese takeout, we are stir-frying our own zucchini and drizzling it with the walnut oil we drove five miles to procure. Like our mothers and grandmothers, we fall prey still to the seductions of housekeeping—to Martha Stewart's promise of decorative pumpkin lanterns and Rachael Ray's lure of Garlic-Sherry Burgers with Stilton and Pub Browns with Horseradish Sauce. Yet these things take time that working mothers simply don't have. A recent issue of *Everyday Food*, for instance, offers a sigh-inducing recipe for Harvest Vegetable Pancakes with Greens and Goat Cheese. So light. So lovely. I tried it. An hour and a half later, I had a burnt and bedraggled creation that proved far too crunchy to eat. My mother, by contrast, being older and wiser, opens a can of Campbell's cream of mushroom soup, mixes it with a package of Lipton's chicken noodle soup, and calls it a day.

Every so often, my mother will remark that she doesn't know how women of my generation get by. We're so tired, she'll note, so busy. We are doing everything that women of her generation wanted and yet weren't able to achieve.

And then she'll sweetly tell me that my car could really use a wash.

The Madness of Mothering

Meanwhile, much of what's driving our contemporary frenzy is the advent of übermothering. Parents today, and mothers in particular, are no longer just caring for their children, or even doting upon them. Instead they are investing massive amounts of time in managing their children's lives, from the mobiles they watch in infancy to the triple majors they pursue in college. Seduced yet again by the cult of perfection, busy women—accomplished women, ambitious women—are heaving themselves onto their offspring, investing considerable chunks of their time, talents, and energy in the productions formerly known as kids.

Once upon a time—in, say, the golden days of the 1950s—the barriers between children and their parents were rigid and fairly wide. Parents were expected to love their children, of course, and to tend to them, but it was a hands-off kind of loving that was generally presumed, and a minimal amount of tending. Indeed, according to the bible of midcentury childrearing, Dr. Spock's *Common Sense Book of Baby and Child Care*, "Bringing up your child won't be a complicated job if you take it easy, trust your own instincts, and follow the directions that your doctor gives you."[25] It wasn't quite the Victorian standard of children being seen but not heard, but neither was it a close and cuddly kind of love. Dr. Spock told his parents to be firm with their children rather than indulgent. To listen to them, but also to clearly lay out the rules. "It is easy," Spock warns, "to fall into the habit of saying 'Do you want to get into your high chair and have lunch?' . . . The trouble is that the natural response of the child . . . is 'No' . . . It is better not to give him a choice."[26] June Cleaver, the archetypal wife of midcentury America, was a Spockian mom; so were Donna Reed and Carol Brady. Indeed, the Spockian mom hews fairly closely to the Good Wife ideal: the toys are in place, the home is tranquil, and the kids are washed, combed, and smiling. Just look at how the mothers of *Mad Men* are portrayed. They're spending so much time playing cards and mixing martinis that they can barely *find* their children.

Today, by contrast, good mothers are expected not only to be able to find their children (which is surely a good thing) but indeed to be with them nearly every moment of the day, planning their activities, prompting their curiosity, and tending to their every need. Poor Dr. Spock has been relegated to the attic, replaced by counselors such as Penelope Leach and William Sears, who preach a far more intensive and all-consuming style. According to Leach, for example, the "pain of separation" that occurs each time a mother leaves her child with a new babysitter is akin to the "grieving of a baby who loses her one and only special person."[27] According to Sears, good mothers practice "attachment parenting," a "close attachment after birth and beyond [that] allows the natural, biological attachment-promoting behaviors of the infant and the intuitive, biological caregiving qualities of the mother to come together."[28] And Leach and Sears are hardly alone.

Indeed, beginning in the 1980s, American mothers were suddenly subjected to a barrage of hands-on parenting primers. Responding, perhaps, to the relative austerity of the Spockian style or, more cynically, to the flow of women into the workforce and the corresponding backlash it provoked, experts from across the spectrum were loudly urging parents—that is, mothers—to devote themselves more wholeheartedly to the active raising of their children. To read to them constantly. Talk to them constantly. To make eye contact and appropriate playdates and complicated Jell-O molds in the shape of the American flag.* Or as one helpful article cheerfully exhorted, "toys aren't just things. They're vehicles for learning, for entertainment, and for making lasting memories—which is why a poor choice is disappointing and a good one is worth all that time in the store."[29] Across popular magazines and in respected academic journals, in television shows and documentary films, motherhood at the turn of the twenty-first century was consistently being portrayed as an epic war of the wombs, a full-time, all-out marathon of nurturing in which only the "good" (read: focused, devoted, energetic) parents had any chance of producing a "good" (read: healthy, smart, attractive, and presumably bound for Harvard) child.[30] And mothers, as a result, were on the firing line, responsible for the advanced art of raising perfect offspring. Or, as Susan Douglas and Meredith Weaver write in *The Mommy Myth*: "Your kids were in a highly individualized do-or-die race to the top, and if they couldn't do square roots or diagram sentences by age four (let alone distinguish Schubert from Beethoven) it was a reflection on you: on your genes, of course, but also on whether you had been an attentive, intellectually nurturing mother or a lazy, ignorant slut of a mom."[31]

When I was growing up in the 1960s, I took ballet lessons every Monday afternoon in the basement of the local Masonic temple. We had recitals once a year, with costumes (tutus and butterfly wings) sewn by the mother of one of my friends. When I was older, I learned to lifeguard at the YMCA and, briefly, took a Saturday morning class in jewelry making. My parents participated fully in these events—which meant, generally, one car pool a week throughout my childhood, a few ballet recitals, and a drawerful of bracelets concocted from spoons.

My children, by comparison, have endured a veritable cruise ship's worth of activities nearly since birth. Both boys, before kindergarten, had participated in soccer, T-ball, swimming, and art. They joined Cub Scouts soon after and made a lot of things with clay. For several

*Seriously. See the All-American Flag Mold at www.kraftbrands.com.

summers in a row, they went to a theater program that staged a full-length play every week with each child appearing in an equally starring role. (This was a rather soul-defeating structure for Son Number One, who was quite a talented actor, and utterly terrifying for Son Number Two, who wasn't.) Son Number One learned to play the piano and guitar; Son Number Two variously studied piano, trumpet, and drums before realizing that he had no musical ability and turning instead to running and wrestling. My daughter, who joined the family at six, rapidly made up for lost time by joining children's chorus, girls soccer, and the local ballet Nazis. Each of these involved at least one practice/rehearsal/warm-up a week, plus regularly scheduled and constantly rescheduled games/tournaments/performances. There were outfits for each activity, of course, plus celebratory banquets, teacher/coach thank-you parties, and endless opportunities for parent volunteers. One year, I crashed the minivan into a telephone pole during a mad dash to replace the marionette outfit (silly me) with the ladybug. That's when we gave up ballet.

Like any parent, of course—like any addict—I could have just stopped. Could have cut back on the sports, or the music, or the art, as my kids' inherent skills (or lack thereof) began to manifest themselves. Should have stopped, probably, the moment I learned that my husband had spent two full evenings, and hired one of his coworkers, to build a model car for the Cub Scouts' Pinewood Derby competition. But we didn't, of course. Because, like most middle- and upper-middle-class parents these days, we were determined to be the Moms and Dads Who Care. The moms and dads who, raised on a diet of Leach and Sears and La Leche League, truly believe that we owe it to our children to spend all our time on them. Or, more cynically, that if we spend all this time and invest all this energy, we will guarantee that our children, and thus ourselves, turn out to be perfect.

Two questions, though, arise. Is this frenzy any good for our children? And what is it doing to us?

Let me start with the latter, since the answer is so obvious. Simply put, it's exhausting us. As Judith Warner argues in *Perfect Madness*; as Susan Douglas and Meredith Michaels show in *The Mommy Myth*; as countless articles on "intensive mothering" and the "new momism" have described, parents in the twenty-first century, and mothers in particular, are literally draining themselves to entertain and educate their kids.[32] They are cutting back on leisure time, cutting back on civic time, cutting back on time spent with their spouses. In 1965, for instance, married mothers reported having roughly thirty-six hours a week of free time; by 2000, that number was down to thirty-two hours, with women spending, on average, 60 percent less time working with civic organizations and 60 percent less time reading.[33] Mothers in 2000 reported getting only 54.8 hours of sleep a week, on average, three hours less than they had enjoyed in 1975.[34] They report having sex less frequently and always feeling rushed.[35] And their overall level of satisfaction—that joy that was supposed to come from Sears's promised release of mothering hormones and Leach's mother-infant bonding— hasn't budged a bit. Indeed, women in the United States are statistically less happy today than they were in the 1970s.[36]

All of which might be worth it if extreme parenting led to extremely happy—or well-adjusted, or successful—kids. Yet the data here are wholly inconclusive and likely to stay that way. Are some of today's hyperparented kids getting into Harvard and Yale? Yup, and it's pretty much the same number of kids who got into Harvard and Yale in the 1960s and the 1930s.[37] Are some becoming brain surgeons and concert pianists and world-class golfers? Yup, and those numbers haven't budged much either. What has changed is the percentage of kids on Ritalin (4.8 percent of all children aged four to seventeen); the percentage of kids with autism (1 out of every 110); the percentage of kids with asthma (14 percent of all children under the age of seventeen).[38] In 2011, 26 percent of seniors at the Bronx High School of Science, one of the most elite schools in the country, described themselves as drug users or former drug users. Thirteen percent admitted to drinking too much. And this is at the very top of the educational pyramid.[39]

Moreover, it's not clear that all the activities crammed into children's lives are paying off for them as expected. Did my second son really benefit from dragging a trumpet around for two years? I don't think so. Did my daughter gain much from her mother-induced time in the chorus? Probably not. And what about the summer camps? The enforced community service? The "learning trips" to China? As a mother, I can attest that these things are fine. Indeed, I must confess that my daughter is "learning" in Shanghai as I write this. As a college president, though, someone who oversees the review of roughly six thousand carefully crafted applications every year, let me promise you: *We don't care.* Show me that your kid is great at math, or that she truly loves to play the cello. Tell me he edits the high school literary magazine and has an extensive stash of nineteenth-century Russian novels. But expensive trips to far-flung poverty? Fifty-two activities scattered across the seven days of the week? Honestly. It doesn't help. Give me a kid with a passion for learning, a kid who has demonstrated some measure of autonomy and motivation. Give me a kid who knows his or her mind. But these things are harder to come by if the child has been tutored and handheld from birth.

So what does it buy us, in the end, all this kangaroo sleeping and toddler yoga and Baby Einstein flash cards? It means hours and hours, years and years, of a woman's life; years of carpooling and bake sales, of tear-inducing recitals and, if you're really, really lucky, a few great moments of joy. It means kids who will grow—inevitably, God-willingly—and leave you, probably without becoming the cancer researchers or peace prize winners you always thought they'd be. And it isn't their fault, of course. It's yours. Because you're the one who thought you could make them perfect.

Please Don't Feed the Animals

Finally, even as women today are aiming to have jobs and families, even as they are knitting cheerleading costumes for Amanda while doing Gabe's algebra homework, they are also expected—or at least themselves expect—to take care of the men in their lives, those wonderful, coparenting, dentally oblivious, rodent-ignoring men we choose to call our husbands.

Marriage has never been easy. If it were, as Katharine Hepburn once remarked, they wouldn't make you sign a contract. It has never been easy, presumably, to bind oneself to one person forever; to share finances, meals, children, old stories, and germs till death do you part. That's why we still sign contracts, why marriage remains a legal state as well as a personal one. Because, unlike weddings and sex, marriage is hard. It is hard to organize a life with one person, day after day, for de-cades. Hard to be a good husband or a good wife.

In the past, at least, expectations were straightforward. As Engels noted, marriage was primarily an economic relationship designed, as described in chapter 5, to preserve private property and sustain family lines. Within these parameters, husband and wife hewed to clearly prescribed, widely acknowledged roles. His was to father the children (a biological act) and provide for them (a commercial one). Hers was to birth the children (biology again), nourish them (a social relationship, prodded by biology), and provide their father with sex. Maybe not the most romantic of relationships, but at least one with well-defined rules. So clear and concise were these rules, in fact, that they saw most of humankind through the Middle Ages and the Industrial Revolution; through massive changes in demography, technology, and communi-cation. Continents were conquered, railroads built, the sun stopped revolving around the earth. But the laws of marriage didn't change: one man, one woman, one set of rules and responsibilities.

And then, of course, in the blink of a historical eye, everything turned upside down. Women streamed into the commercial labor force, joining men in (and displacing men from) jobs that were once wholly theirs. Wives were less present at home and less willing to devote themselves to household duties. Men and women were less accustomed, suddenly, to monogamy, and bombarded by new opportunities for both sex and baby making. We are so used to describing this revolution that we for-get just how radical—how truly revolutionary—it was. Yet in less than two generations, nearly everything we once knew about husbands and wives was gone, swept away by new rules and new expectations. Of equality. Independence. Shared parenting and no-fault divorces.

No wonder we're so confused.

Today, women—and men—are grappling with an evolving kalei-doscope of desires and expectations, many of which are wholly contra-dictory.

- We want to be fully involved in the care of our children without compromising our time spent at work, with our spouses, and on ourselves;

- We want to have free, frequent, and noncommital sex for ten or twenty years of our lives, and then monogamous, passionate, and equally frequent sex ever after;
- We want Martha Stewart's media empire and her hand-crocheted doilies, but not her painful divorce;
- As women, we want men who love our bodies and our minds, who treasure our independence but still put gas in the car;
- We want our husbands to bathe, diaper, and tend to the children, but only if they do it as well as we do;
- We want to earn our own income and achieve pay equity with men, but we prefer our husbands to earn more than we do;[40]
- And even if we are working as truck drivers or management consultants, as welders or CEOs, we still want to be regarded as decent homemakers, as good mothers and good wives.

How can we ever square the circle on all these desires?

One place to start might be with the raft of self-help books devoted to these issues. Heirs to the Good Wife's Guide, books such as *Maintain a Keeper* and *Becoming the Woman of His Dreams* litter the (few remaining) shelves of American bookstores and feature prominently on bestseller lists. Interestingly, the vast majority of these titles address themselves to women rather than men. And scarily, most adhere to a starkly conservative line, essentially exhorting women to revert to the Good Wife's rules. In *The Proper Care and Feeding of Husbands*, for example, Dr. Laura Schlessinger perkily tells her readers (millions of whom also tune into her internationally syndicated radio show) to "forgive their husbands . . . for being men."[41] Women, Schlessinger scolds, are unhappy because they are self-centered; because they are focusing on what "their men can do for them, and not what they can do for their men."[42] The simple remedy, therefore, is to treat husbands better, to "roll over in bed, close your eyes, give him a big hug, and remember that, without him, you are only a sorry excuse for a person."[43] Not exactly Gloria Steinem stuff. Similarly, in *The Surrendered Wife*, author Laura Doyle advises her readers to relinquish any effort to control their husbands and to focus instead on becoming vulnerable, trusting, respectful, and grateful.[44] Remember, she writes, to "respect the man you married by listening to him. Give up control to have more power.

Abandon the myth of equality. Say yes to sex. Let him solve your problems."[45]

It is easy to dismiss these texts as reactionary dross, part of the ongoing backlash against feminism in general and working mothers in particular. Which is, of course, exactly what they are. Schlessinger is explicit in her accusations, claiming that women's unhappiness is a "result of the women's movement, with its condemnation of just about everything male as evil, stupid, and oppressive."[46] So is Suzanne Venker, author of *The Flipside of Feminism*, who argues vehemently that "feminism has been the single worst thing that has happened to American women."[47] Tracee Stukes, author of *Maintain a Keeper*, more colloquially dismisses feminism as "this new age woman crap." And then she advises her readers simply to "snap out of it, girlfriend, and cook for that man."[48] Ah, yes, if only Betty had known.

Yet the sheer popularity of the feed-and-love-your-husband message—Schlessinger's book, her tenth, sold over a million copies; Doyle's inspired an entire movement in which wives from across the country met in groups to discuss their surrenders—suggests that they cannot, or at least should not, be ignored by those of us who find them distasteful. Because at some basic level, the message of marriage and motherhood that second-wave feminism meant to convey—that women could have families and careers, satisfied husbands and minds of their own—has not taken root among millions of American women. And even those who devoutly wanted to believe in feminism's domestic message, including committed younger feminists like Naomi Wolf and Stephanie Staal, have publicly, poignantly, admitted to struggling with the messy realities of modern marriage. After the birth of her first child, for instance, Wolf describes how her husband suddenly seemed to be pulling back from his formerly feminist convictions and slipping into a more traditional male role. "Our generation," she writes ruefully, "did not think we were marrying breadwinners; we thought we were marrying our best friends. But the husbands were pulling rank in a way that best friends don't do. Simply put, the men were good husbands, loving, faithful, and kind, but they had at some level that seemed not very important to them, but very important to women, sent the message 'I love you, but in some fundamental ways we will live our lives my way' . . . It just wasn't quite fair, and it wasn't going to be quite

fair, ever."[49] Similarly, Staal, once a successful reporter, finds herself—
just like Schlessinger's listeners and Doyle's "unsurrendered" wives—at
home with a toddler, resentful, exhausted, and angry all the time at a
husband she had once adored. "We talked about [our daughter] and
little else," she recalls. "We no longer looked each other in the eye. The
causes and symptoms of what seemed our impending marital break-
down were, I suppose, more intricate than that, but a few years into
marriage and parenthood, and we had both grown distant and resentful, each of us bearing a thousand tiny wounds."[50]

Presumably, women like Wolf and Staal, like me, like nearly every
bright and ambitious young woman I've taught over the past twenty-
five years, are not simply going to turn our collective backs on everything we've wished for and expected nearly since birth. We are not
going to quit our jobs and renounce our desires and head home to feed
our husbands. But, burned now by the very real contradictions of our
expectations, we also need to acknowledge that the solutions we once
embraced are not enough. Or, more precisely perhaps, that they never
really existed after all. The secure and affordable day care, for example.
The flexible working hours and multiple career paths. The husbands
who would ditch the remotes to lunge eagerly after dirty socks. It's
been fifty years, after all, since Betty Friedan first insisted that women
move out of their kitchens and into the mainstream of life. *Fifty years*.
My entire life.

And there's still so very far to go.

In Praise of Muddling Through

So what, then, are we to do? Is there any way of redressing the domestic
contradictions that feminism has wrought?

One obvious possibility would be to give up on men, at least in the
form of husbands. And of course many hard-core feminists have done
that, either by eschewing heterosexual marriage as an institution or by
eschewing men altogether. That works, but it's not very palatable to
those of us who still like the creatures—no, love the creatures—dirty
socks and all.

A second option would be to give up on children, or at least on

those we call our own. This, quietly, is an option that many successful women have adopted, either intentionally or not. As Sylvia Ann
Hewlett found in a recent study, between a third and a half of all successful career women in the United States do not have children.[51] And
as several commentators archly noted in 2010, the two most recent female appointees to the Supreme Court, Sonia Sotomayor and Elena
Kagan, are both childless.[52] As with giving up on men, though, this
seems an awfully draconian solution, and one that won't appeal to the
vast majority of women. Most women, as described in the previous
chapter, want children. They want to raise their children, and educate
their children, and participate in their children's childhoods. They just
don't want to give up everything for them.

Finally, the third obvious solution is the one put forth by Schlessinger and Doyle, the one that urges women to escape from their contradictions and return to the home. And it is, to be honest, a seductive
call. Particularly on those days when the boss is cranky, the traffic is
slow, and your high heels are killing you. But it would be a tragedy to
steal from women the victories they have so painfully wrought. And a
disaster to deny the world their energies and talents.

So we can't, just can't, go back to the hearth. We need some way of
moving forward, even if it involves creeping, inch by inch, in those
ever-painful heels.

As a first step, let me suggest that the quest for perfection simply
must end. Clearly, as humans, we have a desire to be better. That's what
has brought us evolution and iPads and other good things. But women
of the postfeminist years have taken this quest to the brink, truly, of
madness. It isn't really our fault. It's not that we just blithely raised
our expectations, or indulged in a media-induced fantasy of perfect
housekeeping, child rearing, or marriages. It's that we were brought up
to believe—told, in fact, essentially promised—that we could have it all.
That as women who had finally been freed from the constraints of our
foremothers, we were almost obligated to have it all. Or at least try very
hard to get it.

And so we good girls of the 1970s, 1980s, 1990s, and 2000s are trying really, really hard. We are trying to prove—to ourselves more than
others—that we have picked up the torch that feminism provided. That
we haven't failed. And yet, in a deep and profound way, we are failing.

Because feminism wasn't supposed to make us feel guilty. It was supposed to free us. It wasn't supposed to prod us into constant competitions over who is raising better children and getting less sleep. And, most critically, it wasn't supposed to chain us back to the hearth but propel us into the world of critical thought and action. The personal, remember, is political. Or at least it once was.

So we need to stop trying to be so damn perfect. Especially in those areas like cupcake making and nursery découpage where, to be honest, the stakes are pretty low. As a generation—maybe even as a nation now—we are keeping our houses too clean, our kids too hypoallergenic, our families too well costumed and organized. We are not helping our children or our marriages. And we're certainly not helping ourselves.

When I look back on more than twenty years of juggling, the joys I remember most perfectly didn't come from moments of perfection: not the perfect chocolate layer cake, or the perfect school report card, or the perfect Halloween costume. (In fact, we had the perfect Halloween costume just once. It was a little robot suit, made lovingly by my husband for our three-year-old son. It had lights that actually blinked and shiny gold paint. The lights terrified him, though, of course, and he cried miserably the whole evening.) No, the real joys were serendipitous, hatched when I least expected them and wholly unorganized. Watching as my infant son burst into spontaneous laughter for the first time, rolling on the floor in glee. Spying as my daughter, adopted just months before from a Russian orphanage, crept quietly downstairs on her first Christmas morning. Seeing my younger son sprint effortlessly across the finish line. And the mad dashes across airports or shopping malls to get to wherever I was supposed to be? The heroically organized birthday parties with fishing games and matching shark goodie bags? I honestly don't remember much of those at all.

As Courtney Martin and Judith Warner have separately argued (Martin from the perspective of adolescent girls, Warner from that of young mothers), women of the postfeminist generation have misinterpreted feminism's call for liberation for a much more subversive quest for control. Feminism, in other words, was meant to be about expanding women's roles and choices; about giving them the freedom, for the first time in history, to participate with men as equals, and to use their minds and bodies and talents and energies as they desired. Yet somehow this expansive and revolutionary set of *political* goals has been squeezed—or hijacked or mistaken—into something much more narrow and personal. Rather than trying to change the world, women are obsessed too often with perfecting themselves. Rather than seizing the options and challenges that society presents them, they are focused on controlling what they think they can: their bodies, their children, their homes.

Which brings me to my second proposal. And that is that women of my generation and younger must revisit and resuscitate the political agenda laid out by our feminist forebears. Even if women (like me) don't believe that government can ever fully solve the problems that women face every day in their kitchens and laundry rooms, we need at least to demand that government be part of the solution, that our leaders and legislators consider the small things they can do to alleviate the complicated burden of America's working families. Things like tax incentives for on-site day care, expanded options for after-school programming, and more consistent licensing of child care providers. We need to press—at the state or local level, if the federal proves too cumbersome—for more gender-neutral family policies, like Sweden's much-touted extended paternity leave. And we may need to put aside some of the broader issues that divide women in the United States to find common ground on more mundane, but perhaps more tractable, issues.

Similarly, we need to find ways of regaining the fast-fading art of organizing—coming together around issues of joint concern. If you Google the word "organizing," or search for it on Amazon, what pops up instantly are books and articles on organizing *things*: your closets, for example (*From Closet Clutter to Closet Control: Four Steps to Organizing Your Clothes*) or your home (*A Ready Reference Guide with Hundreds of Solutions to Your Everyday Clutter Challenges*). What falls far, far behind are texts on organizing *people*, guides that might advise us on how to work together. Once upon a time, of course, this was the whole focus of the emerging women's movement—bringing women together, raising their consciousness (even the word sounds quaint now), and organizing them to stand and work together. Yet somehow we've lost this urge, burying it instead under the quest for self-perfection—to have,

for instance, the most beautiful home rather than the safest neighborhood, or to fight for your kid's SAT scores rather than for the local
public school.[53]

Sadly, this embrace of the individual seems only to be growing
stronger. At the national level, we are witnessing a resurgence of liber-
tarian policies and a spreading political disdain for any sort of communal action. And in thousands of local communities we see women
dedicating vast amounts of energy to their kids, their homes, their careers, their pet causes, their book groups—and not very many joining
forces to fight for something together. It needn't be anything particularly elaborate. How about babysitting collaboratives for worn-out
moms, for example? Or potluck suppers, that relic of our grandparents'
age? How about all the parents in a school district together petitioning
for child care at open school nights? Or school calendars published far
enough in advance that parents can actually plan around them? We
could work together more often to try to make things happen; to try, as
a group of mothers or friends or colleagues or neighbors, to make the
life we share a bit easier for us all. And yet too often we do not. Why?
Because we're too busy trying to be perfect.

As I was writing this chapter, I received a phone call from a professional acquaintance, someone I knew in passing but not very well. He
was a young man in his early thirties who had just completed his doc-
torate in neurobiology. He already worked in one of the country's top
stem cell laboratories and was heading, shortly, to another lab to complete his postdoc. If someone ever finds a cure for Alzheimer's disease,
it might well be him. He had a three-year-old daughter at home, and a
two-month-old infant. His wife was returning to work in a month and
he—not she, *he*—had contacted me about some housing issues they
were having. As we spoke, his little girl was clearly whispering in his
ear, trying to catch his attention. When she became increasingly per-
sistent, he calmly withdrew from our conversation to attend to her.
"Daddy," I heard her say, "Daddy, I'm doing a project on teamwork
now, and I need your help." He promised to be there in a moment.

I think there may be hope.

8

CRASHING INTO CEILINGS: A REPORT FROM THE NINE-TO-FIVE SHIFT

Nine to five, for service and devotion
You would think that I would deserve a fair promotion
Want to move ahead but the boss won't seem to let me
I swear sometimes that man is out to get me.

—Dolly Parton, "9 to 5," 1980

Several years ago, I was participating in a performance review for one of my colleagues. She was a very successful woman: razor-sharp, always working, and never afraid to speak her mind. Since moving into this position, she had fired several long-standing employees and prodded dozens more into action. She had set performance targets, revamped databases, instituted new practices. All highly professional. All fulfilling the expectations of her job.

But she was miserable. Not because she didn't enjoy the job, or because she wasn't feeling satisfied with her work. No, she was miserable because people didn't like her. The consultant who was overseeing the review, a tiny, buffed woman in a silk leopard print blouse, posed the question as sensitively as she could. "Debora," she asked, "do you *like* Pam?"

Caught utterly off guard, I responded honestly. "Look," I said, "I spent seventeen years at Harvard Business School. I never worried about whether I liked people or not. I just had to work with them."

"Ah," the consultant sighed. "I think it's a woman thing. We girls need to feel loved. We like to like our colleagues. We want to be friends." *And that,* I groaned silently, *may be precisely our problem.*

Over the past five decades, American women have participated in one of the most stunning labor migrations in history.[1] Since the 1960s, the ranks of working women have climbed steadily—rising from 35 percent of the labor force in 1960 to 47 percent in 2008—and included significant forays into what were once all-male bastions of power. In 2008, 34 percent of lawyers in the United States were women, as were 30 percent of the country's doctors. Women constituted 61 percent of the nation's accountants and auditors and 25 percent of its architects. Yet, as countless studies have noted and bemoaned, women are still sorely underrepresented at the top of the professional pyramid: only 15.2 of the board members of Fortune 500 corporations, 16 percent of partners at the largest law firms, 19 percent of surgeons. Indeed, there seems to be some sort of odd demographic guillotine hovering between 15 and 20 percent, some force of nature or discrimination that mows women down once they threaten to multiply beyond a token few.

The literature on this topic is vast. There are volumes devoted to accounting for the female differential in specific sectors or industries, and earnest reports condemning the inequities that poor working women undeniably face. There are analyses of structural barriers and psychological ones, of the barriers that men and society put in women's way, and of the steps women can take to surmount them. Many of these treatments focus either on the hostility that often still greets women's advancement, or on the obstacles that women, and particularly mothers, regularly confront: inferior child care, inflexible working hours, a lack of mentors and role models.[2] All of these reports essentially agree that women pay a disproportionate price for trying to juggle kids and career, and that many high-powered men remain subtly antagonistic to working with and promoting the women who surround them.

Both of these points are indubitably true. But the issues that confront women who work encompass more than just family juggling and old-fashioned norms, more than maternity leaves and mommy tracks and men who don't play nice. Instead, they include more subtle and intangible factors, many of which may stem from underlying differences in how women tend to work and organize themselves professionally.

Or to put it more bluntly: before, say, the 1980s, it was totally appropriate for women to blame men for holding them back, and entirely sensible for women to lobby for the kind of regulatory changes that would enable them to advance through the ranks of power. The good news is that the women who made these arguments and fought for these changes succeeded. They wrested open the men's clubs and Ivy League universities, passed equal-pay legislation and Title IX funding. They won maternity leaves in nearly all workplaces and on-site child-care in some.[3] The bad news, though, is that these tangible victories have not brought women nearly as far as one might have hoped. Instead, as just noted, they're stuck. Stuck in the 16 percent power cranny. Stuck in the "women's chair." Stuck, far too often, in a room still packed with white men. Or, as one woman, head of a prestigious girls' school, moaned to me recently, "I read these statistics and I feel like I'm back in 1962. We haven't gotten anywhere."

In this situation, it's tempting to blame the things we've been blaming for decades. The men. The rules. The jokes. But the very stickiness of women's status—the fact that we're stuck across the board at this infernal 16 percent—suggests that something more fundamental may also be at play here. Something that goes beyond the usual suspects and into the core of women's working lives. Maybe, for example, women are opting out of certain career tracks that subsequently close off other opportunities. Maybe they are choosing careers that, in retrospect, demand more juggling than is reasonable to undertake. Maybe they are running headlong into the wrong kinds of workplaces, or marriages, or lifestyles. And maybe in our quest to nurture girls and hear their voices and raise their self-esteem, we have actually failed to provide them with the appropriate tools for success.

For seventeen years, I enjoyed the mixed blessings of being one of a very small handful of women working in a particularly male institution. In 1991, when I joined the faculty of Harvard Business School, men outnumbered women by two to one in the student body and four to one among the senior faculty (both of these figures still roughly hold true). Male students at the time saw nothing wrong in circulating sign-up sheets for striptease parties during class; male faculty would occasionally, and with good-natured grins, attribute female faculty members' teaching ratings to their legs, or their smiles, or their eyes. For all those years, I swam through that testosterone, eventually settling comfortably into my own female niche: the first woman to be tenured in my department; the first to be called upon when there was something critical and public—a panel, a dinner, a breakfast, a committee— and they "really needed a woman." And then, in 2008, I left Harvard for Barnard College, moving from a business school to a liberal arts college and, much more significantly, from a workplace dominated by men to one run almost wholly by women. It wasn't a change necessarily for the better. Or the worse. But it was most definitely a change, and a big one at that.

Indeed, as I've jetéd from one end of the gendered-workplace spectrum to the other, I've become increasingly convinced that organizations run (or at least dominated) by women are different from those run or dominated by men. Not better or worse, again. But different. And different in ways that demand scrutiny. Because if organizations reveal the gender biases of those who control them, then historically male places (like Wall Street, or automobile manufacturers, or oil rigs) will naturally tend to be harder on women, and to promote only those women who, in essence, behave "like men." Which helps to explain why so many sectors of the modern economy get stuck at female participation rates of 15 to 20 percent. These are the women who either naturally, or by the sheer force of will, learn how to operate in what remains a male-dominated, male-driven environment. Their presence, however, does not mean that women have actually entered into this club on equal footing, which is why the numbers prove so resistant to change. Conversely, once an industry or organization becomes dominated by women (as has been the case, for example, in both veterinary medicine and obstetrics), the norms of the workplace become feminized to some extent, displaying characteristics (such as consensual decision making and greater risk aversion) more associated with women's management styles. Venture capital firms run by women, for example, may be less inclined to invest in high-risk, untested businesses. Women's colleges may have a harder time asking their alumnae for financial contributions.

Again, these differences do not imply normative values; it's not that an organization dominated by women is any better or worse than one dominated by men. But if women—in general, and in the aggregate—tend to lead differently than men, then it is critical for us to understand what these differences are, and how they are likely to play out in the workplace and across women's lives. If women tend to make different career choices and prefer different kinds of working environments, then we need to understand the shape of these decisions and how they affect women's power and prestige. And, most critically, if women really have succeeded—and they have—in dismantling the tangible barriers that once blocked their paths to professional success, then we need to concentrate on the intangible and often invisible barriers—on those last pesky, impolitic, and sometimes personal factors that separate working women from where they are and where they want to be.

The 16 Percent Delusion

At every women's conference, in every think tank report, at every celebration of Women's History Month or International Women's Day, the same data are repeated. I've said them so many times myself that I can reel them off from memory. But they are crucial, and they bear repeating once again. Only twenty-one companies on the Fortune 500 list are run by female chief executives.[4] Only 16.6 percent of these companies' board members are women.[5] Women account for only 16 percent of partners at the largest law firms in the United States, and only 19 percent of the country's surgeons. Across the board, women earn on average twenty-three cents less than men for every dollar that they earn.[6]

Two things, of course, leap out from this rather depressing list. First, that the numbers are so similar across even hugely different industries (movie directors and accountants, for instance). And second, that the vast bulk of them seem stubbornly cemented at around 16 percent. It's as if some evil grim reaper came regularly to mow down any female who dared to peek her head above the mandated allotment. *Women? Yes, we love them. Please, give us more. Oh, no; no, wait. Not that many more . . . there seems to be a mistake . . . BEGONE!*

What makes this accounting even more dismal is that it is no longer credible to blame the proverbial pipeline. For decades, after all, the dearth of women at the top of organizations could easily be explained by the dearth of women anywhere in the organization. No female surgeons? Well, of course not, if there are no women in medical school. No female law partners? Wholly predictable if there are no female associates. But the pipeline to the top has been full now, or at least plentiful, for over twenty years. In 1984, the year I entered graduate school, 31 percent of graduating physicians were female, as were 36 percent of graduating lawyers and 37 percent of newly minted Ph.D.s. By 1994, women constituted fully 50 percent of graduating physicians, 46 percent of graduating lawyers, and 48 percent of Ph.D.s. Theoretically, all of these women have now been in the workforce for somewhere between fifteen and twenty-five years, more than enough time for them to have soared, crawled, or shouldered their way to the top. But they haven't. Instead, as the oft-repeated numbers show, women's position in the ranks of power has hardly surged ahead. Think about it. In 1980, there were eighteen women in Congress (3 percent) and two in state governorships. Now there are ninety-eight (18 percent) and five, respectively. In 1980, there were 58 female mayors of major American cities; now there are 217.[7] Yes, women ran (unsuccessfully) for both president and vice president in 2008, but women also ran (unsuccessfully) for president in 1964, and vice president in 1984. Without question, women have advanced professionally since the days of the feminist revolution, but that advance has been slower—much, much slower— than anyone really expected.

To get a more nuanced sense of where, and how, women are getting stuck, it's useful to look at a few fields where the deceleration has been most pronounced. In law, for instance, women seem particularly prone to being jammed into the 16 percent cranny. Since the 1980s, as noted above, women have been filing into law schools, accounting for more than 40 percent of law degrees by 1986.[8] Yet the percentage of female partners at major law firms has remained stubbornly set at around 16 percent, and the average compensation of a male partner is still almost $90,000 higher than that of his female counterpart.[9] As a result, according to Judge Judith Kaye, the first female chief judge of the State of New York, "what the profession still lacks is a critical mass of women to mentor junior associates approaching pivotal points in their careers, to ensure not only implementation of diversity programs but also accountability with regard to these programs, or to influence firm-wide decisions from the management ranks. The statistics tell us that we are definitely not there yet."[10] Similarly, while women have proliferated across the lower and middle tiers of finance, they show few signs of achieving anything close to equal representation at the top: only 2.7 percent of CEOs, 16.6 percent of executive officers, and 18 percent of board directors.[11] When I asked Ina Drew, former chief investment officer at JPMorgan Chase, and one of the banking sector's highest-ranking and longest-serving women, how to explain this discrepancy, her answer was succinct: "The top echelons of finance still lack mentors that women desperately need . . . If women remain unfulfilled by their positions without the potential for growth and discouraged by male aggression, the discrepancies will persist."

My friend Jill is a case in point. Born on a farm outside Lincoln, Nebraska, Jill attended college on a full ROTC scholarship. She studied Chinese as an undergraduate, earned a black belt in karate, and eventually became an ordnance officer in the Army. For four years, she dismantled bombs, and managed troops, and served on security detail for the White House. Needless to say, this is not a woman who scares easily, or who shies away from hardship. Jill married Paul, a classmate from ROTC, and helped support him through medical school. Then she entered law school, moved to Michigan, and gave birth to three kids—all in fairly rapid succession. For a while, it worked. Paul put in long hours as a newly minted orthopedic surgeon; Jill opened a small private law practice; and they hired a nanny they liked. Slowly, though, the troubles crept in. Paul was on call many nights and weekends, leaving Jill to juggle the kids, the errands, and the housework. Her cases were intriguing, but limited by her inability to bring on additional partners or devote more than fifty hours a week to the job. Their parents lived far away, and Jill never quite found the energy to put three toddlers in the back of the car and make the long drive back to Lincoln. So she slowly wound the practice down, throwing herself into volunteer work and her sons' tennis teams. Now the boys have graduated, though, and the big house is empty. Jill travels some, and works out, and tends to her increasingly far-flung family. But she rues the career she didn't have, and the regrets that hound her frequently. "This isn't what they gave me a degree for," she confided recently. "Somewhere, I screwed up."

My friend Shireen's regrets, meanwhile, are of a different sort. Petite and vivacious, she is one of those rare women who always manage to look both casually dressed and meticulously put together. Shireen went to business school in the early 1980s, when women were still rare among the ranks of MBAs. She graduated near the top of her class and took a fast-paced job in media marketing. She also met and married a fellow student, a hardworking son of Mexican immigrants who joined a media conglomerate as well. Shireen and Miguel worked happily together through the first few years of their marriage, grabbing takeout, skipping weekends, and sharing stories. They worked through the arrival of baby number one, and baby number two. After about eight years, however, and the arrival of baby number three, Miguel's career march accelerated. Suddenly, he was working hundred-hour weeks and shuttling back and forth among the company's expanded global operations. Without much fanfare, Shireen quietly stepped down. "What was I going to do?" she recalls. "Leave the kids with nannies around the clock?" So she took on all the child care, and the housework, and the increasingly large role of becoming a corporate wife. Today, even with her kids now grown and out of the house, Shireen maintains a breakneck schedule. She serves on several nonprofit boards and is involved with a score of local charities. She and Miguel have a strong and happy marriage. But she wears a veneer of wariness, a wariness that stems from suspecting what others want of her, and why. "People always say that they want me for my brains or my energy," she says with a smile. "But I know what they mean. They want Miguel's money. And the funny thing is," she continues, "that I really do have a lot of brains and energy. Or at least I once did."

Where women have made significant strides, for better or worse, is at the lower end of the pay scale and professional spectrum, in areas such as nursing, hairdressing, and middle school teaching, where women wholly dominate men.[12] As reported in the 2009 Shriver Report, fully half of all workers in the United States are now female, and mothers contribute to their family's earnings in nearly two-thirds of American households. Mothers are the primary breadwinners, in fact, in four out of every ten households; and half of these mothers are single.[13] These are important facts to consider, and complicated to think through. Because what does it really mean to have a household run by a single mother earning, on average, only $36,000 a year?[14] Or to have two working-class parents holding down jobs and struggling to afford day care for their kids? The good news is that millions of women—black, white, Latina, and Asian—are financially independent, working in full- or part-time jobs to support themselves and their families. The bad news, though, is that many of these women are only barely hanging on, operating along the bottom of the social and economic pyramid, where women have long struggled and from which they were supposed to have escaped.

And certainly, some have. In 2009, women entrepreneurs ran more than 10 million businesses with combined sales of $1.1 trillion.[15] As of 2007, firms owned by women in the United States employed 7.6 million people.[16] But the aggregate numbers—that darned list of statistics again—makes clear that most positions of power in this country (and indeed, around the world) are still persistently held by men. Women are flocking into college, into graduate programs, into entry-level and midlevel positions across every conceivable industry—but they are falling out well before they reach the top.

Why?

It isn't legalized prejudice anymore. It isn't barriers on the way in. And it's not just men being mean. Indeed, most men in visible positions of power today are almost desperate to have some reasonable number of women in their ranks. So what accounts for the bottleneck? For the clogged pipeline, the glass ceiling, the pervasive code words meant to capture the reality that women are simply getting stuck?

Clearly, painfully, they're getting stuck because so many of them are choosing to stop. Women are not getting fired from midlevel positions at accounting or law firms; they are not disproportionately being denied tenure at major research universities. They are deciding, like Jill and Shireen, that they need to stay at home, or work part time, or step away from the fast track. Individually, each of these women's moves may make great sense. Together, though, they have created a landscape where women are still scarce, and where the clashing visions between what is and what was expected to be makes them feel scarcer still.

Of On-Ramps, Off-Ramps, U-Turns, and Dead Ends

In 1989, Felice Schwartz wrote a wildly popular (or at least wildly well read) article in the *Harvard Business Review*. Entitled "Management Women and the New Facts of Life," the article argued that if corporations wanted to retain their best and brightest female employees, they needed to create a more flexible and family-friendly workforce, one that offered young mothers a variety of ways to structure their working hours and their careers.[17] High-potential women, Schwartz suggested, fell naturally into one of two camps. In the first were "career primary women," women who essentially behaved like men at work and were willing to undertake the same set of trade-offs. These women were almost certain to remain single or at least childless, Schwartz predicted, and to demand only that their employers "recognize them early, accept them, and clear artificial barriers from their path to the top."[18] In the second camp were "career-and-family women," women who wanted children *and* a career, and who, unlike both men and "career primary women," were willing to trade some of the demands of promotion for the freedom to spend more time with their children.[19]

Schwartz, a devoted feminist who had founded the women's advocacy group Catalyst, never actually used the term "mommy track." But as her piece went viral (and this in the days before social media!), others rapidly coined the phrase and attached it to her argument. The mommy track, in common parlance, became the less arduous path women took when they wanted to stay in the workforce but not sacrifice their entire lives to it. The mommy track was what allowed employers to retain the women they had recruited, trained, and invested in. And the mommy track turned out to be a great dead end.[20]

In theory, keeping mothers in the workforce demands little more than flexibility; a certain willingness, as Schwartz initially suggested, to give career-and-family women "the freedom to take time off—a couple of hours, a day, a week—or to do some work at home and some at the office."[21] In theory, talented women on a mommy track could telecommute or job-share; they could work twenty (or thirty-five) efficient hours every week, staying current and valuable in the workplace without necessarily devoting every ounce of their being to its demands. In theory, the mommy track should work, both for women and their employers.

In practice, however, few organizations have found ways to carve their most important positions into anything other than full-time chunks. Today, for example, more than twenty years after Schwartz published her article, there are still only eight scientists working part time at the National Science Foundation (NSF).[22] Only 13 percent of women lawyers work part time, as do 2 percent of female financial managers.[23] When prodded, representatives from these organizations say all the right things. Remarking upon the intensity and importance of his agency's work, for example, the senior human resource specialist at the NSF explained that "you can imagine that the task of determining which projects are funded, distributing the awards, and monitoring and reviewing compliance . . . is daunting to say the least. Because of that, most of our employees are full-time professionals."[24] But at the end of the (full eight-hour!) day, the facts speak for themselves. At HSBC, a major global bank, 8.3 percent of all employees work part time; at one of their leading competitors, the number is a rather stunning 1.1 percent. Even at Barnard College, a place run largely by and for women, only 11 percent of the college's staff members were working less than full time in 2011. Again, it doesn't seem that the human resource departments of any of these organizations are consciously choosing against part-time positions. On the contrary, most HR managers (who tend to be disproportionately female) explicitly embrace the idea of part-time work and flexible employment. But when it comes to putting actual bodies in actual jobs, full-timers simply tend to dominate. As a result, while the number of women who work part time is statistically quite high (roughly a quarter of all female workers), the vast majority of these part-timers are clustered at the lower end of the economic spectrum, working as cashiers, waitresses, and sales assistants.[25]

Many women who have left the full-time workforce, of course, predict that their hiatuses will be brief. Most women, in fact, and particularly high-earning, high-achieving women, presume that they will leave their jobs for just brief periods of time, returning in full force once their maternity leaves expire, or their children set off for preschool, or their husbands return from that overseas assignment. Yet, as Sylvia Ann Hewlett found in a 2005 study, most women who pull blithely into a career "off-ramp" find the road back far more treacherous than they had anticipated. Positions disappear; salaries plummet;

professional relationships grow stale. And at the end of the day, only 40 percent of women who try to return to full-time professional jobs actually manage to do so.[26] The rest settle into early retirement, or slower-paced, lower-ranked jobs.

Exploring these on-and-off patterns has become a cottage industry of sorts—and a nasty one, at that. In 2003, Lisa Belkin wrote a piece for *The New York Times Magazine* that sketched the lives of eight formerly fierce women. All had undergraduate degrees from Princeton. All had equally impressive graduate degrees (in law, English, business); all had charged eagerly into their chosen profession. And all, after marriage and a couple of kids, had, as Belkin dubbed it, "opted out." Instead of racing to the office in the morning, they were watching their toddlers and drinking lattes at Starbucks; instead of staying on the fast track, or even the mommy track, they were hitting the treadmill at the gym. None of these women had been pushed from their professional perches. They had simply opted out, choosing a life—of children, motherhood, wifedom—they found more appealing. "I don't want to be famous; I don't want to conquer the world; I don't want that kind of a life," asserted Sarah McArthur Amsbary, a former theater artist with a master's degree in English. "I don't want to be on the fast track leading to a partnership at a prestigious law firm," echoed Katherine Brokaw, a former lawyer. "Some people define that as success. I don't."[27] Dipping into her own story—as a hard-charging reporter who had eventually decided to freelance instead—Belkin raised the same concerns, the same choices, as those of her subjects. "I was no longer willing to work as hard," she recalls, "for a prize I was learning I didn't really want."

Two years later, another reporter at the *Times* wrote a similar piece, focusing now on even younger women, women who were deciding to opt out before they had even begun. In the article, reporter Louise Story told the tale of Cynthia Liu, a smart, disciplined, and talented sophomore at Yale, who, at nineteen, was already planning to devote at least a chunk of her life to being a stay-at-home mom. "My mother's always told me that you can't be the best career woman and the best mother at the same time," Ms. Liu confided. "You always have to choose one over the other." And Liu apparently was not alone; according to Story, 60 percent of the women she polled at Yale reported that they, too, planned to cut back or stop working entirely once they had children.[28] "I'll have a career until I have two kids," predicted Angie Ku, another Yale student covered in the story. "It doesn't necessarily matter how far you get," she reasoned. "It's kind of like the experience: I have tried what I wanted to do."

The response to both pieces was immediate, long-lived, and vicious. After Belkin's piece ran, the *Times* reportedly received more mail—angry mail, from angry women—than it had ever before received about a single story.[29] "I found the article depressing," wrote one self-proclaimed "old-fashioned feminist." "The personal is political. Remember that?" enjoined another.[30] Katha Pollitt, a leading feminist writer, repudiated Belkin's statistics (or, more accurately, lack thereof), arguing in *The Nation* that Belkin's subjects represented at best a "blip," a tiny downtick in working mothers driven, most likely, by a weakening economy.[31] Likewise, the *Times* was deluged in 2005 by furious responses to Story's piece, with women writing to complain about the students' self-indulgence and passivity.[32] Even now, eight years since the article's publication, women regularly regale me with their reactions to it, describing everything from violent rage to a guilty sigh of relief.

It's not surprising that the opt-out debate pushes every nasty button in the world of warring women. Because in trying to define a complex, highly idiosyncratic decision, writers like Belkin (unwittingly, perhaps, and unfortunately) tend to split women into two camps: Those Who Do (work at meaningful jobs that utilize their talents and contribute to the national well-being) and Those Who Don't. Those Who Do (love their children and care about their emotional development) and Those Who Don't. Adding insult to injury is the oft-bemoaned fact that the women in these stories are invariably well educated and well off, able to agonize over choices that poorer women never have the luxury of being miserable about. Unlike Katherine Brokaw, for example (the former lawyer profiled in the *Times* piece), most women in the United States (never mind the world) don't have a fulfilling job and lucrative salary to walk away from.[33] Unlike my friend Shireen, most women can't build a wholly satisfying life around the philanthropy that their husband's wealth provides. Indeed, for women on the lower end of the socioeconomic spectrum, the choice between staying in and opting out is no choice at all. They stay in the workforce because they have to, and they pay probably the harshest penalties of all.

Yet there's something very real about the opting-out portrayal; something that transcends class distinctions and tiffs about lifestyle choices. And that's the fact that women—given the choice about their lives and careers—are making these choices differently than men. In the aggregate, and given a certain measure of financial security, they are making the choice between work and family in favor of the latter. According to one study, only 62 percent of the women who received MBAs from the University of Chicago between 1990 and 2006 were working full time ten years after graduation.[34] According to another, half the women in each incoming class at a major professional services firm had left the firm—and indeed the workforce—within five to seven years of their arrival.[35] In 2000, when the U.S. economy was booming, 22 percent of American women with professional degrees were not in the labor market at all.[36]

Anecdotally, many of these women report that they leave reluctantly, pushed by the sheer impossibility of trying to juggle family and career, rather than being pulled by the sweet scent of their baby's newly washed skin. Indeed, in a famous rejoinder to the opt-out kerfuffle, the noted legal scholar Joan Williams argued that the real story (overlooked by the media) was that the contemporary workplace remained mired in the patterns of the 1950s workforce, and that employers were simply unable and unwilling to deal with the phenomenon of working mothers.[37] Her conclusions were further borne out in a 2004 study of forty-three professional women, nearly all of whom reported leaving the workforce, not out of any lighthearted sense of choice, but rather because the "amount, pace, and inflexibility" of their work simply would not, and could not, accommodate their family responsibilities.[38] For these women, as the study's authors note, "there was no 'Eureka!' moment, no final straw, but rather the gradual accumulation of often overlapping workplace pushes and family pulls that led them to quit their jobs."[39]

Yet detailing these often-excruciating tensions still does not explain why women respond differently to them than men. Why women are the ones opting out and pulling back far more frequently than their presumably equally entangled, similarly educated husbands. Here are my two answers (based, I confess, entirely on speculation).

Number 1: the women simply jump first.

And number 2: they jump particularly quickly when they are not passionate about their work.

Or, to put it slightly differently: when the choice is between compromising a job and compromising a family, women seem more inclined to focus on the family, men to stick with the job that pays the bills. Perhaps this goes back to our vestigial roles as feeders of children and killers of meat. Perhaps it is the media, still hammering stereotypes into our brains. Perhaps it is the modern workplace's stubborn refusal to create schedules or structures that are even vaguely conducive to the rhythms of family life. But when push comes to shove—and it can, and it will—women are the ones who more often walk away. Not necessarily because their husbands push them to. Or because their employers are unwilling to accept a modicum of flexibility. No, they go because the kids are weary and the dinners are rushed and the job, after ten or twenty years of working, has ceased to deliver the thrill it once did. If a job is truly satisfying to a woman, or if she needs the income it provides, she will strive to stay in the workforce. But if she doesn't need the income, and she doesn't love the job, it becomes tougher and tougher for a working mother to undertake all the juggling that comes with her role.

This mismatch between jobs and desire seems to vary not only with time and gender, but across industries as well. Specifically, there are some fields from which women seem to flee in droves: law, consulting, banking. And some fields in which they seem to stay: medicine, academia, entrepreneurial ventures. Typically, the reasons cited to explain these patterns are the obvious ones—fields like consulting and corporate law, for example, are frequently described as being too demanding on young mothers' time and too "male" in their knee-jerk behavior patterns. ("Once the babies came," you'll frequently hear, "she just couldn't rationalize being away that long." Or "After a while, she didn't want to deal with the jokes, and the leers, and the guys all heading out to Hooters together.") When women leave these fields, therefore, it is easy to see their departures as somewhat predictable, even expected. Which to a large extent is true. Commodity trading floors are still rough-edged, often raunchy, places. Would-be partners at major corporate law firms work insanely long hours. But let me suggest two other reasons that may explain the patterns of opting out we see across industries. The first has to do with the men women marry; the second, with the desires they have.

Let's start with marriage. Interestingly, in a world increasingly dominated by match.com and JDate, in a world of sexual equality, working women, and casual sex, men and women still tend toward spouses who are roughly like them. That is, lawyers marry lawyers and doctors marry doctors. Movie stars marry movie stars, and teachers, in the aggregate, marry teachers. As a result, many professional women find themselves married to men with roughly similar educational backgrounds and earning potential.[40] And as these potentials play themselves out over the course of a life, couples seem to make different kinds of choices, choices that are quite sensible when seen as aggregate patterns. Specifically, women who marry men who make a great deal of money leave the workforce at higher rates than women married to men who make less money. It doesn't seem to matter, statistically at least, how high the woman's salary is, or how stellar her academic credentials. If her husband is earning a particularly high salary—the salary, say, of an investment banker or corporate lawyer—she is more likely to leave than if her husband is earning even the moderately high salary of a professor or medical doctor.[41] Admittedly, this element of opting out is limited to the elite of the elite: to incredibly well-paid women leaving incredibly well-paid jobs because they have husbands earning equally incredible salaries and working equally insane hours. But it accounts for a fair amount of the highest-profile outflow of women—women who, like my friend Shireen, find themselves in marriages in which there's simply too much money and not enough time for the wife to keep working. Where money is tighter, by contrast, women keep working.

These patterns are relatively easy to identify. What is harder, and what I suggest with considerably greater trepidation, is that women may also leave careers that feel less satisfying to them, or that they entered somewhat haphazardly. The default case here is medicine, an area in which women's professional ranks (30 percent of physicians practicing in the United States) line up fairly well against their numbers in graduate school (48 percent of medical degrees awarded in 2010).[42] Now, it's possible that women stay in medicine because they have organized their lives (through flexible hours, larger practices, more predictable specialties) in a workable way.[43] It's probable that they stay, in part, because they tend to marry doctors, and a one-doctor household (remarkably) no longer guarantees a spot among this country's upper middle class. But it's also possible that women stay in medicine because that's where they've always wanted to be. Few people, of any gender, enter medical school on a whim. Even fewer stay for the eight to twelve years it requires, and pay (or borrow) the roughly $180,000 it costs, if they don't see medicine as both a dream and a calling—something they want so badly that they're willing to undertake the significant sacrifice it entails.

In other fields, by contrast, the outflow of women may be partly explained by the more haphazard route through which they entered. Take law, for instance. As noted above, the disparity between women with law degrees and women in the top echelons of the legal profession is particularly stark: women currently receive around 50 percent of law degrees but account for only 16 percent of partners at major law firms. Again, much of this discrepancy is due, no doubt, to the extraordinary hours that partners (and associates) are expected to bill, and to the law firms' unwillingness to create viable part-time or flex-time options. Some may be attributable to the fact that partners at major law firms can easily earn $600,000 or more—more than enough for a family to support even the most lavish lifestyle on a single salary. Yet, based wholly on the anecdotal evidence of having spent two decades around college-age students, I can't help suspecting that many women leave the law because they never fully embraced it in the first place. Instead, a bright young woman (or man) may decide to apply to law school because it seems a solid and respectable next step after college, a choice that few parents would advise against. The hardworking student may do well at law school, may join the law review and land a great job after graduation. But if a young woman never really loved the law (or accounting, or finance), if she never truly reveled in the day-to-day work, then it will be harder and harder for her to embrace the trade-offs that these professions require, and easier and easier, over time, to pull back.

In May 2011, Sheryl Sandberg, the chief operating officer of Facebook, gave the commencement address at Barnard. It was a gutsy speech, and she knew it. Because rather than falling into the traditional platitudes

of graduation, and rather than following the predictable route of urging the newly minted young women graduates to follow their dreams
and seek their passion, Sandberg, one of the country's most successful
female executives, explicitly told the Barnard graduates not to compromise their careers. "Women," she cautioned them, "almost never make
one decision to leave the workforce. It doesn't happen that way. They
make small little decisions along the way that eventually lead them
there. Maybe it's the last year of med school when they say, 'I'll take a
slightly less interesting specialty because I'm going to want more balance one day.' Maybe it's the fifth year in a law firm when they say, 'I'm
not even sure I should go for partner, because I know I'm going to want
kids eventually.' These women don't even have relationships, and already they're finding balance, balance for responsibilities they don't
have. And from that moment, they start quietly leaning back."

Sandberg—a wife and mother of two—pulled no punches in telling
the young women what to do. "Do not lean back," she urged. "Lean in.
Put your foot on that gas pedal and keep it there until the day you have
to make a decision, and then make a decision. That's the only way,
when that day comes, you'll even have a decision to make."[44]

If Women Ran the World: Voices of Power and Persuasion

Around 2009, the world was suddenly awash with a particular sort
of heroine. Armed with sensible heels and sheer intelligence, she de-
scended upon the planet to clean up the mess unleashed by men. In
Iceland, a handful of female politicians and businesswomen seized
control of that country's financial system, wrecked and bankrupt over
the past several years by a bevy of male bankers.[45] In Liberia, President
Ellen Johnson Sirleaf set out to mend a nation broken by decades of war
and civil strife. In Germany, Chancellor Angela Merkel worked to restore not only her country's economy but all of Europe's as well. In the
United States, reeling still from the calamities of the 2008 financial
crisis, a small but mighty group of women were dubbed the new sheriffs of Wall Street: Sheila Bair, Mary Schapiro, and Elizabeth Warren.[46]
Hillary Clinton was tapped to right the United States' foreign policy,
Samantha Power to refine its humanitarian goals. When Dominique

Strauss-Kahn, director of the IMF, was indicted for the attempted rape of a hotel chambermaid, all of Europe lobbied for a woman, Christine Lagarde, to replace him. And Lagarde was quick in touting the advantages of being female. "Gender-dominated environments are not good," she argued, "particularly in the financial sector, where there are too few women. Men have a tendency to . . . show how hairy-chested they are, compared with the man who's sitting next to them. I honestly think that there should never be too much testosterone in one room."[47]

Possibly, the timing of these various promotions was wholly coincidental. Possibly, it was the birth pangs of a genuine female elite—the daughters of feminism finally thrust into power. And possibly it was because, in a time of turmoil and despair, society at large was explicitly searching for a different kind of power, and a different tone of voice.

For centuries, women were presumed to be not only inherently inferior to men, but qualitatively different as well—more fragile, more vulnerable, and far less inclined to lead anything more complex than a household. Such views reached a pinnacle of sorts during the Victorian era, when women were reconstructed as "domestic angels," genetically predisposed to cook, clean, and raise the children—and otherwise stay clear of men's affairs. In an 1872 Supreme Court case, for instance, Justice Joseph Bradley ruled that "the natural and proper timidity and delicacy which belongs to the female sex evidently unfits it for many occupations of civil life." Going on, the good judge opined that "the harmony, not to say identity, of interests and views which belong, or should belong, to the family institution is repugnant to the idea of a woman adopting a distinct and independent career from that of her husband."[48]

As droves of women started to chafe at their enforced domesticity, however, and to flow into the colleges and jobs that were increasingly available to them by the turn of the twentieth century, prevailing views on women's nature began to modify somewhat, acknowledging, albeit begrudgingly, that women could occasionally find a place and a voice outside the domestic realm. Yet even the most enthusiastic of women's advocates still saw women's roles as essentially shaped and constrained by their inherent femininity—by the sheer fact, in other words, that their bodies and minds worked differently than men's. "In the government of the physical world," wrote Mary Wollstonecraft in her path-breaking

Vindication of the Rights of Woman, "the female in point of strength is, in general, inferior to the male. This is the law of Nature."[49] Accordingly, even as women sneaked into formerly all-male bastions such as law or medicine, even as they ran small businesses or organized their communities, they were presumed to do so in a "womanly" fashion—speaking softly, tending to others, and never seeking power for its own sake.

All this changed, of course, with the advent of feminism. Suddenly, women were not only barging into positions once reserved strictly for men, but they were barging in on the men's terms, insisting on wholly equal and nondifferentiated treatment. Indeed, attacking the rhetoric of "separate but equal" that was also being dismantled in the civil rights arena, second-wave feminists argued passionately against any special or distinctive treatment of women, any hint that women in the workplace might behave differently than men. Critically, the scholars and activists who promoted this argument were not just advocating that women be taken seriously or that they be allowed into once-male spheres. They were arguing that the entire history of women's inequality was due, not to any inherent differences between the sexes, but rather to centuries of structural oppression imposed by men. Or, as Simone de Beauvoir put it: "Representation of the world, like the world itself, is the work of men; they describe it from their own point of view, which they confuse with absolute truth."[50] Women, in other words, were not essentially different from men, not gentler, or kinder, or inherently more focused on their offspring. They had simply been forced into these roles by men.

This view of inherent equality has permeated public discourse since the late 1960s. Under Title VII of the Civil Rights Act of 1964, employers are prohibited from discriminating on the basis of sex, even if such discrimination were to take the form of favorable or protective treatment for women.[51] Under the terms of the Pregnancy Discrimination Act of 1978, women who give birth are not actually treated as women giving birth per se, but as individuals undergoing a medical event.[52] And under the terms of the Family and Medical Leave Act of 1993, caregiving, even to a newborn child, is explicitly defined as a gender-neutral activity, with provisions for unpaid leave extended equally to men and women. Under U.S. law, therefore, any hint of women's distinctiveness has been essentially banished, replaced by the belief that women, given the same opportunities, will behave more or less like men.[53]

In the wake of the financial crisis of 2008, however, a renegade, slightly retrograde view has started to emerge.[54] What, some observers have wondered publicly, if women in the workforce don't behave exactly like men?[55] What if women leaders, in particular, don't lead exactly like men? And what if those characteristics, rather than consigning women to domestic chores, actually made them highly prized members of social organizations?

Clearly, this is dangerous ground to tread. Because if it's acceptable to claim that women are different in a good way, then it's just a hop, skip, and jump back toward defining them as different in a bad way. If we attribute any particular characteristics to women as a group, aren't we just reducing them to the same sorts of social stereotypes that feminism so successfully toppled?

Yes, admittedly, there are real risks in heading down this path, and real potholes—both practical and theoretical—to avoid. But there are also intriguing strands of research that seem foolish to ignore. Since the early 1990s, for example, the Georgetown University professor Deborah Tannen has been demonstrating persuasively that men and women in the workplace communicate differently. According to her now-voluminous studies, men in group settings strive generally to preserve status, while women try to gain intimacy and closeness.[56] Women, that is, try to get people to like them. They ask for resources and favors less frequently than men, try not to appear to be acting aggressively, and tend to share power rather than seizing it.[57] Which means that women can appear to lack authority in the workplace—but, also, potentially, that they can be more inspiring and transformational leaders.[58]

Others, meanwhile, have tackled the tricky issue of gender difference from more peripheral, though no less fascinating, directions. Boris Groysberg, for instance, is a former colleague of mine who set out in the early 2000s to tackle a fairly standard business question: Why, he asked, do the star performers at certain investment banks not remain stars once they've transferred to other, similar firms? As a good student of organizational behavior, Groysberg was expecting to find factors that related to the structure of the organizations—hierarchies, for example, or channels of information. What he found instead, though, was that one of the most important predictors of success, and one of the most important differentiators in a person's career, was gender. Simply put, male stars who changed firms failed to perform as well as they once had, while female stars did just as well or better. Further research convinced Groysberg that the women were not inherently more talented than the men, or even simply luckier. Instead, even as women were building careers at their first firms, they were also—either consciously or unconsciously—building networks and relationships outside the firm. When they left, they took those networks with them and benefited from them. Men, by contrast, tended to spend their time and social capital building relationships inside the firm—grabbing a beer with the boss, say, or golfing with the team. When they left, these relationships died, along, apparently, with their once-stellar performance.[59]

In a similarly orthogonal vein, John Coates and Joe Herbert, researchers in neuroscience at Cambridge University, launched a study in 2008 to examine the relationship between testosterone and risk taking. Working only with male subjects (because they had no explicit intent to study gender differences), they assembled a group of seventeen volunteers, all working as financial traders in London. Each morning for eight days, Coates and Herbert measured the traders' testosterone levels.* And each afternoon, they recorded their daily trades. What they found was stunning, if not entirely surprising: the more testosterone a man had, the more profitably he traded. Higher levels of testosterone literally appeared to make men more willing to take risks, while lower levels made them more cautious.[60]

Finally, one of my favorite bits of recent research comes from Muriel Niederle and Lise Vesterlund, economists at Stanford and the University of Pittsburgh, respectively. In 2007, they put eighty college students in a room and asked them to complete a series of arithmetic problems. In the first round of the experiment, the students, half male and half female, were split into groups and compensated according to two different payment schemes: half were paid a piece rate of fifty cents for each correct answer, and half were paid a competitive rate in which the highest scoring student (in a group of four) received two dollars for each correct answer. There was no mention of gender, and the men and

---

*They took saliva samples twice per day, testing for both testosterone and cortisol.

women scored equally well. In the second round, the students were offered a choice between the two payment schemes: either fifty cents for
each correct answer, again, or two dollars per correct answer to the top
scorer. Theoretically, both men and women should have responded
similarly to this choice, with the highest scorers from round one selecting the competitive payment scheme and the lowest choosing the more
secure piecemeal option. Instead, though, the group split markedly
among gender lines, with more men choosing the competitive scheme
(73 percent) and more women selecting the per-puzzle rate.[61] Men
chose risk, in other words, even when logic dictated against it. Women
chose security even when the risks were low.

A handful of studies, of course, does not a movement unmake. And
given the prejudice, discrimination, and structural obstacles that have
surrounded women for centuries, it would be exceedingly foolhardy to
leap blithely toward a belief that women are somehow organically destined to behave differently in the workplace than do men. To do so
would risk going back to a world in which women were routinely suspected of being kinder, and gentler, and more caring. Of being less fit
for the rough-and-tumble of working life.

Yet it's not clear (at least to me) why being supportive of women's
ambition necessarily means denying the possibility of biologically or
hormonally driven implications. Are all women, under all circumstances, predestined to behave in certain ways or perform certain functions? Of course not. But are women, in general, more or less likely to
evince particular characteristics? Maybe. And if those characteristics
can be usefully harnessed—if they can, in fact, help us to define models
of work and leadership that might fit more comfortably around more
women—then they almost certainly demand some measure of scrutiny.

Looking back over the past twenty years of my own life, I find it
impossible not to believe that men and women tend to manage things
differently. Not better. Not worse. But differently. My evidence on this
point is wholly anecdotal, of course, but it comes in wave after wave,
and hits me whenever I venture from a male-dominated organization
(Harvard Business School or the board of Goldman Sachs) to a female
one (Barnard College or the board of my daughter's all-girls school).
Some of the differences are wholly trivial. At Harvard, no one ever noticed anything about my wardrobe; at Barnard, every suit and handbag

is well known and under constant appraisal (one alumna even wrote formally to complain about a dress I had worn to a reunion). At Harvard, a colleague once suggested that I end class by jumping out of a cake. At Barnard, that just doesn't happen. The jokes vary dramatically in male- and female-dominated offices, as do the offhand references, the out-of-office gatherings, and the simple rhythms of day-to-day life. (At Barnard, I have two desk drawers reserved for gifts of chocolate and nice notes. At Harvard, I think I kept spare batteries there.)

Other differences, though, are both subtler and more substantive.[62] In an organization dominated by men, in my experience, decisions tend to be made through fairly predictable, relatively hierarchical channels. The lines of power are clear and well defined, and once policies have been set, they are presumed to be permanent. In an organization dominated by women, by comparison, streams of power and influence are considerably more fluid, flowing not just from the top down, but in often-invisible eddies around the center. Decisions are taken more slowly and with a more conscious sense of their impermanence. To give one relatively minor example: when Harvard Business School changed its website some years ago, I was a senior member of the faculty and the chair of a department. Yet my involvement with both the decision and the design was minimal, limited to a handful of conversations around the new site's implementation. At Barnard, by contrast, a 2011 decision to redesign the website was met with a veritable storm of opposition and input. There were listening sessions and consultations, working groups and committees. And when the community still expressed its disapproval with the final design, we pulled the website, had more consultations, and eventually redesigned it. Was one route better than the other? I don't know. HBS got its website up and running faster and more efficiently. Barnard got a better website in the end. Same decision, but a wholly different dynamic.

Similarly, organizations run or dominated by men seem to be less concerned than those run by women with achieving internal consensus. Men, to put it bluntly, are comfortable with exerting authority over dissent; women, less so. At Harvard, and in male environments generally, I would say, people are accustomed to and accepting of disagreement—even all-out, pitched-battle disagreement. The case in point here is Larry Summers, the University's controversial president from 2001 to 2006. Summers adored disagreement, in my experience, and loved nothing more than a good argument. He didn't necessarily care what people thought of him, or what he thought of them. The argument, the logic, was what mattered.* At Barnard, by contrast, and in organizations more dominated by women, dissent is a bad thing, something to be avoided or patched up. People don't want to fight, don't want to be angry, and certainly don't want to be disliked. Again, I wouldn't argue that either end of the spectrum is better or worse than the other. But they are different.

Finally, as Niederle and Westerlund's academic research so powerfully suggests, organizations run by women tend to be more cautious than those run by men. Which makes great sense. If men are by nature more inclined to take risks (particularly financial ones) and women less so, then groups of men will tend to cluster around risky behaviors while groups of women avoid them. We see evidence of these patterns across the financial sector and in other areas (gambling, online poker, motorcycle jumping) where the bets are large and the risks tangible. There are very few women, still, in hedge funds and venture capital, and yet a disproportionately large number of women (Sherron Watkins at Enron, Brooksley Born at the Commodity Futures Trading Commission, Coleen Rowley at the FBI) who have acted in recent years as whistle-blowers, calling attention to dangerous behaviors that others chose either to participate in or ignore. Interestingly, women seem more inclined to take the personal downside risks that whistle-blowing entails and less inclined to take the big upside risks that came to dominate global financial markets in the 1990s and 2000s.

Recent years have seen a surge of interest in measuring, or at least defining, the "gender dividend." Driven by both the relentless flow of women out of leadership positions, and the small but heady number of women (Clinton, Pelosi, Merkel, Sotomayor, Lagarde) reaching for the very top, researchers have tried to identify—analytically and apolitically— just why it matters at all. Are organizations qualitatively different if more women are involved? Do they perform better? Or maybe worse?

*And, in the end, what precipitated his downfall.

The answer, for the moment at least, is that we really can't tell.[63] Some studies triumphantly find an uptick in stock prices when women join corporate boards; others find no relationship at all. Some see a link between business performance and the percentage of female executives; others don't. Surveys of governance suggest tantalizing links between the number of female legislators and the kinds of laws they pass, but they don't reveal much about the inherent quality of this legislation. And thus we are left—statistically at least—still in the dark, unable to prove the merits of having more women aboard.

For me, though, the case for including women—in all organizations, across all levels, and into the very highest reaches of power—rests not on data, but on common sense.[64] Women account for 49 percent of this world's population. They receive 58 percent of college degrees in the United States; 48 percent of medical degrees; 50 percent of Ph.D.s. They tend to manage themselves and their organizations through different channels than men, bringing different perspectives and priorities into play. It is simply absurd to leave these talents on the sidelines, particularly when those proverbial few good men are getting harder and harder to find.

Slogans for My Tombstone

Frequently, women who've achieved some measure of professional success are asked—in public and private, at conferences and cocktail parties—the identically worded question: "How do you do it?"

Often, there is an odd emphasis on the second word—how *do* you do it?—as if to underscore the oddity of doing "it" at all, or to insinuate that any woman doing "it" (whatever "it" may be) either has a magical bag of tricks at her disposal, or is actually forsaking some other great responsibility in pursuit of the miraculous "it." I hate the query and the connotation behind it.

But the phrase I hate even more, the phrase that's been lobbed at me dozens—no, probably thousands—of times is that tuckaway clause, slipped in sotto voce when the speaker thinks either that I'm not listening or that I don't care: "And," he (or sometimes she) will say, "and, umm, I don't mean to disparage or anything, but we also really need a woman..."

Really need a woman. Indeed. Usually that means that they don't actually *need* a woman at all, but they think that others will expect a woman to be there (on the stage, or committee, or board) and are therefore under pressure to produce one. Usually it means that there aren't enough women in the pool from which they're drawing, and that the few of us who exist will therefore be asked to do double or triple duty. Sometimes, being the woman means that great things fall at your feet. More often, though, it means yet another Saturday afternoon or Thursday evening spent showing up to make someone else look better.

Because the issue, of course, is not about pulling token women into public places to pretend that their presence is more widespread. The issue is about making it easier for all women to have the jobs and careers they want, and for all organizations to benefit from the diversity of perspectives that women tend to bring. I realize this is easier said than done. I realize that women across the United States and the world remain stuck in the 16 percent cranny, stuck in on-ramps that don't advance and mommy tracks leading nowhere.

But it doesn't have to be this way. Women *can* have kids and professional lives, healthy marriages and productive careers. Organizations can have employees who are devoted to their work and their families and who bring the diversity (not only of gender, but of race and class and ethnicity, too) that any organization needs to thrive. At the risk of sounding unnaturally optimistic, let me suggest that we already know how to do these things. Major firms such as Deloitte Touche have dramatically increased the number of women in their ranks, and boosted their own performance as a result.[65] Several top-tier law firms have instituted formal, firmwide diversity programs that have helped to propel women into their highest echelons.[66] It's just that the numbers here remain relatively small, while expectations have become sky-high.

And this, once again, may be part of the problem. Today, women are expected not just to get a job and keep a job, but to flourish in whatever career they have chosen, to rise through the ranks happily, and to maintain a partner and children along the way. They are expected, moreover, to raise those children perfectly (see chapter 7), to stay awake for sex (chapter 3) and to look like Beyoncé as they do it all (chapter 4). *This* is the part that's not do-able. And so is the expectation that women in complex organizations will behave exactly like men, picking up their preferences, their management styles, and their reservoirs of Australian rugby trivia. No, in the aggregate and in general, women in professional organizations will manage themselves slightly differently than men—more cautiously, perhaps, more inclusively, and with a preference for consensus over conflict.

Being realistic about these issues will certainly not banish the problems and tensions that working women face. But it does suggest a way forward that is more promising than male bashing and more fun than whining. Specifically, young women need to be realistic about the careers they desire and the trade-offs they will inevitably have to face. Want to be an investment banker or a technology entrepreneur? That's fine. But assume ninety-hour work weeks and, if you want children, more than full-time child care. Assume you'll work nights and weekends and that the guy across the hall will have an easier time than you. Assume the baby will come down with croup the night before your major presentation and have a backup plan in place. If you don't want to live like this—and let's be honest, most people don't—then don't become an investment banker or technology entrepreneur. Pick a more flexible career or one with more reasonable hours. But for heaven's sake, don't go into a field without first understanding the rules of the game and considering deeply whether you want to play by them.

Meanwhile, women of all ages need to be realistic about their strengths and weaknesses, about what they bring to the table and what they don't. Men, in general, tend to understand that there is only so much they can do at one time and so many skills they can master. So if the budget report is due tomorrow, the lawn can go unmowed. Women, by contrast, try to keep everything going well and at once—all the plates spinning, all the kids happy, all the clothes clean. If they are in male-dominated organizations, they also often try to adjust their behaviors, chameleon-style, to conform to the environment that surrounds them. I've seen myself do this a thousand times. If I'm working for someone who loves a good argument, I'll argue right back. If a decision comes down through clearly marked channels, I'll stifle my inherent tendency to question it. The problem, though, is that chameleons only live for so long, and eventually most women—most people—will only be comfortable in a setting that accords with their values and rewards their strengths. For women, this means finding organizations that fit their own styles rather than accommodating to alien environments or presuming the power to change them singlehandedly. And for organizations, it means that "fixing the women's problem" is not about fixing the women, or yanking them onto committees, or placating them with yet another networking retreat. It's about fixing the organization— recognizing a diversity of skills and attributes, measuring them in a concrete way, and rewarding people accordingly.

Recently, I found myself going back, yet again, to one of my best employees. "Robert," I said, "I hate to ask you to take on another burden. I know how busy you are. But this task force is really important. I know you'll do a great job and, umm, I really need a man."

It felt good.

9

Memories of My Waist

Long before the eventual mutilation, woman is haunted by the horror of growing old . . . when the first hints come of that fated and irreversible process which is to destroy the whole edifice built up during puberty, she feels the fatal touch of death itself.

—Simone de Beauvoir[1]

I know older men in comedy who can barely feed and clean themselves, and they still work. The women, though, they're all "crazy." I have a suspicion—and hear me out, because this is a rough one—that the definition of "crazy" in show business is a woman who keeps talking even after no one wants to fuck her anymore.

—Tina Fey[2]

Many years ago, I had a friend named Josie. She was in her late seventies by the time I knew her, frail and weakened by decades of battling the aftereffects of polio. She was tiny and gray, a grandmother several times over and the exceedingly proud possessor of one great-grandchild. She and her husband had been married for over fifty years. They had survived childhood poverty, the Depression, World War II, and a series of unspoken personal trials. Josie was one of the feistiest women I've ever known—always probing and cheerful and determined to do whatever she set her mind on—but since I met her when I was twenty-two, she was also, to me, just *old*. So I was shocked one day when she confessed over tea that she felt like a teenager. "I know this will sound odd," she said, "but I still can't get my head around my age. I know what I look like, and how I feel, but when I see myself in my own mind, I'm still eighteen. Which makes all of this stuff," she gestured around her, "seem silly."

At the time, I couldn't have agreed more. Because Josie was dying—she knew it—and "this stuff" was the hospital, the doctors, the various tubes that she indignantly sported. How silly, indeed, to have your mind stuck in such a distant past, in a person who hadn't existed for so many years.

Now, though I'm still far short of Josie's years, I know exactly what she meant. When I see myself and define myself, I'm somewhere between twenty-four and twenty-seven. I'm a young mother and a woman just starting out on her career. I am someone for whom facial creams are a protection against future wrinkles rather than a cover-up of what's already there. And I'm someone who still thinks I'll be in better shape next year. 'Cause that's what resolutions are for, aren't they?

Most women I know share this mental metric. Our bodies are growing older, but our minds and identities are resolutely stuck somewhere in the past—at a point, generally, when our breasts were firmer, our lips fuller, and our dating prospects pretty good. Or, as Lori Gottlieb notes in her recent book, *Marry Him*, "everyone in my age bracket looks old to me because when I picture myself, I view a mental image of me at thirty. I haven't recalibrated the image to reflect what I look like today." Maybe men feel this way, too. My husband denies any ache that could possibly be attributed to pushing his body where it once easily went. My friend Paul, who just turned sixty, admits that he's astonished every morning to see his father peering out at him from the mirror.

But age, like so many things, seems to fall harder on women. My husband, who sports a full head of curly white hair, is constantly being told by strange women how handsome he is. Paul is married to a woman twenty years his junior. Women of a certain age, by comparison, slowly get used to having the compliments—and the men—fade away. In our minds and photographs, we stay young and lithe and attractive, peering out, like Josie, at all that lies ahead. From the other side of the looking glass, though, we are simply old.

Part of what drives this fixation and frustration with age, of course, is the media, which often seem physically incapable of portraying an attractive woman above the age of thirty. Yes, yes, Meryl Streep has recently broken the age barrier by looking lovely in at least twenty films made since she turned fifty. And Diane Keaton has managed to find work well into the ice age of her sixties. But female Hollywood stars above the age of thirty-five are exceedingly rare. Men, by comparison, can age with grace, dancing the tango (Richard Gere in *Shall We Dance*), fighting evildoers (Harrison Ford as Indiana Jones), and bedding goddesses as they run (James Bond, everywhere). With a few high-powered exceptions, television news channels have largely banned women (but not men) over thirty-five from their broadcast studios, while style and fashion magazines specialize in nubile teenagers posed to look older. What's a woman to presume? Obviously, that beauty lasts only slightly longer than puberty.

Meanwhile, women pushing into their forties and fifties are also dealing with the basic inequities of biology. By the age of thirty-five, the average woman's fertility has plummeted. By forty-four or so, most women are physically unable to conceive children, and by fifty nearly all have undergone the hormonal changes wrought by menopause: sagging breasts, drying skin, declining bone density. All of this is bad enough, fodder for sitcom laugh lines and witty birthday cards. But the real toll of menopause is emotional rather than physical; tied not just to how a woman looks, but to the powerful and unspoken links between looks and reproduction. Because the dominant images we hold of women—not only in the pages of *Vogue*, but on the walls of the Louvre and the rock drawings of ancient civilizations—are of women as mothers. The woman in our collective imagination is a producer and tender of children, armed with the assets—breasts, hips, eggs—that make her not only capable of this task but also attractive to the men who must participate in at least the first stages of it. Once this function ceases to exist, women's lives, in a harsh Darwinian sense, are over. Maybe that's why Josie, who married in her teens and soon had two children, always saw herself in her early twenties. Maybe that's why I, who had my first child at twenty-six, still see myself at that age, when everything felt possible.

Yet no matter how we see ourselves, and how many creams we lather upon our faces and thighs, all women—me, Josie, even Angelina Jolie and Kim Kardashian—will inevitably, ineluctably, age. Our faces will wrinkle. Our bodies will sag. Our loving toddlers will become raging teenagers who see our clothes, our music, and our sexuality as horrifyingly and embarrassingly *old*. We will settle, more or less comfortably, into the choices we made or had thrust upon us—this mate, these children, this job and home and community—and watch our other choices melt irretrievably into fables. The man I might have married but didn't. The children I lost or didn't have. The opportunities I let slip away. If feminism was largely about giving women choices, then age is in some ways the cruelest slap, slyly removing possibilities as time passes by.

And herein lies the irony. By blessing women with so many options, feminism also—unwittingly and unwillingly—raised the bar on women's lives and expectations. It pushed girls to excel at school *and* sports; encouraged young women to seize control of their love lives, their sex lives, *and* their careers; and urged young mothers to juggle the demands of work *and* family. All the time, all around them, women heard the newfound siren, seducing them with dreams of glory. And it wasn't just wealthy white women or overeducated liberals. Sarah Palin, self-styled hockey mom of five, governed a large state and shot wild animals for fun. Michele Bachmann, lawyer, small business owner, and congresswoman, gave birth to five children and fostered twenty-three others. *Twenty-three*. Oprah. Condi Rice. Wonder women, all. Piano-playing, Zen-meditating, home-schooling, free-throw-shooting, Ivy League–attending wonder women who saw their choices and grabbed them all. Yet along with the siren of success—in notes both lower and higher, swirling from everywhere and everything—women heard the ancient chants, the ones that had never gone away. Be beautiful. Be sexy. Be fruitful and multiply without ever gaining a stretch mark. Make every man who sees you fall in love, but then choose one—only one—to love and cherish till the end of your days. Practically, the choruses should have clashed. They should have erupted into a cacophony of impossible aims, dragging women away from the absurd idea that they actually could have it all. At once. For themselves. Forever. Yet women today have heard these clashing melodies all their lives. They have absorbed and devoured them in ways that sweet Josie, born tough and hard and practical in 1913, could never have imagined. And so when they look back over their lives, or catch themselves in the mirror of middle age, they are inevitably disappointed. Because how, with an infinite array of life choices, did they somehow get it wrong? And why, with Botox and face lifts and serial spinning, must they still look so old?

Anatomies of Age

There is, of course, a central problem with aging: it doesn't end well. For women and men, for all of us acquainted with this thing called life, the arc of aging is our most inevitable bond. We are born, we age, we die. Nothing in the infinity of variation that defines us—our gender, our wealth, our luck, our species—makes so much as a dent in this most relentless trajectory. We are born, we age, we die. Aging is inherent in life itself, a permanent marker of both our presence and our mortality. Or, as Bob Dylan put it more bluntly: "he not busy being born is busy dying."[3]

For women, though, the process of aging has always been a bit more poignant, and considerably more precarious. There are some societies— such as the Iroquois and ancient China—in which women of a certain age were traditionally awarded a modicum of respect, and others in which aged women were even considered the heads of their matrilineal clans.[4] Between the eleventh and thirteenth centuries in parts of Europe, a surge of young men who aspired to the noble classes gave older, wealthy women a window of advantage: seeking entry to higher society, aspiring young men would court aging women (usually widows) with love poems and acts of chivalry, hoping to earn their approval and thus their access to social power.[5] But the norm has been for older women either to slink into the shadows or to assume a mischievous, even evil, cast.[6] Ovid's *Amores*, for instance, portrays age in the form of Dipsas, a drunken, white-haired hag who counsels young women to trade their beauty for money before it is too late; Chaucer's Wife of Bath (the model for legions of subsequent literary portrayals) mourns her youth while gloating, rather bawdily, about the five husbands she has married and seen to their graves.[7] During the Middle Ages, when life expectancy was only about thirty or forty years, women were considered old by thirty, dismissed by society and disdained by potential suitors.[8] During that time as well, tens of thousands of older women were accused of being witches, and then tortured or killed for their purported sins. Frequently, these "sins" revolved explicitly around sexuality and fertility; they were "sins of nature," linked to the myriad ways in which women could induce or thwart reproduction.[9] According to the *Malleus Maleficarum* (*Witches' Hammer*), for example, a fifteenth-century publication that became the central text of Europe's witch trials, all witches had the ability, among other evils, to make men impotent; to perform castration; and to "destroy the generative force in women."[10] Women incapable of bearing children anymore, in other words, and women presumed not to be having sex, were seen only as meddlers in these vital affairs, diabolically concocting schemes and potions to destroy others' reproductive lives. "Once they are old," intoned one Spanish friar, "and men pay no attention to them, women have recourse to the devil to satisfy their appetites."[11]

Matters changed somewhat (as they so frequently did) during the Victorian era, when a general embrace of family and femininity served to usher in the newly cast figure of the benevolent granny. We see her as the matronly Mrs. Pryor in Charlotte Brontë's *Shirley*, in the two benevolent grandmothers (Peter's and Clara's) who provide comfort and compassion to the orphaned young Heidi.[12] This new type of old woman was quiet and domesticated, as spiritual as her medieval counterpart was sexual. But other than knitting and cooking and dispensing sage advice, she didn't actually *do* very much. Rather, while grandfathers got to chop logs and drive trains, grandmothers (even of the figurative sort) were relegated to the sidelines, "condemned," as one midcentury observer noted, "to unpaid good works, for the church, for its missions, for homes for unwedded mothers and their unsanctioned babies, to meddle around with moral uplift or sew pinafores for the heathen in far-away lands."[13]

Today, of course, old age is a constantly moving target and aging women play far more public and pervasive roles than in the past. Christine Lagarde became director of the International Monetary Fund at fifty-five. Nancy Pelosi, sixty-seven in 2007, opened her first session as Speaker of the House surrounded by her eight grandchildren. Angela Merkel, at fifty-seven, was still negotiating around the clock to try to save the euro. In less hallowed halls, women who might once have retired to needlepoint and tea sandwiches are instead volunteering for

Doctors Without Borders and climbing Mount Everest.[14] Hell, they're even having babies—according to a 2011 article in *New York* magazine, eight thousand babies in the United States were born in 2008 to women over the age of forty-five; 541 of these were born to women over *fifty*.[15] When I call my own mother, instead of rattling off a list of medical ailments, she typically mentions that she just returned from her daily four-mile walk and then drags me through her week's social calendar: tutoring, bridge, a few concerts, and a quick dash downtown to the museum. It's exhausting just to listen to her.

This triumphant new old-ageism displays its pride nearly everywhere. "Forget Bingo!" urges one news story, "80 is the new 30."[16] HOW TO LIVE TO BE 100, promises another.[17] And my personal favorite: "If your erection lasts more than four hours, call your doctor."[18] It's as if an entire generation, having listened far too intently to Pete Townshend's plan to "die before I get old," has decided, quite simply, not to age.

And some of this, of course, is real. Average life expectancy in the United States today is 78.7 years. For a man who has already attained the age of fifty, it is 79.6; for a woman, 83.2.[19] Diseases that once claimed hundreds of thousands of lives a year—notably smallpox and tuberculosis—have, thanks to better drugs and health care, been pushed nearly into oblivion. Others, such as diabetes and cardiovascular disease, can be managed so effectively that they are now considered chronic conditions rather than life-threatening ailments. So dramatic are these developments that some in the health care field (still, albeit, on the margins) now claim anyone alive today can (with the proper provision of vitamins, or minerals, or exercise, or attitude) live to the age of one hundred.[20] Or, as the critic Katha Pollitt quips, "Old is the new young!"[21]

And yet. Ask any (honest) fifty-year-old if she really, truly, feels the way she did at seventeen. Ask any passerby if that fifty-year-old—even a well-coiffed, well-dressed, well-exercised, Botoxed fifty-year-old—looks even vaguely the way she did at seventeen. Or thirty. Or even forty. Because the aging process doesn't stop. It can't. As our bodies' cells mature, the individual molecules—of proteins, lipids, and nucleic acids—slowly accumulate a roster of tiny damages. The telomeres at the end of each chromosome shrink over time, reducing the cell's ability to replicate or divide. So, inevitably, in all humans lucky enough to live long enough, the most basic building blocks of the physical body eventually begin to malfunction and decline.

Slowly, stealthily, these changes start to manifest themselves on the public side of the body. The accumulation of sun exposure pops up as small darkened patches on the skin—"age spots." The gradual loss of collagen and elastin draws elasticity from skin cells and causes the dreaded crepey neck and sagging arms of middle age. All of this is totally natural, the simple toll of biology and gravity over a certain number of years. But it hits women hard. Or, as Nora Ephron lamented in a wonderful 2006 essay,

> Oh the necks. There are chicken necks. There are turkey gobbler necks. There are elephant necks. There are necks with wattles and necks with creases that are on the verge of being wattles. . . . You can put makeup on your face and concealer under your eyes and dye on your hair, you can shoot collagen and Botox and Restylane into your wrinkles and creases, but short of surgery, there's not a damn thing you can do about a neck.[22]

It's easy (and probably healthy) to laugh. It's okay for younger women to dismiss their mothers' concerns, or to try at ever-younger ages to ward off the aging process. But for the women affected—which is, after all, all women of a certain age—it's just no fun. Because no matter how good they feel, no matter how successful they've been or how wonderful their husbands and talented their children, part of their identity has long been attached to their looks. And as those looks change, so, subversively, do they.

Curses: A Brief and Grumpy Survey of Menopause

For most women, what really brings these changes to the fore—what forces them to realize and wrestle with aging—is menopause, "the change" that tends to occur smack in the middle of middle age.

In practical terms, menopause should be a really good thing.[23] After decades of bleeding and worrying, decades of lugging around a veritable arsenal of birth control and "hygiene" products, postmenopausal women should be able to yank a whole slew of concerns off their to-do lists. No more tampons and condoms. No more week counting and mood swings and studiously avoiding white for four to seven days a month. Biologically, menopause at last puts women roughly on a par with men, freeing them from the bleeding and breeding that have long set them apart. Margaret Mead, for example, described reveling in what she called a "post-menopausal zest"[24]; Elizabeth Cady Stanton, at fifty-three, wrote of how the "vital forces" once contained in her reproductive organs had begun "flowing" instead to her brain, prompting her to launch a career as a lecturer.[25]

Yet it is precisely this freeing that seems also to occasion a deeply reflective moment for many women.[26] For centuries, many scientists presumed a direct link between a woman's uterus and her brain, a chain that connected her reproductive abilities with her cognitive ones. No wonder, then, doctors hypothesized, that women undergoing menopause experienced mood swings, and no wonder that postmenopausal women often succumbed to what was described as "nervousness" or "involutional melancholy."[27] In the 1920s, as science unlocked the complex mechanics of estrogen and other hormones, doctors saw more clearly how this link might operate, and how powerful it could be: once their bodies were deprived of estrogen, women were condemned not only to cease reproduction but also to lose the other physical benefits— firm breasts, supple skin, a libido—that estrogen provided. Not surprisingly, doctors cautioned, women undergoing these changes could easily become depressed, or even mad.[28] Several decades on, Freud and his disciples took these concerns one notch further, arguing that menopause meant not only a physical change but an emotional one as well, reawakening in women both the castration complex (desire for a penis) and an Oedipal urge (desire for sex with a younger man). The only solace for such women was to redirect their sexual energies toward asexual pursuits, such as doting on their grandchildren.[29]

A personal caveat is in order here. I haven't experienced menopause yet, much less the infirmities that attend real old age. But writing from the midlife perspective of my midforties, and writing from a particular perch that surrounds me with both the constant company of very young women and the less frequent but very regular company of much older women, I suspect that the real trauma of menopause lies in what it biologically means: the end of childbearing.[30]

As explored already in chapter 6, all women, regardless of their race, creed, color, or religion, are born, physiologically, to breed. That is our biological purpose. It is why we have breasts and wombs and ovaries. Men, too, of course, are programmed to reproduce, but because their biological function focuses on the conception of the child, the bearing and rearing of that child seem somehow less hardwired into male behavior. Or at least that is the way society has largely interpreted gender roles—not just in the age of corporate-driven advertising, but indeed throughout history. Look at art. Women are presented overwhelmingly as mothers—Mary and the Christ Child, scores of medieval homemakers rocking cradles and nursing infants—or as objects of (male) desire. Men, by contrast, are workers, or warriors, or gods. One rarely sees portraits of men with young children, or indeed of men adopting anything like a fatherly pose.[31]

Whether this categorization—women as mothers; men as active members of society—is driven by biology or patriarchy or (most likely) a combination of both, does not really matter. Because at the end of the day, what affects women is how they feel. And most women, regardless again of who they are and what they do, experience a deep-seated desire to produce a child. To mother. To push back the hands of a biological clock that stops, inevitably and irretrievably, at some well-marked point in their lives. For men, both puberty and age arrive somewhat stealthily, heralded only by wisps of facial hair and then the creeping signs of baldness. For women, they come (quite literally, sometimes) in a flash: periods start and then, roughly forty years later, they stop. Women can conceive and carry children and then they cannot. Even if an individual woman's fertility is actually more complicated (fertility generally declines well before menopause), there is still a distinctive cut-off point. Once a woman has undergone menopause, she can no longer even fantasize about bearing a child.[32] And so a part of her life is simply over.

For many women, of course, this passage is liberating, because not being able to conceive children also means not having to worry about conceiving them. Yet the milestone itself is still meaningful, proof that some chunk of life has now passed and that some of its most powerful options are no longer possible. "What happens to the heart," muses one husband whose wife learns she is too old to conceive, "when a woman's reproductive time runs the course of its season? How do you reconcile this severance?"[33]

For me, having been lucky enough to raise three children, the moment was oddly connected to thoughts of rigatoni. For years, I had gamely tried to skip whatever meetings were taking place that day to join my kids' classes for the inevitable Thanksgiving celebration. I had pasted what felt like millions of faux feathers on turkeys traced around small hands and strung yards and yards of rigatoni "wampum." I wore more necklaces made of macaroni than I can recall, and taped dozens of holiday projects, heavy with pasta and glue, to the refrigerator door. And then one day, without really thinking about it, I realized that my days of rigatoni were over. That no child of mine would ever again lug home a handmade Thanksgiving creation, or a smushed ceramic mug, or a Popsicle-stick picture frame. An entire era had passed, and I could never get it back or do it over. Marriage isn't like that, because if you're lucky, it goes on. Relationships and jobs evolve naturally over time, always allowing for the prospect of something different, and something new. But having a child—a small child, the kind of child you picture when you think of a "child"—just ends. And a woman who sees that milestone, and marks it irrevocably with her menopause, recognizes that the end of her children's childhood is, in some ways, an ending of herself.

Poststunning

What makes menopause even crueler for most women is that its advent also brings subtle, but real, changes to their physical appearance. The causality isn't entirely direct: entering menopause doesn't cause wrinkles or gray hair. But the hormonal changes that accompany menopause, along with the basic trajectory of midlife aging, wreak a steady assault on some of women's formerly most erogenous zones. Or, as Simone de Beauvoir expressed it, "Whereas man grows old gradually, woman is suddenly deprived of her femininity; she is still relatively young when she loses the erotic attractiveness and the fertility which, in the view of society and in her own, provide the justification of her existence and her opportunity for happiness."[34] Now this, recall, is *the* Simone de Beauvoir; the Simone de Beauvoir who, in the very same book, exhorts women to separate their identities from their biological makeup. The Simone de Beauvoir who famously wrote that "[the] body is not enough to define [a] woman."[35] Yet, peering down the barrel of her own middle age (Beauvoir was forty-nine when *The Second Sex* was published), the author laments the physical changes that steal an aging woman's femininity. "What is to become of her when she no longer has any hold on him?" she wonders aloud, "helplessly look[ing] on at the degeneration of this fleshy object which she identifies with herself. She puts up a battle. But hair dye, skin treatments, plastic surgery, will never do more than prolong her dying youth."[36]

In general, feminism has been quiet on the subject of aging.[37] Perhaps because the movement was dominated in the 1970s by mostly younger women, perhaps because its theoretical and political impulses were so tightly linked to the topics of sexual and reproductive choice, feminism was largely focused on the issues of younger women. It was about the power of gaining access and having choices rather than the pangs of watching those choices slide by. It was about cherishing the pleasures of one's body rather than watching that same body sag. It was about youth. So it's no surprise, then, that feminism discovered aging relatively late in its own evolution—right about the time, in fact, that some of the most ardent second-stage feminists stumbled into personal second stages of their own.[38] Beauvoir tackled the ostracism of the elderly in *The Coming of Age* (1970), a book in which she argues for the acceptance of age. Betty Friedan explored the aging process in *The Fountain of Age*, published when she was seventy-two.[39]

Where mainstream feminism has long overlapped with aging, though, is around the problem of beauty.[40] As chapter 4 described, after all, feminism was supposed to knock beauty off the pantheon of women's assets. It was supposed to free women from a male-designed, media-driven image of what they should look like and replace that (unattainable, unhealthy) vision with a more realistic portrayal. It was supposed to make women feel good about who they were and what they did rather than how they looked. And had that goal been achieved, it would have been revolutionary for older women, none of whom, of course, can ever hope to look the way they did at sixteen. Yet instead, bizarrely, the pendulum seems to have swung in precisely the opposite direction. Rather than women of all ages being appreciated for their good deeds and inner beauty, rather than ideals of attractiveness being widened to apply to a broader swath of women, global standards of beauty have actually narrowed over the past four decades, settling around an ideal that is generally young (the average model is sixteen years old), thin (fashion models weigh roughly twenty to twenty-five pounds less than average American women of their height), and androgynous. No curves, no wrinkles, and no gray hair. White is allowed, but only if it's long and flowing and of a white that basically looks like a more exotic blond.[41]

Even worse is the expanding arsenal of cosmetic products and surgical techniques that theoretically promise to defy age. Far from achieving Naomi Wolf's vision of smashing a beauty myth built around men's institutions and power, we live now in an age of age defiance, in which women are expected to remain wrinkle-free nearly until death and any visible sign of aging is taken as a character defect. Look, for example, at the "older" model below: she has no facial creases and the hair and body of a teenager. The one defiant stripe of white is the only thing that marks her, even vaguely, as mature. Or look at photos of Diane Sawyer and Katie Couric, high-profile newscasters who have far outlasted most of their female peers. Both are uncommonly attractive, blessed with looks that defy the years. Even Oprah Winfrey and

Cindy Joseph, a sixty-one-year-old supermodel

Martha Stewart, famous for their folksy and down-home style, share
not a wrinkle between them. And these women are in their late fifties
(Oprah) and early *seventies* (Martha).

Rather than freeing women from the traditional constraints of
beauty, therefore, the postfeminist era has somehow imposed higher
standards and greater expectations—expectations that now extend well
into what might once have been considered an older woman's dotage.
With tummy tucks and spinning classes, a middle-aged woman can
theoretically erase any sign of the children she's borne or the fat that
her body naturally produces around the onset of menopause. With Botox
and fillers, she can "look years younger even in fluorescent lighting."
And because these things are available—in the United States, women
underwent 1.3 million cosmetic procedures in 2010—they become expected. If a woman *can* deny age, in other words, then she should.[42]

These exhortations reach a particularly feverish pitch around the
face—that unmaskable, unavoidable, front-and-center window to the
soul.[43] Once upon a time, women wore their wrinkles as badges of experience or, more realistically perhaps, as inevitable markers of time's
passage, as natural and unstoppable as age itself. In 1922, for example,
one plastic surgeon dismissed even the idea of using surgery to erase
the signs of age: "I would not touch any woman at any price who
came to me and asked me to remove the legitimate trace of her years,"
he thundered. "A woman of forty years of age, or more, ought to be
ashamed to have a face without a wrinkle."[44] Today, by contrast, wrinkles for women are more akin to clothing lint—an annoyance to be
avoided and removed. The options for their removal are legion, and
growing all the time. Xtend Life Age Defense Active Day Cream, which
women as young as twenty should carefully apply each morning. Organic kale and raw green chili peppers, said to provide the vitamin C
necessary for collagen. Botox, to eliminate laugh lines, frown lines, and
crow's feet. Restylane, for filling folds and wrinkles. Eyelid lifts, lip
augmentation, buttock implants. Even food companies are now getting
into the business, with products like the Beauty Booster, a burgundy
liquid "loaded with antioxidants and minerals and tasting of the sweet
fruit that inspired it."[45] To some extent, of course, this is all just snake
oil, high-tech promises to play off the vanity that has long assailed
women. In ancient Egypt, Cleopatra doused herself with an oily balm

Pears' Soap advertisement, 1888

extracted from sheep's wool.[46] In Victorian London, the Pears' Soap company swore that its cleanser could keep a middle-aged woman looking like a teenager.[47] Presumably, neither of these concoctions did very much, other, perhaps, than giving the user either the scent of lamb chops or relatively clean skin.

In contrast, though, and for better or for worse, most of the twenty-first-century potions and procedures actually work. By paralyzing the facial muscles into which it is injected, Botox does (for some period of time) erase wrinkles. By pelting the face with a high-pressure spray that removes the outer layers of skin, microdermabrasion creates (again, for some period of time) a smoother, softer complexion. And by slathering the skin with moisture and blocking it from the sun, most age-defying creams and serums provide at least some measure of wrinkle relief.

The question, though, is at what cost. To avail herself of these new-found fountains of youth, a typical middle-aged woman can now easily spend upwards of several thousands of dollars a year investing in her complexion ($700, on average, for a single treatment of the filler Radiesse; $400 a shot for Botox; $2,200 for laser skin resurfacing).[48] Add this to the beauty counter she's already got going (mine is 282 hours a year), and a fifty-year-old woman, ostensibly still in the prime of her professional life, is actually committing some not insignificant percent of her waking hours and disposable income to banishing frown lines from her brow. Moreover, and more insidiously, by spending this time and this money and this energy, women are consistently adding to a veritable arms race of enforced youth, a contest driven not just by genes and luck anymore but increasingly by money, connections, and time.

Again, as in so many areas of female obsession, one is tempted to say simply, "stop." Just stop it. Brush your hair, dab on a bit of makeup, maybe, but leave the fillers and the toxins, the brow lifts and the hugely expensive creams alone. I can say it. I can scream it. I can mean it. Yet when I look around any room these days with women over forty, I know that nearly every woman there—with precious few exceptions—is indulging, at least, in a little Botox. Yes, these women tend to be wealthy, and many of them occupy high-profile positions. But that should, in theory at least, push in the other direction. These are women recognized for their accomplishments, women who have already succeeded in politics or academia, media or philanthropy. Most of them are devout feminists, fully committed to women's rights and gender equality. Still, they fill and lift, discreetly banishing lines in an effort to deny time.[49]

Because at the end of the day, despite what feminism hoped for and what so many women wish were true, women care about their looks. Care way more than men. It may be biology, still rewarding women with the attributes—bountiful breasts, smooth skin, eternal youth— that imply fecundity. It may be society, twisting little girls nearly from birth to believe they are pretty. And it may be patriarchy, with generations of men accustomed, almost subconsciously, to instantly assess a woman on the basis of her looks. In any case, though, the results are the same: because women are so deeply attuned to their physical attractiveness, particularly their sexual attractiveness, any change in what my college roommate always blithely referred to as her "assets" becomes a topic of concern. And if a woman can address these concerns, then frequently, increasingly, she does. Indeed, insofar as feminism freed women to seize control of their own bodies, so, too, oddly, may it have freed them, or compelled them, to extend that control into areas and across decades that were never really intended.

At a dinner party recently, I was chatting with the woman on my left. She is brilliant, a well-regarded professional, and a mother of three. She is also uncommonly beautiful. We were talking about the 2011 uprisings in the Middle East; about the connection between art and revolution; and about the need for more women to seize the reins of political power. Then we shifted to the fiscal crisis in Europe, and, briefly, to Angela Merkel, the pioneering German chancellor. I mentioned the extraordinary negotiation she was involved in, trying, simultaneously, to save the currency union in Europe while maintaining her own party's position. "But don't you think," my companion mused, "that she should get some Botox? All those wrinkles are so disconcerting. I mean, really." Really indeed. Some months later, I gave a speech on feminism at a women's university in Seoul. The audience was enthusiastic, expressing their concern for women's rights and their commitment to ridding Korean women of a still-pervasive double standard. After the lecture, when a national TV station had asked me to join their program the following morning, one of my hosts pulled me aside. "You can't go on TV looking like that," she said. "You have way too many wrinkles for a woman your age. You need to do something tonight. Really."

I was reminded in both instances of an event I attended several years ago. It was a big black-tie affair, full of serious people. At the outset, my husband and I ran into an older couple we knew well; the man had been a professor and mentor of mine for decades. "You look stunning," he said, in the rich European voice that generations of students had come to love. "So do you," I replied. "No," he stated slowly. "We do not. We are distinctly poststunning." Not wrinkled. Not old. Not coy. Just honest: we were stunning once, and now we are post.

Alone Again

For many women, the fears of middle age play out within the context of a now-protracted relationship. Coming into their fifties and sixties, demographically speaking, over 90 percent of American women are or have been married, roughly half in unions that have stretched by this point across several decades and children, across heartache and infidelities and a love long past its first blush.[50] For them, middle age is marked by the looming question of retirement, by the acknowledgment of choices taken and passed by, and by the reality of children sprung suddenly into adulthood. Some claim that it is the happiest time of their lives. Writing at the edge of her sixties, for example, the author Anna Quindlen reports that "what I've found is that if you push most women a little harder, almost everyone eventually gets past the hip replacement and the crepey neck and winds up admitting that they're more contented now than they were when they were young . . . perhaps if we think of life as a job, most of us finally feel that after fifty we've gotten good at it."[51]

Yet even if they have mastered life by their fifties, many women enter this phase of the game alone. Some have been widowed. Indeed, in 2009, roughly 20 percent of American women over the age of fifty were widows—blunt evidence of the demographic fact that women are simply more likely to survive their husbands than to be survived by them.[52] Others have either left their partners or divorced. According to the most recent data, 36 percent of once-married women were divorced by the time they hit their forties, and 41 percent had divorced by their fifties.[53]

After years or decades of marriage, then, a considerable chunk of American women become single in middle age. Some make this leap by choice, others through loss. But it is a dramatic shift for nearly all. Because being single at fifty-two is different from being single at twenty-five. It is different for women than for men, and for those who become single later in life rather than slipping into it early on. Like menopause, the end of a long-term relationship often brings a new-found freedom, releasing a woman from decades-old patterns of worry and responsibility. But it can also be an excruciatingly painful change, leaving women both economically vulnerable and socially isolated. Because while both patriarchy and feminism suggest multiple roles for young women—the ingénue, the mother, the goddess, the whore— neither has much to offer a suddenly single, emotionally drained postmenopausal mom.

At the risk of veering too far into anecdote, I must report that nearly a dozen of my own friends have entered this phase in the past two years. All of them are well-educated women between thirty-five and fifty. All were raised in feminism's wake and tasted its many freedoms. All married men they truly loved and raised healthy, happy kids. They had good educations and serious jobs—a physician, a lawyer, a literary agent, a designer. And then, in the space between one Christmas and the next, they were single. Living in small apartments a town or two over from where they'd tended their own gardens. Rearranging the books and photos; venturing, gingerly, online.

Take my friend Shelly. After college and the Peace Corps, she met and married Frank, who worked briefly at the State Department before becoming an executive with a high-tech company. They raised three children together and renovated a rambling Victorian house. Slowly, in between playdates and PTA meetings, Shelly earned a graduate degree in social work and opened a small practice, mostly providing marital counseling to low-income couples. She and Frank underwent a fair amount of counseling themselves, dabbling in couples therapy and family therapy and individual Jungian analysis. There were some problems—Shelly had had a difficult childhood, and they didn't always agree on how to parent—but these seemed relatively minor, the normal chaff of complicated lives. Then, one day in late fall, after Shelly had told Frank that their counseling wasn't working, he said that he wanted to leave. "Just like that," she said. "I'd been threatening to walk for years, I know, but I never thought it would be him, and that he'd just do it." They told the kids over Christmas and then, gently and amicably, went to IKEA to outfit a second, smaller place. The idea was that the kids would stay put while Shelly and Frank rotated between the big old house and the new small apartment. It was all very sane, very gentle, very free.

And then Shelly found herself, at fifty, learning how to recarve a life. Frank, within four months, was eagerly dating again. She was not. Frank embraced his time with the kids, earning kudos all around from being an involved, committed dad. Shelly felt awkward, worrying about spoiling her children when she was with them and about abandoning them when she was not. And her financial situation had changed dramatically, of course. Because Frank had been the major breadwinner during their marriage, she had few independent assets and would depend, upon the divorce, on receiving a lump sum payment of sorts from the sale of what had once been "theirs." But because she was in the workforce and earning a decent salary, she was also prepared to become financially independent after the divorce, rejiggering her life and expenses to accommodate a substantially lower annual income.

Other women, of course, face much harder realities. In fact, divorce is one of the worst calamities that befall women in middle age, packing both a psychological and financial wallop.[54] According to recent data from the U.S. census, recently divorced women are more financially strained than others in the general population, experiencing higher rates of poverty, lower incomes, and greater reliance on public assistance.[55] According to a British study, separated wives saw an immediate decline in their incomes of 22 percent, while separated husbands saw a *rise* of 13 percent.[56] For women who originally left the workforce to focus on the home front, the fallout from divorce can be particularly treacherous. With children still to tend to in many cases, and no recent history of employment, they find themselves juggling a broader array of problems with fewer economic resources. Moreover, and more maddeningly, because many stay-at-home moms had solid academic credentials and extensive work experience before they chose to stay at home, courts often presume they will become financially self-sufficient and treat any potential alimony payments accordingly.[57] In one recent case, for example, a judge awarded a woman who had been married for forty years only four years of alimony, suggesting, as she recalls, "that I go for job training when I turned sixty-seven." Her husband, she continued, "got to take his girlfriend to Cancun" while she got to sell her engagement ring to pay the roofer.[58]

Meanwhile, for women like Shelly, who liked being married and having a spouse, dating over fifty is a whole new game. Some of the news is good: with the proliferation of online sites like over40andsingle .com and datingsecretsfordivorcedwomen.com, women can search for men in the privacy of their own homes, looking in particular, say, for a man with (or without) kids, or even a married man just interested in sex. Women can employ hands-on dating agencies or scroll through a seemingly endless list of options on sites like match.com. But for middle-aged women online, the math of mating is excruciatingly bad. Most men over fifty want to date (or at least sleep with) women no older than forty. Most prefer "slim" or "athletic" builds. Recently, a divorced investment banker boasted joyfully to me about his online skills. He wouldn't go out with any woman over thirty or under five feet seven. (He himself was neither young nor tall.) He wouldn't see (umm, that is, sleep with) any woman more than once. And he was teaching his tactics to all the other single men he knew, jokingly contemplating that he might even open a little consulting business on the side.

Not all men are like him, of course. I know another man, twice divorced, who carefully screens his online options for what might be considered more reasonable attributes: similar interests, a solid education, a limited gap in age. His biggest problem is numbers. Last I heard, he was combing carefully through more than a hundred possibilities, trying to prune his short list down to no more than five.

In biological terms, neither of my acquaintances is particularly unusual. In fact, anthropologists and evolutionary biologists have long noted the gender inequities that manifest themselves across age. Across cultures, men tend to mate with younger women and to prefer a larger and larger age gap as they themselves grow older. Men consistently rate physical attractiveness as more important in a potential partner than do women; and, in those cultures where they still put an actual price on brides, they pay accordingly more for younger women.[59] To quote my daughter's favorite phrase, "It's not fair." But these are the preferences that seem, still, to mark our affairs.

What this means for Shelly, though, and for millions of suddenly single middle-aged women like her, is a serious rejiggering of expectations as they near their golden years. These are women, demographically speaking, who grew accustomed to a fair amount of casual sex early in life. Now, their sexual encounters are going to be less frequent, and their partners—demographically speaking again—considerably older. These are women who grew up amid the cacophony of choice, women who had more education, more career options, and more reproductive choice than their mothers could have conceived of. And yet while their mothers' generation retired quietly to play bridge and mind the grandkids, this generation has a less clearly trodden path. If she's lucky and healthy, a woman like Shelly can reasonably expect to spend nearly four decades in her postmarried, postmotherhood life. Should she try to hit the replay button and settle down again? Embrace her single status and focus on herself? Or forge new bonds with friends and professional colleagues and family? The options, once again, are many. The choice among them is bewildering.

When my grandparents retired, they moved en masse to Florida, taking the car, the dog, and their entire circle of friends to the same anonymous strip mall town outside Pompano Beach. They watched each other's grandchildren grow and compared notes over neatly divided egg salad sandwiches. They went to each other's funerals and witnessed their wills. When my maternal grandmother, widowed in her fifties, needed to buy a new car or fix a leaky faucet, it was my paternal grandfather who stepped into the role. "But how?" my children asked recently. "Why was he there?" Because he just was. Because they all lived in the same building and checked in on each other every day. My generation, Shelly's generation, isn't going to Pompano. We are not going to wrinkle; we are not going to dine at the early bird buffet; and we are certainly never going to stop having sex. But what, then, do we do?

In 2010, there were 21.8 million women in the United States over the age of sixty-five. Fifty-eight percent of them lived alone.[60]

The Lupine Lady

Recently, I met a woman named Gretchen, who had just moved to New York. She was a friend of a friend, and so on a frigid January day, we ducked into a bad Chinese restaurant to become acquainted and compare notes. After forty years of marriage, she said, she and her husband had decided to divorce. "The kids were grown," she explained between slurps of roast pork noodle soup, "and we suddenly had all this time on our hands. It wasn't nasty or anything, but we realized that our interests were too different." She quit her job, sold most of her belongings, and rented a small one-bedroom apartment. Other than her grown daughter and me she didn't know anyone in the city.

I felt for her, and worried how she was going to find her way. Turns out I shouldn't have. Six months later, Gretchen was reveling in her new job, her new friends, her new life. She was prowling the ethnic markets of the Lower East Side for dinner rather than lugging home bags of groceries to feed a mob; she was spending time with a newborn grandchild and joining female friends to attend concerts, readings, and lectures. After she held a small party in her even smaller apartment, the thank-you notes from her guests spoke of the easy camaraderie she'd built. "With your generous spirit you bring us together to shed light on our lives and on the world," wrote one new friend. "You are a connector of people and a melder of relationships par excellence."

I don't know Gretchen well. Maybe she cries every night into too many glasses of Chardonnay. Maybe she pores fruitlessly over datingsecretsfordivorcedwomen.com and pines for another man. But I somehow suspect not. Because she seems, later in life, to have discovered what feminism intended to be about, or at least a piece of what it promised to the generations who followed blindly in its wake. The freedom to live one's life apart from any prescribed pathway. The ability to love men and children and jobs but not lose one's self to them. The opportunity to embrace choices rather than just have them.

As my generation passes into middle age, and eventually toward whatever we will eventually call real old age, it will inevitably encounter— indeed already is encountering—the Great Boomer Problem. This is a problem caused not only by the massive demographic bulge that the Boomers have created, nor by their considerable drain on the country's Social Security and health care resources.[61] It is also a problem of expectations. Because this is a generation, of course, raised on youth and beauty and sex. A generation that sincerely thought—still thinks, judging from the barrage of hip replacements, lip enhancements, and sexual dysfunction ads—that it will never age. Or at least that aging won't mean having to grow old. Yet, if we're lucky, we will grow old, and it won't be pretty. We will become infirm and wrinkled and less mobile. Our minds will wander; our bodies will sag. Our children, if we're lucky again, will leave us and make lives of their own. And those we cherish most will eventually be gone.

We can deny this process, as a generation or as individuals, or we can begrudgingly come to acknowledge it. Even accept it, realizing that there's no way to make old perfect. Which is, of course, true of every other stage in life as well.

There are many books on how to grow old. Cheerful ones, like Anna Quindlen's recent and wonderful *Lots of Candles, Plenty of Cake*. Angry ones, like Margaret Morganroth Gullette's *Agewise* and Susan

Jacoby's *Never Say Die*. And more self-help tomes than any human could possibly read in a lifetime: *The Art of Growing Old, How to Succeed at Aging Without Really Dying, From Age-ing to Sage-ing*. My favorite, though, isn't a book on growing old at all. It's a children's book called *Miss Rumphius*.[62]

I can't recall when I first stumbled upon it, but I have had it now for at least twenty years. I read it over and over again to each of my kids, and used it as the basis for both a colleague's farewell party and a commencement address. I still can't get past page fifteen without crying.

Miss Rumphius tells the tale of Alice Rumphius, a girl born sometime, it appears, in the 1880s or 1890s. As a child, she passes time in her grandfather's workshop, helping him fashion figureheads for the prows of ships and painting the skies in the background of his landscapes. She becomes a librarian, "dusting books and keeping them from getting mixed up, and helping people find the ones they want." Then, when she turns what looks to be around thirty (with auburn hair pulled into a bun and a muff to keep her warm), she sets off to see the world.

From Miss Rumphius, *written and illustrated by Barbara Cooney*

She climbs tall mountains where the snow never melts, sees lions playing and kangaroos jumping. "And everywhere she met friends she would
never forget." In the Land of the Lotus-Eaters,[63] though, she tumbles
from a camel, hurts her back, and has to return home. So she moves to
a cottage by the sea, healing slowly with a cat by her side. And as she
recuperates, Miss Rumphius takes a look at her life. "There is still one
more thing I have to do," she says. "I have to do something to make the
world more beautiful." The next summer, when she can walk again,
Miss Rumphius buys five bushels of lupine seed (she has always loved
lupines the best) and scatters it around highways and lanes, "around
the schoolhouse and back of the church." Some people, the narrator
recalls, "called her That Crazy Old Lady."

By the next spring, there are lupines everywhere, and then more
and more each year as Miss Rumphius grows to become "an old, old
woman." Now, the narrator reports, "they call her the Lupine Lady."

It is only a child's book, I know. Hardly the stuff to wave before the
likes of Friedan, Dworkin, and Beauvoir. But Alice Rumphius, in a
wholly unassuming way, lays out a plausible dream for women. To be
free, wholly free, as little girls, building ships and painting imaginary
worlds. To have careers and friends that make them happy. To see the
world. And then, before they die, to do something to make that world
more beautiful.

At the very end of *Miss Rumphius*, the book's author reveals her
voice. She is "little Alice," the great-niece, presumably, and namesake
of Miss Rumphius. The original Alice is very old now; perhaps, her niece
ruminates, "the oldest woman in the world." But she has left behind a
story, and a legacy. Which may, in the end, be the best we all can do.

10

KISSING CHARLIE GOODBYE

Oh yes, I am wise
But it's wisdom born of pain
Yes, I've paid the price
But look how much I gained
If I have to, I can do anything
I am strong
I am invincible
I am woman

—Helen Reddy, "I Am Woman," 1972

It ain't easy walkin' in stilettos
But somebody gotta do it
Spend a day in my shoes
Then see what the hell I go through
It's so rigorous
Doing what I do
Always on point
Always on cue
Life's so hectic
Call it a zoo
Think you understand?
If only you knew

—Jordin Sparks, "I Am Woman," 2011

In 2005, I was teaching a first-year class at Harvard Business School. As usual, slightly under a third of my students were women. As always, I was the only female professor they had.

So one evening, my female students asked me and one of my female colleagues to join them for cocktails. They ordered a lovely spread of hors d'oeuvres and white wine. They presented each of us with an elegant lavender plant. And then, like women meeting for cocktails around the planet, they—well, we, actually—proceeded to complain. About how tough it was to be so constantly in the minority. About how the guys sucked up all the air around the place. About the folks in career services who told them never to wear anything but a good black pantsuit to an interview.

Over the course of the conversation, though, things began to turn. The women stopped talking about their present lives and started to focus on their futures, futures that had little to do with conferences or pantsuits and everything to do with babies, and families, and men. One woman, a quiet but steely Korean, declared that she was planning to abandon any hope of a family to focus on a career. Two young Europeans speculated about trying to blend their personal and professional lives. But most of the others were frankly intending to work "for a year or two" and then move into motherhood. These were some of the smartest and most determined young women in the country. They had Ivy League degrees, for the most part, and were in the midst of paying over $100,000 for an MBA. And yet they were already deeply concerned about how they would juggle the course of their lives and surprisingly pessimistic about their chances of doing so. The next day, one of them, already married to a high-powered husband, pulled me aside and asked, "Did we disappoint you yesterday?" Although every bone in my body urged me to be nice, to confirm the life she had already chosen for herself, the Charlie side of me took over. "Yes," I confessed, "you did. I wanted you to want more." And then, immediately thereafter and ever since, I have felt guilty—about pushing her and them, about blaming them somehow for failing before they even began, about thrusting my own expectations on a younger generation of women.

Ever since the publication of *The Feminine Mystique*, American women have been haunted by the problem of more. Spurred by Friedan's plaintive query *Is this all?*—inspired by feminism's struggle for expanded rights and access—seduced by Astronaut Barbie—we have stumbled into an era of vast and towering expectations. Little girls want to be princesses. Big girls want to be superwomen. Old women want and fully expect to look young. We want more sex, more love, more jobs, more perfect babies. The only thing we want less of, it seems, are wrinkles. None of this, of course, can be blamed on feminism or the feminists. Or, as one former radical gently reminded me recently, "We weren't fighting so that you could have Botox." Yet it was feminism that lit the spark of my generation's dreams—feminism that, ironically and unintentionally, raised the bar on women so high that mere mortals are condemned to fall below it.

In its original incarnation, feminism had nothing to do with perfection. In fact, the central aim of many of its most powerful proponents was to liberate women from the unreasonable, impossible standards that had long been thrust upon them. Betty Friedan, for instance, strove explicitly in *The Feminine Mystique* to free women from society's expectation that they be perfect mothers and housewives. Gloria Steinem, in her notorious *Playboy* exposé, sought to end women's role as mere sex objects for men.[1] Andrea Dworkin and Naomi Wolf aimed, respectively, to free women from male oppression and the unattainable norms of beauty perpetuated by a male-dominated society.[2] Other feminists, meanwhile, labored always in the trenches of the real, fighting to give women decency—decent rights, decent health, decent relationships—rather than anything that ever approximated perfection.

As feminist ideals trickled and then flowed into mainstream culture, though, they became far more fanciful, more exuberant and trivial—something easier to sell to the millions of girls and women entranced by feminism's appeal. While activists like Gloria Steinem and Robin Morgan were fighting for affordable child care and equal pay in the early 1970s, for example, network television was giving birth to Rhoda and Mary Tyler Moore—working women, yes, and independent-minded, but tethered not at all to the worries of the world or the needs of any nonexistent children. While Kate Millett and Andrea Dworkin were advocating for reproductive rights and a more realistic view of women's bodies and sexuality, Hollywood was creating the Bionic Woman and Charlie's angels—women with rights and bodies, admittedly, but lives so fantastic that they blew poor June Cleaver away. It is easy, in retrospect, to say that women growing up in this world should have seen through the fantasy to the underlying struggle, that they—we—should have realized the myths of Charlie (both the angels and the perfume) and fought from the outset for the real rights of women. But most of us didn't, not because we were foolish, necessarily, but because it's hard, coming of age, to embrace the struggles of your parents' generation. And so we embraced the myth instead, planning, like Atalanta, to run as fast as the wind and choose the lives we wanted.

Over time, however, the myths began to multiply and collide, convulsing into a giant and incoherent chorus of "more." Feminism created the hope that women could work in once-male-dominated fields such as law and medicine and politics; Hollywood upped the ante with shows like *Murphy Brown* and characters like Clair Huxtable, women who worked at the very tippy-top of these professions and had children, looked fabulous, and somehow managed to find the time for romantic encounters.[3] Feminism fought for contraception and a woman's right to choose; magazines like *Cosmopolitan* and *Glamour* trumpeted the attractions of casual sex—all the time, all-orgasmic, and all without commitment. Feminism urged women to overthrow the patriarchy and join a global struggle; L'Oréal and Lancôme reminded them to do so with dewy skin and dusky eyes. Unconsciously, even sometimes unwillingly, the feminists' aspirations became fixed in the minds of every woman brought up in their shadow.* But so, too, did the more trivial stuff, the unwritten expectations that feminism's fight for women's liberation somehow unleashed.

Meanwhile, none of society's earlier expectations of women disappeared as a result of these cultural changes. Yes, advocates fought in the 1970s to give women control over the timing of their pregnancies and the manner of their children's birth. But there was nothing they

---

*They also became fixed in the minds of the population at large. As one leading early feminist recently reminded me, even Dick Cheney now regularly says "he or she" when referring to people in the abstract.

could do to change the underlying biology. For obvious reasons, women still bear the full physical burden of pregnancy and childbirth. They still carry the bulk of the responsibility for contraception and reap the immediate consequences of conception. Less obviously, and for more complicated reasons, women remain sexualized to an extent that men rarely are, and they feel the impact of their physical attractiveness in a much more direct and pervasive way. This aspect of women's lives might well have been eviscerated by the feminist and sexual revolutions. In fact, eliminating women's status as sexual icons for men was one of these revolutions' earliest goals.[4] But it didn't happen. Instead, looser norms of sexual conduct, combined with the exploding realm of digital media, have brought us to the world of *Toddlers and Tiaras* and pervasive online pornography. Not only are women's bodies arguably more objectified than ever, but the object of all this desire has been airbrushed and Photoshopped nearly beyond recognition, pushing women toward standards of bodily perfection that are literally no longer human.[5]

The result of these conflicting pressures is a force field of highly unrealistic expectations. Almost by definition, a woman cannot work a sixty-hour week in a high-stress job and be the same kind of parent she would have been without the sixty-hour-a-week job and all that stress. She cannot save the world and look forever like a seventeen-year-old model, or bake a perfect cheesecake the night before a major presentation. No man can do this; no human can do this. Yet women are repeatedly berating themselves for failing at this kind of balancing act, and (quietly, invidiously) berating others when something inevitably slips. Think of the schadenfreude that erupts every time a high-profile woman hits a bump in either her career or her family life. Poor Condoleezza Rice, left without a boyfriend. Sloppy Hillary, whose hair is wrong again. Bad Marissa Mayer, who dared to announce her impending pregnancy the same week she was named CEO of Yahoo.[6] She could not pull it off (snicker, snicker). She paid for her success. She *Could. Not. Do. It. All.*

Of course she could not do it all. No one can. No one does. Yet women today are laboring under an excruciating set of mutually exclusive expectations; a double or triple whammy of hopes and dreams and desires. To be madonna and whore. Mother and wage earner. Smart but not arrogant. A leader but not a bitch. And because they can't possibly be all those things at once, women are retreating to the only place they can, the only realm they have any chance of actually controlling. Themselves.

More specifically, rather than focusing on the external goals that might once have united them, women are micromanaging the corners of their lives and, to a somewhat lesser extent, those of their children. Think about it. When was the last time a woman bragged to you—even spoke to you—about a protest she joined or a community group she had helped organize? When was the last time a woman told you about her kids' homework or her own extreme juggling? A while ago on the first one, probably; yesterday on the second. How many stories will you find in women's magazines about the pursuit of anything other than bodily or familial perfection? Not many. Here is a random tally, pulled from the newsstands in July 2012: "The Wonder Woman Philosophy of Staying Young." "Superpowered Skin Care: The Most Effective Wrinkle Fighters." "Set Your Mood to Sunny: 4 Happiness Helpers." "Busy Women's Beauty Tricks." A better world or neighborhood: 0. A better you: 16.[7]

To be sure, this turn to the personal is not restricted to women. Instead, it follows a trajectory that can be traced back to Woodstock, or, more precisely, to the jagged route that befell the members of the Me Generation. Once upon a time, the children of the Eisenhower years rebelled against the confines and conformity of their own upbringing. Born in postwar prosperity, raised in a segregated world of gray-flanneled, martini-sipping cogs, they strove to shake up that world and make it better. To include women and people of color within the ranks of power; to throw off the strictures of corporate control; to end a senseless war in Vietnam. So they protested and fought for the rights of a newly constructed individual in a more liberal and open world. A world, in the words of the student activist Tom Hayden, where "men have unrealized potential for self-cultivation, self-direction, self-understanding, and creativity."[8] A world, as it trickled down to the ears of the next generation, where everyone was free to be . . . you and me.

And to a large extent, it came to pass. Nixon fell. The war ended. Civil rights became law at last, and the battle for individual rights—for women, for gays, for black and brown Americans—was engaged and largely won. But along the way, the struggle for individual liberties was transformed into the mantle of individualism, and the free love of the late 1960s and early 1970s gave way swiftly to the free market of the early 1980s. Ronald Reagan was elected in 1980, after all, just eleven years after Woodstock. Margaret Thatcher came to power in 1979.* Together, and backed by a free-market ideology that riffed oddly but powerfully upon the individual rights ideology of the Woodstock years, they oversaw a sea change in political views. The rights stayed, thankfully, but the focus shifted, from social change to individual good, from the needs of the group to the desires of the self. Or, as one former Woodstock participant recently noted, "It's all of a piece. For hippies and bohemians as for businesspeople and investors, extreme individualism has been triumphant. Selfishness won."⁹

Just as Reagan and Thatcher led the fight to privatize markets, so, too, have women raised after the 1960s led the charge to privatize feminism. It's not that we're against feminism's ideals. Indeed, younger women are (not surprisingly) far more likely to be in the workforce than were their mothers.¹⁰ Younger women are wholeheartedly devoted to birth control and to sexual freedom.¹¹ As noted at the outset of this book, they comprise a majority of this country's college students and a growing chunk of its professional class. Sixty-six percent of mothers with children younger than seventeen work outside the home, a stunning reversal of the stay-at-home malaise that engulfed Friedan and her peers.¹² Yet because these women are grappling with so many expectations—because they are struggling more than they care to admit with the sea of choices that now confronts them—most of them are devoting whatever energies they have to controlling whatever is closest to them. Their kids' homework, for example. Their firm's diversity program. Their weight.

My generation made a mistake. We took the struggles and the victories of feminism and interpreted them somehow as a pathway to personal perfection. We privatized feminism and focused only on our dreams and our own inevitable frustrations.

Feminism was supposed to be about granting women power and equality, and then about harnessing that power for positive change. It

---

*A tremendously important woman, of course, who is rarely discussed by feminists.

was, as Andrea Dworkin wrote, "a political action where revolution is the goal . . . part of a planetary movement to restructure community forms and human consciousness so that people have power over their own lives, participate fully in community, live in dignity and freedom."[13] Yet rather than embracing these political objectives, younger generations of women have largely turned away from feminism's external and social goals and instead turned in on their own lives, focusing, say, not on better neighborhood schools, but on their own children's SAT scores; not on social equity writ large, but on the professional advancement of small and highly specific groups of women. Rather than trying to address the world, we are trying to control our own small pieces of it.

So what, then, do we do?

Two generations after *Roe v. Wade*, two generations after Title IX and sexual liberation, four decades after the debut of Charlie, we are still circling around the same maddening questions. Can women really have it all? Is the myth of Charlie ultimately just an illusion, or is there another way, a real way, for women to balance their personal and professional lives? Can the lofty aspirations of the early feminists—for equality, opportunity, choice—be meshed with their daughters' stubborn yearning for more traditional pleasures like white weddings and monogamy? And can women pursue their dreams—*all* their dreams— without losing their sanity?

Yes, I would argue, they can. But not in the mythical mode of Charlie, or along completely gender-blind lines. Women, in other words, are not perfect, and they are not identical to men. They are instead physical and social beings, marked by flaws, programmed to reproduce, destined to age, and generally inclined to love. Any approach to women's issues must start from the reality of women's lives rather than from an idealized or ideological view of who they should be and what they should want. It must start, in other words, by killing Charlie and other myths of female perfection, replacing them with more attainable and flexible dreams—dreams that acknowledge both women's aspirations and the obstacles to them that most women will inevitably confront. This rejiggering does not in any way mean that women should lower their sights or accept anything less than total equality with men. But it does suggest that women's paths to success may be different and more complicated than men's, and that it is better to recognize these complications than to wish them away.

Remembering Biology

To begin with, we need to recognize that biology matters. Women are not in any way physically inferior to men, but they are distinctly and physically different.[14] They have wombs and breasts and ovaries, physiological attributes that—for better or for worse—tend to affect the course of their lives in serious and inevitable ways. Feminism, for many good reasons, tended to downplay these physical differences.[15] But a new look at feminism's issues would suggest integrating biology more explicitly, and acknowledging the not-so-subtle ways in which women's physiology can tend to shape their destinies.

Two areas, of course, are paramount here: sexuality and reproduction. Because although women and men are arguably equally involved in both sex and reproduction, the effects of both these acts fall differently on women, with impacts that stretch across the arc of their lives.

Let's start with sex. As described in chapter 3, most women—not all, but most—approach sexual relations differently than men. They are more interested in romantic entanglements than casual affairs, and more inclined to seek solace in relationships. Biologically, these preferences make sense, since it is women who benefit reproductively from relationships that extend beyond the moment of conception. Sociologically, though, they set the stage for an awful lot of workplace complications.[16] Simply put, if men and women are working together, some subset of them are liable to get involved in sexual encounters. For men—in general, and in the aggregate—the focus of these encounters is likely to be purely sexual. For women—in general, again—there will be more of an emphasis on, or at least desire for, a relationship. Right from the outset, then, this imbalance puts women at a disadvantage. If a woman (and particularly a junior woman) forms a relationship with a man in her office, people will often presume she is having sex with him—the dreaded "she slept her way to the top" accusation. And if she does actually have a sexual encounter, it's unlikely to lead to a longer-term relationship, either personal or professional. To deal with these admittedly awkward possibilities, most organizations have enforced strict relationship policies over the past few decades. Both Columbia and Harvard, for example, have rules that require employees to report any romantic or sexual relationship with another employee to their main supervisor. A major U.S. bank similarly requires that "the relationship must be reported to the next level supervisor or manager as soon as the situation arises."[17] At some level, these restrictions make sense. They seem like the right thing to do. But they don't actually help women. In fact, by rigidly drawing attention to the perils of sexual attraction, they can drive men away from the kind of relationships that would help women advance—the kind of relationships that senior men regularly have with junior men. I will always recall a conversation with a senior executive who openly joked that he would never take a woman on a consulting trip. "My wife would kill me!" he said. "And so," I muttered grumpily under my breath, "your wife is happy, but you'll never promote a deserving woman."

The way out of this mess is complicated but relatively clear. Organizations must be vigilant in promoting policies against sexual harassment and implementing them fully. No employee—male or female, gay or straight—should ever be pressured into having sex against their will, or exchanging sexual favors for the promise of professional advancement. No employee should be the subject of sexual jokes or innuendo. Those who violate these rules should be held fully and transparently accountable. At the same time, though, organizations should also be less puritanical about the possibilities of sex and sexual attraction. Because if all attraction constitutes harassment and all relationships are marked by fear, then women will constantly be at a disadvantage.

Two things will prod this evolution along. First, we simply need to get a larger critical mass of women into the organizations dealing with these tensions. Easier said than done, of course, but the math is straightforward. The more women there are in an organization, the more openly gay men and women—the more diversity—the less potent the sexual pressures will be on everyone. Second, the senior men in any organization need to engage actively and professionally with the women around them. They need to bring them along on trips, take them to lunch, invite them for golfing and to meet their wives. If there's a hint of sexual attraction involved, so be it. Deal with it, and move on. I will always be incredibly grateful to the men (and they were nearly all men) who mentored me early in my career. They did take me on trips, and out for drinks. In a few cases, I suspect there were quiet snickers behind our backs. But they didn't shy away or ever breach the barrier between personal and professional. And I was able to build a career with their help.

Meanwhile, of course, the other physical difference that separates men from women is the act of reproduction, the intimate and complicated process that goes into producing a child. As chapter 6 described, the acquisition of babies shapes women's lives in profound ways, ways that have barely been touched by the otherwise dramatic social changes of the last fifty years. Before women have children, they can compete fairly evenly across most segments of life. They can play sports and be educated and gain access to nearly every job or profession. These are the victories that feminism has wrought. After women have children, however, the lines of their lives begin to depart—slowly, subtly, but still powerfully—from men's. Even if they are lucky enough to have decent maternity leaves and good child care, women quickly find themselves pumping breast milk at the office and lumbering under the effects of too many sleep-deprived nights. They dodge meetings to make doctor's appointments and suffer an onslaught of guilt every time they leave a crying child to attend a boring conference. They get pulled into parent-teacher organizations, elementary school bake sales, and endless rounds of playdates. These are the aspects of mothering that defy government regulation and corporate policy; these are the pulls that feminism forgot. And they are not going away.

To deal with these tensions successfully, therefore, women (and men) need to be far more explicit about recognizing the specific dilemmas of motherhood. Yes, companies can and should strive to create generous maternity leaves and family-friendly workplaces. Yes, governments should aim to provide more accessible and affordable child care. The United States, far behind its peers in both of these areas, could benefit greatly from the kinds of policies that prevail in countries like France, Spain, and Australia, where fully paid leaves of sixteen to eighteen weeks are the norm. In particular, we should consider (at a federal, state, or local workplace level) the now-renowned Scandinavian model, in which both women and men are given generous paid parental leaves, and strongly encouraged to take them.[18]

But at the end of the day, women who juggle children and jobs will still face a discrete and serious set of tensions, tensions that simply don't confront either men (except in very rare cases) or women who remain childless. Women cannot avoid these tensions entirely, but they can make choices—and plans, if they're lucky—that acknowledge them more carefully. Women can choose, for instance, between high-paying jobs in far-off cities and lower-paying ones that might leave them closer to family and friends willing to help with the predictable crises of child rearing. They can choose careers with more or less flexibility, and husbands with more or less interest in shouldering child care responsibilities. They can choose whether to have children earlier in their lives or later, and indeed whether to have them at all. The point, though, is that women need to make these choices and realize their impact rather than simply hoping for the best. Because unless biology truly undergoes a revolution, women will still be having babies rather than men. And having babies imposes consequences that cannot, and should not, be denied.

It is difficult, of course, to parse these consequences early in one's life. A young woman of twenty-two, for example, does not know when she'll meet the partner of her dreams, where her career will take her, or whether, usually, she even wants children. Yet, as I increasingly tell my own students, there are still certain decisions she can start to make, certain bits of information that can help guide a course. First, all young women should know the basic fact of fertility: *it declines*. Rapidly. Starting at about age thirty-five, and then falling pretty quickly off a cliff after that point. This does not mean that women should race out in their twenties and start having babies. But they should know that having babies gets harder in their thirties, and excruciatingly so in their forties. Yes, fertility treatments help. But they are expensive and don't always work. Yes, egg freezing is an attractive insurance plan. But it is expensive, too, not to mention relatively new and untested. The sad truth is that Mother Nature simply designed women to have babies in their twenties: that is when they are most fertile. And so any plan that aims to have children later—after the fun, after the education, after the partnership or record deal or whatever, will always be subject to a certain amount of risk. Meanwhile, there may be some advantages to having one's children younger in life. This, interestingly, is the route carved by the first generation of female pioneers—the Sandra Day O'Connors and Nancy Pelosis and Hillary Clintons, all of whom had their children in their late twenties or early thirties.[19] They didn't have much choice in the matter, to be sure, since they all gave birth before the era of IVF and egg donation. But it is an intriguing model nevertheless, and one that gives women, in theory at least, the chance to chase after toddlers when their own energy levels are high and then send those former toddlers to college in time for their own careers to blossom.

The argument against this model has recently been that it gives women maximum child care responsibilities just at the moment when they tend to have maximum job stress. Or, as a controversial article in *The Atlantic* recently calculated, "if you have children earlier, you may have difficulty getting a graduate degree, a good first job, and opportunities for advancement in the crucial early years of your career."[20] The problem with this math, though, is the same problem that ultimately confounded its author, Anne-Marie Slaughter: the kids grow up and the child care remains. Indeed, many women have found that their child care responsibilities only multiply as the kids get older, migrating into areas that are considerably tougher to outsource to others. Most parents can eventually find child care for their toddlers. Yes, some care is infinitely better than others; some is far more expensive or tougher to secure. But you can find people to watch three-year-olds. They're cute and relatively easy to manage. What's tough is a fourteen-year-old whose first girlfriend just broke up with him. A fifteen-year-old whose math grades are tumbling. A sixteen-year-old who is doing, or selling, drugs. There is no day care left at this stage, no nanny—regardless of the price—who can deal with your kids. And so a woman who has her babies after her career is ostensibly set is only fooling herself that she's over the hard part. Because it's all the hard part.

Young women, all women, need to know this. That is, they need to understand that having children isn't a nine-month or two-year or ten-year project. It is, conservatively speaking, a full-time, twenty-year undertaking. It is wonderful, not only the crawling-drooling-first-words stage, but even the driving-drinking-SAT-taking stage. But it's not a casual commitment, or a short-term assignment that can be neatly scheduled and planned for. It's life, in its messy and most spectacular form. If women want to combine motherhood with a full-time career—or a part-time career, or a deep commitment to anything outside the nuclear family—then they need to anticipate a truly extended period of permanent chaos. Beautiful, crazy-making, totally exhausted chaos. And they need to stop feeling guilty for letting this madness ensue.

Redefining Choice

Which brings me to the second category of things we can do to address the proverbial "women's problem." We can begin to redefine the meaning of choice.

For decades now, ever since the passage of *Roe v. Wade*, the word "choice" has been linked inextricably to the notion of reproductive choice, and to the goal of giving women control over their bodies and reproductive rights. These are huge and important concerns. But choice itself is a much bigger concept and needs to be understood by women in all its infinity and complexity. Today, women in the United States enjoy options that would have confounded their ancestors. They can get married, or not; have children, or not; pursue a profession, or not. They can choose the shape of their noses, the level of their education, the religion of their partner—even, if they want, the musical talents of their child's egg donor. These are the choices that feminism and modernity have created for women, the choices that have catapulted women from a life characterized by the feminine mystique to one of almost infinite possibilities.

The problem, though, is that this multitude of choices can easily feel overwhelming. All too often, even the most talented and fortunate women find themselves paralyzed by the options before them, and by the expectation that they can somehow entertain them all. Rather than delighting in their opportunities, in other words, or seizing the incipient power that has been thrust upon them, women are laboring under the expectation of the ephemeral "all." The expectation not only that they *can* have perfect jobs and children and bodies, but that they *should*.

Thankfully, this problem is not that hard to fix. In theory, at least, it demands little more than a change in attitude, a societal ratcheting down of the great expectations that now engulf women. Critically, this doesn't mean lowering the ambitions of any given woman or of women in general. It just means moving away from the vague but pernicious sense that any individual can have or do it all. In other words, because women today face such a dizzying array of options, they need to be more systematic in recognizing the specific choices they face and the distinctive trade-offs that accompany each one. Harshly put, they need to realize that having it all means giving something up—choosing which piece of the perfect picture to relinquish, or rework, or delay. Having choices means making them, and then figuring out how to make them work.

One way to begin this process is by embracing the concept of "satisficing," an economics term that might best be translated as a combination of cutting corners and settling for second best. What drives the Charlie myth, after all, what defines Barbie and fills the pages of both *Vogue* and *Working Woman* is the ineffable pursuit of perfection. The belief, or more precisely the desire, for women to be all things at once, with equal magic and mastery. Because this myth of perfection remains so strong, even minor departures from it (What? Isaac's Halloween costume wasn't hand-sewn? You *bought* the brownies? With *nuts?*) can send the most confident and mild-mannered women into whirlpools of doubt. This, again, should be a relatively easy problem to fix. Simply put, women need to go easier on themselves, to move from the Martha Stewart world of feminine perfection to a messier and more chaotic reality. They need to pick some areas of their lives where they strive for greatness and others where they settle comfortably for less. They need—consciously, explicitly, and happily—to take whole chunks of activities off their to-do lists and add still others to their to-do-less-well lists. It doesn't really matter which activities an individual selects. Some may choose, as I do, to forget about providing breakfast and lunch, but regularly try to cook (or at least prepare) dinner. Some may develop routines like my friend Sarah, who doesn't cook at all but carefully encloses a handwritten napkin note into each of her daughters' lunchboxes each day. Some may give up all job-related travel that isn't absolutely necessary. Some may take the trips as precious time away and give up long lunches instead. Judith Shklar, the brilliant political theorist who was one of the very first women to be tenured at Harvard, once stunned a graduate school class by admitting—adamantly—that she didn't spend any time at all going to conferences or chatting with her colleagues. "If I want to know what they think," she declared, "I read their books." The trick, she discovered, is precisely to develop tricks, to carve out some kind of shortcuts or solutions that focus finite energies on what will always be an infinite number of demands. Like Shklar, women need to acknowledge that they can't, *won't*, do it all—an admission, by the way, that has never been particularly difficult for men. And once they figure out how to do what matters most, they need to master the equally tough task of not caring so much about the rest.

Inherent in this move away from perfection is an accompanying loss of control. This sounds like a bad thing. It's not. For over a century, admittedly, women have been fighting to gain control—over their bodies, their relationships, their political systems. They have won some major battles in this war (for contraception and abortion rights, for example) and lost others (the halls of political power, as repeatedly noted, remain predominantly male). In the process, though, women have also shifted the locus of their would-be control away from the public sphere and toward the private, focusing, again, on the micromanagement of their own bodies and families. This is the control that has gone too far, the control that leads to anorexia, helicopter parenting, and extreme cosmetic surgery. It is a kind of control that is ultimately useless for the women pursuing it, and even more damaging for the daughters who are watching it and proceeding in its wake. So let me suggest a middle ground.[21] Women should seek empowerment in their lives, but not control. They should be empowered to enjoy their bodies as they desire; empowered to make the choices they prefer; empowered to seek happiness wherever they may find it. But control, like that ephemeral "all" again, is an illusion. Because in the end, the only thing you can really control is your thighs. And they just don't matter that much.

Involving Men

If women are ever to solve the "women's problem," they need to acknowledge that they can't, and shouldn't, do it alone. Men must help. This isn't because women aren't smart enough, or unable to garner sufficient power on their own. It's no longer because women aren't taken seriously or because social structures operate against them. Instead, it's just the basic math. Women account for only 50 percent of the population and far less than 50 percent of the decision-making seats in any organization. If women want to change the world, they need to involve men as well.

Thankfully, the time for this evolution is now ripe. Millions of men have watched their daughters play soccer, their mothers launch companies, their sisters compete in fast-paced jobs. They have invested in female employees who subsequently quit and have wondered, later in their own lives, whether they asked their wives to sacrifice too much on their behalf. Most of these men genuinely want women to succeed. But they don't know how to make the right changes and are generally not party to the conversations—at women's forums and women's colleges, in book groups and bathrooms—that women have among themselves. We need, therefore, to open these conversations and replace the politics of gender with a more reasoned discussion of its practical effects. Rather than endlessly analyzing the problems of "glass ceilings" and "sticky floors," for example, women might usefully advise companies to follow the example of Gerber Products Company, which, more than two decades ago, created a lovely lactation room for its young mothers. Or they could tell them the legend of Elena Kagan, whose first great act as dean of Harvard Law School was to put free tampons in all the school's bathrooms. Men don't like talking about breast-feeding, much less breast pumping. And tampons are just verboten. But tending to these eternal and irrefutable aspects of women's lives is actually a critical part of easing their way in the workplace. Women need to raise these issues with men, and men need to listen.

More broadly, both genders need to be more forthright in discussing the obstacles that women face. All too often, women are scared of raising the topic of gender with men, thinking it will brand them as radicals or troublemakers, while men are terrified of saying or doing anything that might classify them as politically incorrect. The result, of course, is that no one says anything productive at all. Women mutter to themselves about their continued exploitation, men mumble platitudes and hire high-priced diversity consultants, and nothing changes.

Several years ago, Larry Summers infamously speculated, in what turned out to be a public forum, about certain innate characteristics that might be impeding women's success as research scientists. As president of Harvard University, and already under scrutiny for his less than tactful ways, Summers should have known better. He was widely criticized and soon stepped down from his post. But Summers, as many observers have subsequently noted, may well have been on to something important. He couldn't say it, but I can: Women may differ from men in a whole range of important ways. Rather than wishing these differences away, or pretending they don't exist, we need to analyze them, understand them, and then talk to one another about how best to create a world shaped by a diversity of styles and patterns; a world driven by women's skills and interests and passions as much as by men's.

For example, if data show that women, on average, value consensus more than men, and if consensus is something that an organization prizes, then it should find some way of evaluating its employees' consensus-building skills. If women tend to be more risk averse than men, and if risk aversion is a helpful counterbalance to the risk-taking propensities already prevalent in many financial firms, then these firms should explicitly measure and reward successful risk aversion strategies. If women tend to be better mentors, then organizations should evaluate and reward both men and women in this regard. And so forth.

Give 'em the tools and let them figure out how to use them.

Collective Goals and the Pursuit of Joy

Finally, in plotting the way forward it is crucial to remember from whence we came.

Feminism was never supposed to be a 12-step program toward personal perfection. It was about freeing women from the narrowly prescribed expectations that society had traditionally thrust upon them; about giving them the power to shape not only their bodies and their reproductive lives, but their destinies, and that of the world around them as well.

We have come a long way toward that goal in the past forty years.

But, as noted frequently in these pages, we have also lost much of the narrative along the way, neglecting the social goals and purposes that underlay the original struggle. It's time now to go back, to channel the passion of our political foremothers and put it again to good use.* As suggested in chapter 7, we need to focus less of our energies on our own kids' SAT scores and more on fighting for better public schools; less time on competitive cupcake baking and more on supporting those few brave women willing to run for office. We need fewer individual good works and more collective efforts.

Critically, we don't need to reinvent the wheel. Feminism already taught us how to organize, how to agitate, how to petition for things like equal pay and better incentives for child care. We—the women born after feminism's rise, the women who may have discarded or disdained it in the past—just need to get back on that wheel and figure out how to make it work. Moreover, and with the benefits of fifty years behind us, we can also move to what might be considered a softer and gentler form of feminism, one less invested in proving women's equality (since that battle has more or less been won) and less upset with men.

As I was writing this book, one of my most reliable and insightful readers was my friend Richard. A man, yes, and one who harangued me rather constantly about putting men into the argument. As he pointed out, men haven't had it particularly easy over the past half century either. They are the ones who were sent to Vietnam, the ones who died there while women were protesting far more safely back home. They are the ones who lost jobs in the 1980s to a sudden influx of women and who have suffered more recently from the collapse of several historically male industries: construction, automobile manufacturing, electronics. They are the ones who are struggling, as much as their wives and daughters are, to define the workable contours of a radically changed home. Richard, like my husband and most men born since the 1950s, grew up in the cauldron of feminism. His first serious

*I use the phrase "going back" in a very different—but wholly sympathetic—way from Estelle Freedman, who titles her excellent book on feminism *No Turning Back*. My argument, like Freedman's, is that we must continue to push feminism's goals forward; I am just claiming that to do so, we must return to the movement's earliest ideas and ideals. See Estelle B. Freedman, *No Turning Back: The History of Feminism and the Future of Women* (New York: Ballantine, 2002).

girlfriend was a major feminist scholar. His first wife (who, sadly, died young) was a brilliant medical doctor. His second wife, a doctor as well, devotes much of her time to relief work in Africa. Richard is as much a feminist as anyone with a Y chromosome can possibly claim to be. Fifty years ago, though, men like Richard were seen by feminists—had to be seen by feminists—as part of the problem, because they were male, and straight, and therefore part of the patriarchy that feminism was determined to dismantle. That's no longer true. Instead, over the past fifty years, and due in large part to the struggles of feminism, the structures of power have become far more diverse than they once were. Although women (along with blacks, Latinos, gays, young people, and poor people) remain disproportionally underrepresented relative to middle-aged white men, they have nevertheless made great strides—great enough that dismantling a now-evolving patriarchy need not be the central goal of any fight for women's rights. As a result, men like Richard can be part of a feminist solution. And feminists, or anyone who seeks to advance the cause of women, can focus on more practical elements of the problem rather than on a protracted battle of the sexes.

Which brings me to my very last point. When I was writing this book, my working title for many months was *Dancing at Utopia Mall*. As a title, to be sure, it didn't scream its meaning, which was why we ultimately replaced it. But that phrase captured something important to me, something lyrical and poignant that disappears far too frequently from discussions of women, and power, and success. And that something is joy. The feminism that I recall—admittedly, a watered-down, chopped-up, media-manipulated version of feminism—was supposed to be a joyous event. It was about expanding women's choices, not constraining them. About making women's lives richer and more fulfilling. About freeing their sexuality and the range of their loves. Yes, there was pain and sweat along the way to this utopia, but the end point was idyllic, liberating women—*liberating* them—from the pains of the past and the present.

Somewhere, though, the joy fell out of this equation, along with the satisfaction that true choice should bring. If women want to work in high-powered jobs, they should. If they want to work part time, or from home, or not at all if they can afford it, that's perfectly all right, too. If they don't want to be neurosurgeons or look like Barbie or hook up every weekend because it doesn't give them pleasure, then they should consciously and explicitly hold back, choosing not to indulge in other people's preferences. If they like to bake elaborate organic cupcakes, they should. And if they don't, they should send Ring Dings to the bake sale and try not to feel guilty about it.

We need to struggle. We need to organize. And we need to dance.

Fifty years from now, some whiz kid designer will be crafting an advertisement for a new and intoxicating scent. After several prototypes, he or she will stumble upon an equally intoxicating model, a model who captures in an image everything the product is trying to convey. She is female. And successful. And a mother. On whatever screen future advertisements will be displayed, she grabs you instantly and makes you remember. Because, with her hair mussed across her face and laugh lines scampering from her eyes, she is perfect in her own funny and flawed way. Her name will be Charlotte, maybe, or Charlene. And this time, she'll be real.

NOTES

Prologue

1. Boston Women's Health Book Collective, *Our Bodies, Ourselves* (New York: Simon and Schuster, 1973), p. 3.
2. Shelley J. Correll, Stephen Benard, and In Paik, "Getting a Job: Is There a Motherhood Penalty?" *American Journal of Sociology*, vol. 122, no. 5, 2007, pp. 1297–1338.
3. Nancy M. Carter and Christine Silva, "Opportunity or Setback? High Potential Women and Men During Economic Crisis," Catalyst, 2009, www.catalyst.org /knowledge/opportunity-or-setback-high-potential-women-and-men-during -economic-crisis.
4. See Vicky Ward, *The Devil's Casino: Friendship, Betrayal, and the High-Stakes Games Played Inside Lehman Brothers* (New York: Wiley, 2010), p. 148.
5. For a fascinating study of long-term results, see Frank Dobbin, Alexandra Kalev, and Erin Kelly, "Diversity Management in Corporate America," *Contexts*, vol. 6, no. 4 (Fall 2007), pp. 21–27.
6. Catalyst Inc, *2009 Catalyst Census: Fortune 500 Women Executive Officers and Top Earners (2009)*, www.catalyst.org/knowledge/2009-catalyst-census-fortune -500-women-executive-officers-and-top-earners.
7. U.S. Census Bureau, *Income, Poverty, and Health Insurance Coverage in the United States: 2008*, table 6, p. 19.
8. Because sexual crimes are still underreported, these numbers are probably conservative. "Sexual Harassment Charges EEOC and FEPAS Combined: FY 1997– FY 2008," U.S. Equal Employment Opportunity Commission, accessed September 2009 at www.eeoc.gov/stats/harass.html.
9. Diane Kierstead, Patti D'Agostino, and Heidi Dill, "Sex Role Stereotyping of College Professors: Bias in Students' Ratings of Instructors," *Journal of Educational Psychology*, vol. 80, no. 3, 1988, pp. 342–44.

1. Growing Up Charlie

1. Indeed, the commercial became revered as one of the most successful in history. See Geoffrey Jones, *Beauty Imagined: A History of the Global Beauty Industry* (Oxford: Oxford University Press, 2010), pp. 165, 293.

2. Mitra Toossi, "A Century of Change: U.S. Labor Force from 1950 to 2050," *Monthly Labor Review*, May 2002, pp. 15–28.

3. Sheldon Danziger, "Do Working Wives Increase Family Income Inequality?" *Journal of Human Resources*, vol. 15, no. 3 (Summer 1980), p. 445.

4. David Shapiro and Joan E. Crowley, "Aspirations and Expectations of Youth in the United States. Part 2: Employment Activity," *Youth and Society*, vol. 14, no. 1 (September 1982), pp. 36, 45.

5. Joan Kennedy Taylor, *Reclaiming the Mainstream* (Buffalo: Prometheus Books, 1992), p. 92.

6. Shapiro and Crowley, "Aspirations and Expectations of Youth," p. 36.

7. Based on data on the age of birth mothers collected by the Centers for Disease Control and available at www.cdc.gov/nchs/data/statab/t991x06.pdf and www .cdc.gov/nchs/data/statab/t001x05.pdf.

8. U.S. Census Bureau, *Statistical Abstract of the United States: 1999* (Washington, DC: Claitors Publishing Division, 2000), table 1431, p. 879.

9. Despite their perceived perfection, the comforts and luxuries of those suburban towns that flourished in the 1950s and '60s were not as idyllic as they seemed. For more on the dark side of suburbia, see Herbert J. Gans, *The Levittowners* (New York: Columbia University Press, 1982), Stephanie Coontz, *The Way We Never Were* (New York: Basic, 1992), and Kenneth T. Jackson, *Crabgrass Frontier* (New York: Oxford University Press, 1985).

10. In an intriguing recent study, Rebecca Jo Plant also suggests that young mothers of this era were responding to a wave of "anti-Momism," itself a response to a purported bout of overmothering earlier in the century. See Rebecca Jo Plant, *Mom: The Transformation of Motherhood in Modern America* (Chicago: University of Chicago Press, 2010).

11. For a review of these trends, see Claudia Goldin, "From the Valley to the Summit," *Regional Review*, Q1, 2005, pp. 5–12.

12. See Mimi Marinucci, "Television, Generation X, and Third Wave Feminism: A Contextual Analysis of *The Brady Bunch*," *Journal of Popular Culture*, vol. 38, no. 3 (February 2005), p. 518.

13. From "I, Darrin, Take This Witch, Samantha," *Bewitched*, September 17, 1964.

14. For more on this transition, see Bonnie Dow, *Prime Time Feminism: Television, Media Culture, and the Women's Movement Since 1970* (Philadelphia: University of Pennsylvania Press, 1996).

15. See, for instance, "Low-Fidelity Wives," *Cosmopolitan*, January 1969, pp. 77–79, and E. Fishel, "Sex 101: Continuing Education," *Ms.*, September 1975, p. 22.

16. From, respectively, Del Martin and Phyllis Lyon, "Lesbian Love and Sexuality,"

Ms., August 1972, pp. 74–77; Betty Dodson, "Getting to Know Me: A Primer on Masturbation," *Ms.*, August 1974, pp. 106–9; and Barbara Seaman, "The Liberated Orgasm," *Ms.*, August 1972, pp. 65–69, 117.

17. These are only a few of the struggles and victories captured in Freedman's excellent account. See Estelle B. Freedman, *No Turning Back: The History of Feminism and the Future of Women* (New York: Ballantine, 2002).

18. She also had a background in both journalism and leftist politics, facts that she and her supporters rarely mentioned. See Daniel Horowitz, *Betty Friedan and the Making of the Feminine Mystique: The American Left, the Cold War, and Modern Feminism*, 2nd ed. (Amherst: University of Massachusetts Press, 2000).

19. Betty Friedan, *The Feminine Mystique* (New York: W. W. Norton, 2001), p. 21.

20. See Horowitz, *Betty Friedan*, p. 201.

21. Friedan, *Feminine Mystique*, introduction by Anna Quindlen, p. ix.

22. For more on these debates, see Cynthia Harrison, *On Account of Sex: The Politics of Women's Issues, 1945–1968* (Berkeley: University of California Press, 1988), pp. 6–23.

23. Friedan, *Feminine Mystique*, p. 15.

24. Marynia Farnham and Ferdinand Lundberg, *Modern Woman: The Lost Sex* (New York: Harper and Brothers, 1947).

25. Adlai E. Stevenson, commencement address, Smith College, June 6, 1955, excerpted in Harriet Sigerman, ed., *The Columbia Documentary History of Women Since 1941* (New York: Columbia University Press, 2003), pp. 111–15.

26. Estimated from *Statistical Abstract of the United States, 1950–1956* and *1958–1962*, www.census.gov/prod2/statcomp/documents/1962-ol.pdf.

27. As several observers have noted, Friedan's timing was perfect. The strains and pressures that erupted into feminism would almost certainly have occurred without her book, but she published at what was in retrospect exactly the right moment, and *The Feminine Mystique* became (correctly or not) the public face of feminism. See Stephanie Coontz, *A Strange Stirring: The Feminine Mystique and American Women at the Dawn of the 1960s* (New York: Basic, 2011): and Louis Menand, "Books as Bombs," *New Yorker*, vol. 86, no. 45 (January 24, 2011), pp. 76–79.

28. Coontz, *Strange Stirring*, pp. 147–48.

29. NOW mission statement in Miriam Schneir, *Feminism in Our Time* (New York: Vintage, 1994), p. 96.

30. See, for instance, Bonnie Kreps, "Radical Feminism I," in Anne Koedt, Ellen Levine, and Anita Rapone, eds., *Radical Feminism* (New York: Quadrangle Books, 1973), p. 239. For a more general review of the backlash, see Coontz, *Strange Stirring*, pp. 30–31.

31. See "The New Feminists: Revolt Against 'Sexism,'" *Time*, November 21, 1969, pp. 53–56, and "Women's Lib: The War on 'Sexism,'" *Newsweek*, March 23, 1970, pp. 71–76.

32. By 1980, all of the Ivy League was coed, except for Columbia University, which did not begin admitting women until 1983.

33. All of these examples come from Susan Douglas's excellent account of this period. See Susan J. Douglas, *Where the Girls Are: Growing Up Female with the Mass Media* (New York: Times Books, 1994), pp. 166–67.

34. Sara Davidson, "An Oppressed Majority Demands Its Rights," *Life*, December 12, 1969, p. 67.

35. See, for example, Kate Millett, *Sexual Politics* (Urbana and Chicago: University of Illinois Press, 1969), and Andrea Dworkin, *Pornography: Men Possessing Women* (New York: Perigree, 1981).

36. See Davidson, "Oppressed Majority," p. 69, Shulamith Firestone, *The Dialectic of Sex: The Case for Feminist Revolution* (New York: Farrar, Straus and Giroux, 1970), p. 185.

37. Kreps, "Radical Feminism I," p. 239. Another whole segment of feminist thought explored the specific issues facing women of color, poor women, and lesbians, groups whose concerns were often neglected in the broader conversations. Key works in this area include Angela Davis, *Women, Race and Class* (New York: Vintage, 1981); bell hooks, *Ain't I a Woman? Black Women and Feminism* (Boston: South End Press, 1981); and Michele Wallace, *Black Macho and the Myth of the Superwoman* (New York: Dial Press, 1979).

38. Douglas, *Where the Girls Are*, pp. 174–75.

39. See, for example, Suzanne Venker and Phyllis Schlafly, *The Flipside of Feminism: What Conservative Women Know—and Men Can't Say* (Washington, DC: WND Books, 2011).

2. Girls: A Handbook

1. For a full and fascinating history of Barbie, see M. G. Lord, *Forever Barbie: The Unauthorized Biography of a Real Doll* (New York: Avon Books, 1995).

2. Ibid., p. 59.

3. See the discussion in June Statham, *Daughters and Sons: Experiences of Nonsexist Childraising* (New York: Basil Blackwell, 1986). Representative works include H. Biller and D. Meredith, *Father Power* (New York: David McKay, 1975) and M. Lamb, *The Role of the Father in Child Development* (London: Wiley and Sons, 1976).

4. Jean-Jacques Rousseau, *Émile*, translated by Allan Bloom (New York: Basic, 1979), pp. 358, 365.

5. A. B. Barnard, *The Girl's Book About Herself* (London: Cassell, 1912), quoted in Statham, *Daughters and Sons*, p. 22.

6. The classic study of the evolution of childhood, including the differential treatment of boys and girls, is Philippe Ariès, *Centuries of Childhood: A Social History of Family Life*, translated by Robert Baldick (New York: Vintage, 1962). Also, and more broadly, see Carl N. Degler, *At Odds: Women and the Family in America from the Revolution to the Present* (Oxford: Oxford University Press, 1981) and Steven Mintz, *Huck's Raft: A History of American Childhood* (Cambridge, MA:

Harvard University Press, 2004). Note that all of these works argue that child-hood, as a concept, did not really emerge until the sixteenth or seventeenth century. Prior to that time, children—if they survived infancy—blended much more quickly and directly into the adult world.

7. For a more complete description of fetal development, see Lise Eliot, *Pink Brain, Blue Brain: How Small Differences Grow into Troublesome Gaps—and What We Can Do About It* (Boston: Houghton Mifflin, 2009), pp. 19–54.

8. See John Money, Anke Ehrhardt, and D. N. Masica, "Fetal Feminization Induced by Androgen Insensitivity in the Testicular Feminizing Syndrome: Effect on Marriage and Maternity," *Johns Hopkins Medical Journal*, vol. 123 (1968), pp. 105–14.

9. There is an extensive literature on the differences and interplay between sex, gender, and sexuality. See, for example, John Money and Anke Ehrhardt, *Man and Woman, Boy and Girl: The Differentiation and Dimorphism of Gender Identity from Conception to Maturity* (Baltimore: Johns Hopkins University Press, 1972) and Anne Fausto-Sterling, *Sexing the Body* (New York: Basic, 2000).

10. Simone de Beauvoir, *The Second Sex* (New York: Vintage, 1989), p. 267. More recently, a new generation of feminist scholars has also begun to attack some of biology's assumptions about the role hormones play in sexual development. See, for instance, Rebecca M. Jordan-Young, *Brainstorm: The Flaws in the Science of Sex Differences* (Cambridge, MA: Harvard University Press, 2010).

11. Two of the key volumes in this vein include Selma Greenberg, *Right From the Start: A Guide to Nonsexist Childrearing* (Boston: Houghton Mifflin, 1978) and Letty Cottin Pogrebin, *Growing Up Free: Raising Your Child in the 80s* (New York: McGraw-Hill, 1980).

12. Penelope Leach, *Your Baby and Child from Birth to Age Five* (New York: Alfred A. Knopf, 1978), p. 433.

13. See the description in Karin A. Martin, "William Wants a Doll. Can He Have One?" *Gender and Society*, vol. 19, no. 4 (August 2005), p. 458.

14. See Patti Hagan, "Dr. Spock Tells Why He No Longer Sings in Praise of Hims," *New York Times*, October 13, 1973, p. 30. See also Benjamin Spock, *Baby and Child Care* (New York: Pocket Books, 1976), p. xix.

15. Nadine Brozan, "Using Toys to Free Children from the Roles Society Dictates," *New York Times*, May 12, 1971, p. 38.

16. Letty Cottin Pogrebin, "Down With Sexist Upbringing!" *New York*, December 20, 1971, p. 111.

17. Marlo Thomas and Friends, *Free to Be . . . You and Me*, Bell Records, 1972, 33⅓ rpm.

18. From, respectively, Shel Silverstein, "Helping"; Shel Silverstein, "Ladies First"; and Dan Greenburg, "Don't Dress Your Cat in an Apron," in Marlo Thomas, *Free to Be . . . You and Me* (New York: McGraw-Hill, 1974), pp. 60, 39, and 46.

19. Carol Hall, "Parents Are People," in Thomas, *Free to Be . . . You and Me*, p. 48.

20. In academic circles, theories of sex role socialization had likewise fallen out of favor. For a description of this evolution, see Martin, "William Wants a Doll,"

pp. 456–79. For examples of child-rearing advice books that nod to both biology and the potential of socialization, see Louise Bates Ames and Carol Chase Haber, *Your Eight-Year-Old* (New York: Dell, 1989) and Arlene Eisenberg, Heidi E. Murkoff, and Sandee E. Hathaway, *What to Expect: The Toddler Years* (New York: Workman, 1996). Finally, for an excellent survey of the extent to which contemporary parents embrace sex differences, see Eliot, *Pink Brain, Blue Brain*.

21. In one fascinating exception, a Canadian couple opted in 2011 not to reveal the sex of their newborn baby, named Storm. Instead, they declared, they would raise the child to be gender free and to determine whoever, and whatever, he or she wanted to be. See, for instance, "Gender Debate: The Response," *Toronto Star*, May 29, 2011, p. A6.

22. For more, see www.monsterhighdolls.net.

23. Peggy Orenstein, *Cinderella Ate My Daughter* (New York: HarperCollins, 2011), p. 14, and Orenstein, "What's Wrong with Cinderella?" *New York Times Magazine*, December 24, 2006, pp. 34–39.

24. This terrific observation comes from Orenstein, *Cinderella Ate My Daughter*, p. 4.

25. Quoted in Joan Jacobs Brumberg, *The Body Project: An Intimate History of Girls* (New York: Vintage, 1998), p. xxi.

26. Ibid.

27. Authentic Entertainment, "America's Best Pageant," *Toddlers and Tiaras*, TLC, season 3, episode 4, June 22, 2010.

28. Sara Rimer, "For Girls, It's Be Yourself, and Be Perfect, Too," *New York Times*, April 1, 2007, p. 1.

29. Ibid.

30. Ibid.

31. Mary Pipher, *Reviving Ophelia: Saving the Selves of Adolescent Girls* (New York: Putnam, 1994), p. 19. Pipher also builds off Carol Gilligan's path-breaking work on the development of adolescent girls: see Carol Gilligan, *In a Different Voice* (Cambridge, MA: Harvard University Press, 1982) and Carol Gilligan and Lyn Mikel Brown, *Meeting at the Crossroads* (Cambridge, MA: Harvard University Press, 1992).

32. Pipher, *Reviving Ophelia*, p. 19.

33. JoAnn Deak with Teresa Barker, *Girls Will Be Girls: Raising Confident and Courageous Daughters* (New York: Hyperion, 2002), p. 5. For a broader review of this literature, see Natalie G. Adams, "Growing Up Female," *Feminist Formations*, vol. 17, no. 1 (Spring 2005), pp. 206–11.

34. Rosalind Wiseman, *Queen Bees and Wannabes: Helping Your Daughter Survive Cliques, Gossip, Boyfriends, and Other Realities of Adolescence* (New York: Crown, 2002) and Rachel Simmons, *Odd Girl Out* (Orlando, FL: Harcourt, 2002).

35. Mark Kantrowitz, "Backgrounder: Athletic Scholarships," posted to www.finaid.org/educators/20110505athleticscholarships.pdf, March 5, 2011.

36. Betsey Stevenson and Justin Wolfers, "The Paradox of Declining Female

Happiness," *American Economic Journal: Economic Policy*, vol. 1, no. 2 (August 2009), p. 219. Another recent study finds that 56 percent of girls—compared with 40 percent of boys—experience sexual harassment in middle and high school. See Jenny Anderson, "National Study Finds Widespread Sexual Harassment of Students in Grades 7 to 12," *New York Times*, November 7, 2011, p. A14. For the full study, see Catherine Hill and Holly Kearl, "Crossing the Line: Sexual Harassment at School," (Washington, DC: American Association of University Women, 2011).

37. Joan Jacobs Brumberg, *Fasting Girls: A History of Anorexia Nervosa* (New York: Penguin, 1989), pp. 41–60.

38. Ibid.; see also Caroline Walker Bynum, *Holy Feast and Holy Fast: The Religious Significance of Food to Medieval Women* (Berkeley: University of California Press, 1987).

39. http://history.nasa.gov/women.html.

40. Adrian Furnham, Emma Reeves, and Salima Budhani, "Parents Think Their Sons are Brighter Than Their Daughters: Sex Differences in Parental Self-Estimations and Estimations of Their Children's Multiple Intelligences," *Journal of Genetic Psychology*, vol. 163, no. 1 (March 2002), pp. 24–39.

41. In a much-cited study, the American Association of University Women found that by high school, less than a third of girls agreed with the statement "I am happy with the way I am," compared with nearly half of the boys. See "Short-changing Girls, Shortchanging America: Executive Summary" (Washington, DC: American Association of University Women, 1991), p. 4. More recent, and confirming, studies include Franco Cavallo et al., "Girls Growing Through Adolescence Have a Higher Risk of Poor Health," *Quality of Life Research*, vol. 15, no. 10 (December 2006), pp. 1577–85; and Kimberly A. Mahaffy, "Girls' Low Self-Esteem: How Is It Related to Later Socioeconomic Achievements?" *Gender and Society*, vol. 18, no. 3 (June 2004), pp. 309–27. Also Jennifer R. Steele and Nalini Ambady, "Math Is Hard! The Effect of Gender Priming on Women's Attitudes," *Journal of Experimental Social Psychology*, vol. 42, no. 4 (June 2006), pp. 428–36.

42. Julie Zeilinger, *A Little F'd Up: Why Feminism Is Not a Dirty Word* (Berkeley: Seal Press, 2012).

43. Courtney E. Martin, *Perfect Girls, Starving Daughters: The Frightening New Normalcy of Hating Your Body* (New York: Free Press, 2007), pp. 34–35.

44. Letty Cottin Pogrebin, "A Note to Parents and Other Grown-up Friends," in Marlo Thomas, *Free to Be . . . You and Me*, p. 13.

45. See also Laura Hibbard, "Hermione Granger: The Heroine Women Have Been Waiting For," *Huffington Post*, July 14, 2011, available at www.huffingtonpost.com /laura-hibbard/hermione-granger-the-hero_b_898414.html.

46. Maya Catherine Popa, "Sure, He Wanted to Eat Me, *At First* . . . Tracking Abuse in *Twilight*," paper presented directly to author. See also Carmen D. Siering, "Taking a Bite Out of *Twilight*," *Ms.* (Spring 2009), pp. 51–52.

3. Sex and the Social Contract

1. See, for example, Paula England and Reuben J. Thomas, "The Decline of the Date and the Rise of the College Hook Up," in Arlene Skolnick, ed., *The Family in Transition* (Boston: Allyn and Bacon, 2006), pp. 69–79.

2. Laura Sessions Stepp, *Unhooked: How Young Women Pursue Sex, Delay Love, and Lose at Both* (New York: Riverhead, 2007), p. 117.

3. "Dating Is Hell," *Mademoiselle*, November 1986, p. 177.

4. "How to Be a Good Hookup," at www.thefrisky.com/post/246-the-friskys-how-to -be-a-good-hook-up.

5. The considerable literature on sex roles in Athens, as well as across the ancient world, is nicely summarized in Richard A. Posner, *Sex and Reason* (Cambridge, MA: Harvard University Press, 1992), pp. 38–45.

6. Sarah B. Pomeroy, *Goddesses, Whores, Wives, and Slaves: Women in Classical Antiquity* (New York: Schocken, 1975); Beryl Rawson, "The Roman Family," in Rawson, ed., *The Family in Ancient Rome: New Perspectives* (London: Croom Helm, 1986).

7. For more on the role of women during this period, see Ben Witherington III, *Women in the Earliest Churches* (Cambridge: Cambridge University Press, 1988); Jack Goody, *The Development of the Family and Marriage in Europe* (Cambridge: Cambridge University Press, 1983); and James A. Brundage, *Law, Sex, and Christian Society in Medieval Europe* (Chicago: University of Chicago Press, 1987).

8. See Richard T. Vann, "Toward a New Lifestyle: Women in Preindustrial Capitalism," in Renate Bridenthal and Claudia Koonz, eds., *Becoming Visible: Women in European History* (Boston: Houghton Mifflin, 1977), pp. 192–216.

9. Captain Frederick Marryat, *A Diary in America, with Remarks on Its Institutions*, vol. 2 (London, 1839), pp. 246–47. For a discussion of this episode and whether the young ladies were perhaps playing a joke on their British visitor, see Ronald G. Walters, *Primers for Prudery: Sexual Advice to Victorian America* (Englewood Cliffs, NJ: Prentice Hall, 1974), p. 2.

10. John Cowan, *The Science of a New Life* (New York: Cowan and Co., 1873), pp. 116–17.

11. Interestingly, this rise came after a significant dip in the rate between 1800 and 1850. For data and analysis of these trends, see Daniel Scott Smith and Michael S. Hindus, "Premarital Pregnancy in America 1640–1971: An Overview and Interpretation," *Journal of Interdisciplinary History*, vol. 5, no. 4 (Spring 1975), pp. 537–70.

12. By 1850, fertility among American women had fallen from 7.04 children per woman of fertile age to 5.42, a trend that was likely produced by a combination of women's later age at marriage and the spread of rudimentary forms of birth control, including abortion and coitus interruptus. See Carl Degler, *At Odds: Women and the Family in America from the Revolution to the Present* (Oxford: Oxford University Press, 1980), pp. 178–209, and Ansley J. Coale and Melvin Zelnick, *New*

Estimates of Fertility and Population in the United States (Princeton: Princeton University Press, 1963), p. 36.

13. J. Hague to M. W. Foote, 1871, cited in Karen Lystra, *Searching the Heart: Women, Men, and Romantic Love in Nineteenth-Century America* (New York: Oxford University Press, 1989), p. 19.

14. R. Burdette to C. Baker, January 21, 1898, quoted in Lystra, *Searching the Heart*, p. 93.

15. Lystra, *Searching the Heart*, pp. 59–60.

16. Quoted in "A Tale of Not-So-Flaming Youth," *Literary Digest* 105 (May 10, 1930), pp. 69–71.

17. Norton Hughes Jonathan, *Gentlemen Aren't Sissies: A Modern Guidebook for the Young Man About Town* (Philadelphia: John C. Winston Foundation), p. 13, cited in Beth L. Bailey, *From Front Porch to Back Seat: Courtship in Twentieth-Century America* (Baltimore: Johns Hopkins University Press, 1988), p. 67.

18. For an excellent exploration of the drivers and precursors to the revolution, see David Allyn, *Make Love Not War* (Boston: Little, Brown, 2000).

19. Bernard Asbell, *The Pill: A Biography of a Drug That Changed the World* (New York: Random House, 1995), pp. 163–64.

20. See "Birth Control Push," *Wall Street Journal*, November 1, 1963, p. 1, and Sharon Snider, "The Pill: 30 Years of Safety Concerns," Department of Health and Human Services, Public Health Service, Food and Drug Administration, Office of Public Affairs (1992). Some analysts during this period speculated that Searle enjoyed the highest profit margin in the U.S. pharmaceutical industry, an industry already known for generating substantially higher than average returns. See Andrea Tone, *Devices and Desires: A History of Contraceptives in America* (New York: Hill and Wang, 2001), p. 238.

21. Due in large part to their long-standing links with the Roman Catholic Church, many Latin American countries resisted these changes and continued, then and now, to ban abortion. See Estelle B. Freedman, *No Turning Back: The History of Feminism and the Future of Women* (New York: Ballantine, 2002), pp. 238–41.

22. Freud is speaking here specifically about early sexual encounters, but this view seems to permeate much of his analysis. See Sigmund Freud, "The Taboo of Virginity," translated by Joan Riviere and edited by Ernest Jones, *Collected Papers: Authorized Translation Under the Supervision of Joan Riviere*, vol. IV (New York: Basic, 1959), p. 226.

23. Alfred C. Kinsey, Wardell B. Pomeroy, Clyde E. Martin, and Paul H. Gebhard, *Sexual Behavior in the Human Female* (Philadelphia: Saunders, 1953).

24. William Masters and Virginia Johnson, *Human Sexual Response* (Boston: Little, Brown, 1960).

25. Stephen Randall and Editors of *Playboy* Magazine, *The Playboy Interviews* (Milwaukee: M Press, 2007), pp. 153–97.

26. Helen Gurley Brown, *Sex and the Single Girl* (Fort Lee, NJ: Barricade, 2003), p. 4.

27. Brown, *Sex and the Single Girl*, p. 257.

28. Quoted in Allyn, *Make Love Not War*, p. 11.

29. Rebecca Mead, "Still Flying," *New Yorker*, April 14, 2008.

30. Erica Jong, *Fear of Flying* (New York: Signet, 1974), p. 11.

31. Ibid., p. xiv.

32. George A. Akerlof, Janet L. Yellen, and Michael Katz, "An Analysis of Out-of-Wedlock Childbearing in the United States," *Quarterly Journal of Economics*, vol. 111, issue 2 (May 1996), table II, p. 284.

33. Norval Glenn and Elizabeth Marquardt, *Hooking Up, Hanging Out, and Hoping for Mr. Right: College Women on Dating and Mating Today* (New York: Institute for American Values, 2001).

34. Alexa Joy Sherman and Nicole Tocantins, *The Happy Hook-Up: A Single Girl's Guide to Casual Sex* (Berkeley: Ten Speed Press, 2004), p. 4.

35. Andrea Lavinthal and Jessica Rozler, *The Hookup Handbook: A Single Girl's Guide to Living It Up* (New York: Simon Spotlight Entertainment, 2005), p. 3.

36. Elizabeth L. Paul and Kristen A. Hayes, "The Casualties of 'Casual' Sex: A Qualitative Exploration of the Phenomenology of College Students' Hookups," *Journal of Social and Personal Relationships*, vol. 19, no. 5 (2002), pp. 639–61. For more recent, and similar, data, see Paula England and Reuben J. Thomas, "The Decline of the Date and the Rise of the College Hook Up," in Arlene Skolnick, ed., *The Family in Transition* (Boston: Allyn and Bacon, 2006), pp. 69–79.

37. Sherman and Tocantins, *Happy Hook-Up*, p. 5.

38. See Germaine Greer, *The Female Eunuch* (New York: McGraw-Hill, 1966), and Mary Jane Sherfey, "A Theory of Female Sexuality," in Jeffrey Escoffier, ed., *Sexual Revolution* (New York: Thunder Mouth, 2003), pp. 91–99.

39. There are also echoes of a common, if quiet, concern even at the height of the sexual revolution: that men in the movement benefited substantially more than did women.

40. Germaine Greer, quoted in Natalie Angier, "The Transit of Woman," *New York Times*, October 11, 1992, pp. BR1, 32–33.

41. Sherfey, "Theory of Female Sexuality," p. 93.

42. Kate Millett, *Sexual Politics* (Garden City, NY: Doubleday, 1970), p. 62.

43. Janet Reitman, "Sex & Scandal at Duke," *Rolling Stone*, June 15, 2006, p. 76.

44. Stepp, *Unhooked*, p. 37.

45. Paul and Hayes, "Casualties of 'Casual' Sex," pp. 639–61.

46. Ibid., p. 647.

47. Jong, *Fear of Flying*, p. 14.

48. Available at www.psychologytoday.com/blog/teen-angst/201104/hooking-and-friends-benefits-the-modern-day-fairy-tale-0.

49. Akerlof, Yellen, and Katz, "Analysis of Out-of-Wedlock Childbearing in the United States," pp. 290, 295.

50. Quoted in Paul and Hayes, "Casualties of 'Casual' Sex," pp. 658, 654.

51. Robert L. Trivers, "Parental Investment and Sexual Selection," in Bernard Campbell, ed., *Sexual Selection and the Descent of Man* (Chicago: Aldine de Gruyter, 1972), p. 145.

52. Reported in David M. Buss, *The Evolution of Desire: Strategies of Human Mating* (New York: Basic, 1994), p. 82.

53. Glenn and Marquardt, *Hooking Up, Hanging Out*, p. 4. Note that this survey was conducted by an organization with an explicitly conservative agenda, so its findings should be taken with at least a small grain of salt.

54. See Justin R. Garcia and Chris Reiber, "Hook Up Behavior: A Biopsychosocial Perspective," *Journal of Social, Evolutionary, and Cultural Psychology*, vol. 2, no. 4 (2008), pp. 192–208. An additional 45 percent of respondents wanted their hookups to lead either to friendship (28 percent) or further hookups (17 percent). Only 12 percent wanted nothing more.

55. Kathleen A. Bogle, *Hooking Up: Sex, Dating and Relationships on Campus* (New York: New York University Press, 2008), p. 183.

56. *The Rush Limbaugh Show*, February 29, 2012, quoted at http://en.wikipedia.org /wiki/Rush_Limbaugh%E2%80%93Sandra_Fluke_controversy.

57. "Limbaugh's Misogynistic Attack on Georgetown Law Student Continues with Increased Vitriol," *Media Matters for America*, retrieved March 5, 2012, quoted at http://en.wikipedia.org/wiki/Rush_Limbaugh%E2%80%93Sandra_Fluke_con troversy.

58. In 2012, women were equally represented in both major political parties, as well as in both the Tea Party and the Occupy Wall Street movements. See Kenneth P. Vogel, "Face of the Tea Party Is Female," *Politico*, March 26, 2010, available at www.politico.com, and Sarah Seltzer, "Where Are the Women at Occupy Wall Street? Everywhere—and They're Not Going Away," *Nation*, October 26, 2011, available at www.thenation.com.

59. See, for example, Jane Fonda, Robin Morgan, and Gloria Steinem, "FCC Should Clear Limbaugh from Airwaves," CNN, March 10, 2012, available at www.cnn .com, and Erica Jong, "Erica Jong Defends Feminist Revolution," *Daily Beast*, March 27, 2012, available at www.thedailybeast.com.

60. This point was made brilliantly in an op-ed by Frank Bruni. See Bruni, "One-Way Wantonness," *New York Times*, March 13, 2012, p. A25.

61. To protect the privacy of these young women, I have changed all of their names and some of the immaterial details of the evening.

4. Bodies and Other Accessories

1. Germaine Greer, *The Change: Women, Aging and the Menopause* (New York: Alfred A. Knopf, 1992), p. 378.

2. Joyce Tyldesley, *Daughters of Isis: Women of Ancient Egypt* (London: Penguin, 1984), p. 24.

3. Sheila Dillon, *The Female Portrait Statue in the Greek World* (New York: Cambridge University Press, 2010), pp. 1 and 3.

4. Cosmetic surgery figures are from the American Society for Aesthetic Plastic Surgery, reported at www.cosmeticplasticsurgerystatistics.com/statistics/html.

The figure for diet books is for 2006 and comes from *Business of Consumer Publishing 2006* (Simba Publishing). Cited at www.beneaththecover.com/2007/05/14/health-fitness.

5. *Vanity Fair*, November 2009.
6. *Esquire*, November 2009.
7. *Women's Health*, November 2009.
8. Judith Duffett, "WLM vs. Miss America," *Voice of the Women's Liberation Movement*, October 1968, p. 4.
9. The bra burning story stems from an article in the *New York Post*, which started with the provocative lead "Lighting a match to a draft card or flag has been standard gambit of protest groups in recent years, but something new is due to go up in flames this Saturday. Would you believe a bra-burning?" From this speculative sentence, a myth was born. See Lindsy Van Gelder, "The Truth About Bra-Burners," *Ms.*, vol. 3, no. 2 (September 1992), pp. 80–81, and Bonnie J. Dow, "Feminism, Miss America, and Media Mythology," *Rhetoric and Public Affairs*, vol. 6, no. 1 (Spring 2003), pp. 127–49.
10. Robin Morgan, *Sisterhood Is Powerful: An Anthology of Writings from the Women's Liberation Movement* (New York: Vintage, 1970), p. xvi. Morgan's own story is powerful and fascinating. A major child star from the age of two, she renounced her acting career in her late teens and rapidly became one of the leading forces of radical feminism. See Robin Morgan, *Saturday's Child* (New York: W. W. Norton, 2001).
11. See, for example, Harriet Lyons and Rebecca Rosenblatt, "Body Hair: The Last Frontier," *Ms.*, vol. 1, no. 1 (July 1972), pp. 64–65, 131; Judith Thurman, "How to Get Dressed and Still Be Yourself," *Ms.*, vol. 7, no. 10 (April 1979), pp. 49–51, 75–76; and Alice Embree, "Media Images I: Madison Avenue Brainwashing—the Facts," in Morgan, ed., *Sisterhood Is Powerful*, pp. 175–191.
12. Andrea Dworkin, *Woman Hating* (New York: E. P. Dutton, 1974), p. 113.
13. Ibid., p. 116.
14. For an examination of this turnaround, see Susan Faludi, *Backlash: The Undeclared War Against American Women* (New York: Crown, 1991).
15. Calculated in William L. Weis, "When the Forces of Industry Conflict with the Public Health," *AHCMJ*, vol. 1, 2005, p. 116.
16. Data available at www.gallup.com/poll/150986/lose-weight-americans-rely-dieting-exercise.aspx.
17. See "Rating the Diets," *Consumer Reports* (June 1993), pp. 347–547, cited in Laura Fraser, *Losing It: False Hopes and Fat Profits in the Diet Industry* (New York: Plume, 1993), p. 8; and T. Mann et al., "Medicare's Search for Effective Obesity Treatments: Diets Are Not the Answer," *American Psychologist*, 62(3): 2007, pp. 220–33.
18. See Eric Finkelstein and Laurie Zuckerman, *The Fattening of America: How the Economy Makes Us Fat, If It Matters, and What to Do About It* (Hoboken, NJ: Wiley, 2008); and David Kessler, *The End of Overeating: Taking Control of the Insatiable American Appetite* (New York: Rodale, 2009).

19. S. C. Wooley and O. W. Wooley, "Obesity and Women: A Closer Look at the Facts," *Women's Studies International Quarterly*, vol. 2, issue 1 (1979), p. 69. Cited in Naomi Wolf, *The Beauty Myth: How Images of Beauty Are Used Against Women* (New York: Harper Perennial, 2002), p. 187.

20. "The Fat Plateau," *The Economist*, January 23, 2010, p. 33; and Katherine M. Flegal et al., "Prevalence and Trends in Obesity Among U.S. Adults, 1999–2008," *Journal of the American Medical Association*, vol. 303, no. 3, January 20, 2010, pp. 235–41.

21. Fraser, *Losing It*, p. 1.

22. Interestingly, the number of women classifying themselves as overweight has actually begun to shift downward a bit in the past ten years. See Mary A. Burke, Frank Heiland, and Carl Nadler, "Has Overweight Become the New Normal? Evidence of a Generational Shift in Body Weight Norms," Federal Reserve Bank of Boston Working Papers, no. 09-3, April 8, 2009, p. 25.

23. For a fascinating review of these shifts, see Fraser, *Losing It*, pp. 16–49.

24. See Roberta Seid, *Never Too Thin: Why Women Are at War with Their Bodies* (New York: Prentice Hall, 1989), p. 97, and Brumberg, *Fasting Girls*, p. 246.

25. Wolf, *Beauty Myth*, p. 192.

26. For an elaboration of this argument, see Fraser, *Losing It*, p. 7.

27. Data are from the National Eating Disorders Association and are available at www.nationaleatingdisorders.org. Although males also occasionally suffer from these disorders, the number and frequency of cases is substantially lower.

28. Patrick F. Sullivan, "Mortality in Anorexia Nervosa," *American Journal of Psychiatry*, vol. 152, no. 7 (July 1995), pp. 1073–74.

29. For a complete description and definition, see American Psychiatric Association, *Diagnostic and Statistical Manual of Mental Disorders*, 4th ed. (Washington, DC: American Psychiatric Association, 1994), p. 539.

30. "Pro-ana" is shorthand for those who either embrace anorexia or at least claim to be resigned to living with the disease. "Pro-mia" refers similarly to those embracing bulimia.

31. At www.everything2.com/title/how+to+become+a+better+anorexic.

32. The creed appears on many pro-anorexia websites and blogs. See, for instance, http://proanandgirlsruletheworld.blogspot.com/2012/09/ana-creed.html.

33. For a full discussion of possible causes, see Joan Jacobs Brumberg, *Fasting Girls: The History of Anorexia Nervosa* (New York: Penguin Books, 1989), pp. 24–40.

34. See Wolf, *Beauty Myth*, p. 199, and Noelle Caskey, "Interpreting Anorexia Nervosa," in Susan Rubin Suleiman, ed., *The Female Body in Western Culture* (Cambridge, MA: Harvard University Press, 1986), pp. 175–89.

35. See, for example, Susan Bordo, *Unbearable Weight: Feminism, Western Culture, and the Body*, 10th anniv. ed. (Berkeley: University of California Press, 2003), pp. 148–54; Brumberg, *Fasting Girls*, p. 28; Hilde Bruch, *Eating Disorders: Obesity, Anorexia Nervosa, and the Person Within* (New York: Basic Books, 1973); and Albert Rothenberg, "Eating Disorder as a Modern Obsessive-Compulsive Syndrome," *Psychiatry* 49 (February 1986), pp. 45–53.

36. For an excellent history of this period, see Alex Kuczynski, *Beauty Junkies* (New York: Broadway, 2006), pp. 61–78.

37. Gaspare Tagliocozzi, quoted in Sander L. Gilman, *Making the Body Beautiful: A Cultural History of Aesthetic Surgery* (Princeton: Princeton University Press, 1999), p. 68.

38. Robert Gersuny, quoted in Gilman, *Making the Body Beautiful*, p. 249.

39. See Elizabeth Haiken, *Venus Envy: A History of Cosmetic Surgery* (Baltimore: Johns Hopkins University Press, 1997), p. 12.

40. Recounted in Haiken, *Venus Envy*, pp. 76–77.

41. Quoted in Kuczynski, *Beauty Junkies*, p. 73.

42. Haiken, *Venus Envy*, pp. 270–71.

43. Data from the American Society for Aesthetic Plastic Surgery, accessed at www.cosmeticplasticsurgerystatistics.com/statistics/html.

44. Data from the International Survey on Aesthetic/Cosmetic Procedures Performed in 2010, available at www.isaps.org/isaps-global-statistics.html.

45. See Kuczynski, *Beauty Junkies*, pp. 18–32.

46. All quotes from www.drphilipmiller.com, accessed October 26, 2009.

47. Susan Orbach, *Fat Is a Feminist Issue* (London: Arrow, 1988), p. 20.

48. Recounted in Cyndi Tebbel, *The Body Snatchers: How the Media Shapes Women* (Sydney: Finch Publishing, 2000), p. 15. Also Alex Kuczynski, "Plus-Size Models Do an Incredible Shrinking Act," *Milwaukee Journal Sentinel*, April 19, 1998.

49. Wolf, *Beauty Myth*, pp. 11 and 16.

50. Or, as she writes: "There is no legitimate historical or biological justification for the beauty myth; what it is doing to women today is a result of nothing more exalted than the need of today's power structure, economy, and culture to mount a counteroffensive against women . . . The beauty myth is not about women at all. It is about men's institutions and institutional power." Wolf, *Beauty Myth*, p. 13. For other classic arguments along these lines, see Dworkin, *Woman Hating*; Bordo, *Unbearable Weight*; and Sharlene Nagy Hesse-Biber, *The Cult of Thinness*, 2nd ed. (New York: Oxford University Press, 2007).

51. A. W. Mair, translator, *Oppian, Colluthus, and Tryphiodorus* (London: William Heinemann, 1928), p. 555.

52. Courtney E. Martin, *Perfect Girls, Starving Daughters: The Frightening New Normalcy of Hating Your Body* (New York: Free Press, 2007), p. 18.

53. Kuczynski, *Beauty Junkies*, p. 115.

5. Truly, Madly, Deeply

1. For instance: Sheryl Gay Stolberg and Nate Schweber, "State Secret: Chelsea Clinton's Wedding Plans," *New York Times*, July 18, 2010, p. ST1; and Jeremy W. Peters, "Frenzy of Speculation over Clinton's Wedding," *New York Times*, July 29, 2010, p. A18.

2. Stephanie Ellen Byrd, "The Social Construction of Marriage Commitment," *Journal of Marriage and Family*, vol. 71, no. 2 (May 2009), pp. 318–36.

3. Arland Thornton and Linda Young-DeMarco, "Four Decades of Trends in Attitudes Toward Family Issues in the United States: The 1960s Through the 1990s," *Journal of Marriage and Family*, vol. 63, no. 4 (November 2001), p. 1018. See also Andrew J. Cherlin, "The Deinstitutionalization of American Marriage," *Journal of Marriage and Family*, vol. 66, no. 4 (2004), pp. 848–61.

4. Jaclyn Geller, *Here Comes the Bride: Women, Weddings, and the Marriage Mystique* (New York: Four Walls Eight Windows, 2001), p. 31.

5. Germaine Greer, *The Female Eunuch* (New York: McGraw-Hill, 1971), p. 317.

6. Rose M. Kreider and Renee Ellis, "Number, Timing, and Duration of Marriages and Divorces: 2009," *Current Population Reports, P70–125* (Washington, DC: U.S. Census Bureau, 2011), table 6, p. 16, www.census.gov/prod/2011plus/p70-125.pdf.

7. Roughly 70 percent of unmarried eighteen- to twenty-nine-year-olds say they want to get married. See *The Decline of Marriage and Rise of New Families* (Washington, DC: Pew Research Center), November 18, 2010, p. 36.

8. There are some exceptions. See, for example, Debora Cantoni and Richard E. Brown, "Paternal Investment and Reproductive Success in the California Mouse, *Peromyscus californicus*," *Animal Behavior* 54:377–86.

9. See Sarah Blaffer Hrdy, *Mother Nature: A History of Mothers, Infants, and Natural Selection* (New York: Pantheon, 1999), p. 85.

10. See Richard W. Wrangham, "The Evolution of Sexuality in Chimpanzees and Bonobos," *Human Nature* 4:1 (1993), pp. 47–79.

11. See M. L. Crump, "Parental Care Among the Amphibia," *Advances in the Study of Behavior* 25:109–44 (1996). For a fascinating exception to this norm, see J. L. Brown, V. Morales, and K. Summers, "A Key Ecological Trail Drove the Evolution of Biparental Care and Monogamy in an Amphibian," *American Naturalist* 175(4): 436–46 (2010).

12. See Nancy A. Nicolson, "Infants, Mothers, and Other Females," in Barbara B. Smuts et al., eds., *Primate Societies* (Chicago: University of Chicago Press, 1987), p. 330.

13. See Patricia Stuart-Macadam and Katherine A. Dettwyler, eds., *Breastfeeding: Biocultural Perspectives* (New York: Aldine de Gruyter, 1995), pp. 52–54.

14. K. J. Stewart, "Social Relationships of Immature Gorillas and Silverbacks," in M. M. Robbins, P. Sicotte, and K. J. Stewart, eds., *Mountain Gorillas: Three Decades of Research at Karisoke* (Cambridge: Cambridge University Press, 2001), pp. 183–213.

15. Polly Wiessner, "Leveling the Hunter: Constraints on the Status Quest in Foraging Societies," in Wiessner and Wulf Schiefenhovel, eds., *Food and the Status Quest: An Interdisciplinary Perspective* (Providence: Berg, 1996), pp. 182–83.

16. Stephanie Coontz, *Marriage, a History: How Love Conquered Marriage* (New York: Penguin, 2005), pp. 37–38; and Royal Anthropological Institute, *Notes and Queries on Anthropology* (1951), p. 110.

17. Coontz, *Marriage, a History*, p. 24.
18. Ibid. The one exception is the Na people of China; for a description of their social and sexual patterns, see Coontz, pp. 32–33. For more on the basic drivers of early marriage, see David M. Buss, *The Evolution of Desire: Strategies of Human Mating* (New York: Basic, 1994), p. 66.
19. Or, as one anthropologist defined marriage, based on a survey of sixty-two varying practices: "a relationship within which a society socially approves and encourages sexual intercourse and the birth of children." See Suzanne Frayser, *Varieties of Sexual Experience: An Anthropological Perspective on Human Sexuality* (New Haven, CT: HRAF Press, 1985), p. 248.
20. Genesis 5:1–32.
21. For a full description of inheritance laws as laid down in the Old Testament, see Numbers 8:8–11.
22. After repudiating his first wife, he subsequently married eight of his daughters to the rulers of vassal states, presumably buying their loyalty in the process. See Stephanie Dalley, *Mari and Karana* (Piscataway, NJ: Gorgias Press, 2002), pp. 108–9. The full story of the Babylonian king, Zimri-Lim, is recounted in Coontz, *Marriage, a History*, pp. 54–55.
23. See Marvyn Meggitt, *Desert People: A Study of the Walbiri Aborigines of Central Australia* (Chicago: University of Chicago Press, 1965), and Coontz, *Marriage, a History*, p. 41. Coontz notes that cooperation across communities was almost certainly a stronger motive for marriage in early societies than was the division of labor in a two-person household. By marrying their children to neighboring bands or tribes, groups of families could forge "networks of cooperation" that extended far beyond their own limited geographical reach. See Coontz, *Marriage, a History*, pp. 34–49.
24. See the discussion in Philip Reynolds and John Witte, Jr., eds., *To Have and to Hold: Marrying and Its Documentation in Western Christendom, 400–1600* (Cambridge, UK/New York: Cambridge University Press, 2007), p. 48.
25. These laws remained on the Roman books for almost three centuries, when the emperor Constantine revoked them. See Judith Evan-Grubbs, "Marrying and Its Documentation in Later Roman Law," in Reynolds and Witte, eds., *To Have and to Hold*, pp. 43–94.
26. For a purely economic analysis of the marriage contract, see Gary S. Becker, *A Treatise on the Family* (Cambridge, MA: Harvard University Press, 1981), p. 27.
27. Michael Parsons, *Reformation Marriage: The Husband and Wife Relationship in the Theology of Luther and Calvin* (Edinburgh: Rutherford House, 2005), p. 201, and Marilyn Yalom, *A History of the Wife* (New York: HarperCollins, 2001), p. 99.
28. This is one of the central contentions of Stephanie Coontz's wonderful *Marriage, a History*.
29. This question has bedeviled feminists for several generations. For a fabulous description of one early feminist attempt to disrupt a bridal fair, see "Witch Hexes

the Bridal Fair," in Robin Morgan, *Going Too Far: The Personal Chronicle of a Feminist* (New York: Random House, 1977), pp. 80–81.

30. Only 7 percent thought that single people had it easier. See *Decline of Marriage and Rise of New Families*, pp. 33–36.

31. The maxim "A woman without a man is like a fish without a bicycle" is widely attributed to Gloria Steinem. Apparently, though, the original version was penned by an Australian activist named Irina Dunn. Steinem repeated the analogy and popularized it in the United States.

32. See www.bridalassociationofamerica.com/Wedding_Statistics/#marketsummary.

33. www.bridalassociationofamerica.com/Wedding_Statistics.

34. See Chrys Ingram, *White Weddings* (New York: Routledge, 1999), p. 26, and "Statistics on Weddings in the United States," January 10, 2011, www.soundvision .com/info/weddings/statistics.asp.

35. Geller, *Here Comes the Bride*, p. 70. Similar views are expressed and explored in Elizabeth Abbott, *A History of Marriage* (Toronto: Penguin Canada, 2010).

36. Ingram, *White Weddings*, pp. 18 and 23.

37. Geller, *Here Comes the Bride*, p. 18.

38. Catherine E. Ross, John Mirowsky, and Karen Goldsteen, "The Impact of the Family on Health: Decade in Review," *Journal of Marriage and the Family*, vol. 52, no. 4 (November 1990): 1061.

39. Allan V. Horwitz, Helene Raskin White, and Sandra Howell-White, "Becoming Married and Mental Health: A Longitudinal Study of a Cohort of Young Adults," *Journal of Marriage and the Family*, vol. 58 (November 1996), pp. 895–907. Interestingly, the drop in depression after marriage is higher among men; the drop in problem drinking is higher among women.

40. Linda J. Waite and Maggie Gallagher, *The Case for Marriage* (New York: Doubleday, 2000), p. 77.

41. Carmen DeNavas-Walt, Bernadette D. Proctor, and Jessica C. Smith, "Income, Poverty, and Health Insurance Coverage in the United States: 2009" *Current Population Reports P60-238* (Washington, DC: U.S. Census Office, 2010), table 1, p. 5, www.census.gov/prod/2010pubs/p60-238.pdf.

42. Survey of Income and Program and Participation (SIPP), 2004 Panel, Wave 3 (Washington, DC: U.S. Census Bureau, 2009). Wealth Detailed Tables, table 1.

43. See Richard Fry and D'Vera Cohn, *Women, Men, and the New Economics of Marriage* (Washington, DC: Pew Research Center), January 19, 2010. The authors note one interesting exception: married women without a high school education fared worse between 1970 to 2007 than did unmarried women with the same level of education.

44. See Fry and Cohn, *Women, Men, and the New Economics of Marriage*, pp. 5–6.

45. See the discussion in Andrew J. Cherlin, "The Deinstitutionalization of American Marriage," *Journal of Marriage and Family*, vol. 66, no. 4 (November 2004), pp. 848–61; and Arland Thornton and Linda Young-DeMarco, "Four Decades of

Trends in Attitudes Toward Family Issues in the United States: The 1960s Through the 1990s," *Journal of Marriage and Family*, vol. 63, no. 4 (November 2001), pp. 1009–37.

46. See Fry and Cohn, *Women, Men and the New Economics of Marriage*.

47. Lori Gottlieb, *Marry Him: The Case for Settling for Mr. Good Enough* (New York: Dutton, 2010), pp. 43–44.

48. For more on this puzzle, see Cherlin, "Deinstitutionalization of American Marriage," pp. 848–61.

49. Ibid., p. 854.

50. Shulamith Firestone, *The Dialectic of Sex: The Case for a Feminist Revolution* (New York: Farrar, Straus and Giroux, 1970), pp. 118 and 124.

51. Ibid., esp. pp. 3–14.

52. Robin Morgan, *The Anatomy of Freedom: Feminism in Four Dimensions*, 2nd ed. (New York: W. W. Norton, 1994), p. 171.

53. See Hope Yen, "Census: 150,000 Gay Marriages Reported," *Huffington Post*, September 22, 2009, available at www.huffingtonpost.com/2009/09/22/census-gay-marriages-numb_n_294322.html.

54. Quoted at www.lgbtqnation.com/2011/05/gay-couple-together-61-years-still-yearn-for-the-right-to-marry.

55. As the authors of *Why Women Shouldn't Marry: Being Single by Choice* write passionately, "Millions of women today are making the decision to stay single and love it. This is the era of choice." Cynthia S. Smith and Hillary B. Smith, *Why Women Shouldn't Marry: Being Single by Choice* (Fort Lee, NJ: Barricade, 2008), p. 22.

56. "Walters Interviews Gloria Steinem," http://abcnews.go.com/2020/story?id=124030&page=2.

57. Or, as one survey concludes, "While marriage is losing much of its broad public and institutional character, it is gaining popularity as a Super-Relationship, an intensely private spiritualized union, combining sexual fidelity, romantic love, emotional intimacy, and togetherness." See B. D. Whitehead and D. Popenoe, "Who Wants to Marry a Soul Mate?" in *The State of Our Unions, 2001* (National Marriage Project, p. 13), cited in Cherlin, "Deinstitutionalization of American Marriage," p. 856.

6. Mythologies of Birth

1. World Health Organization, *World Health Statistics 2010* (Geneva: WHO Press, 2010), table 9, p. 167.

2. See, for example, Nancy H. Demand, *Birth, Death, and Motherhood in Classical Greece* (Baltimore: Johns Hopkins University Press, 1994), pp. 21–22, and Marjorie Nistak, *Nisa: The Life and Words of a !Kung Woman* (Cambridge, MA: Harvard University Press, 1981), pp. 179–82. Even as recently as the 1850s, the maternal mortality rate in England and Wales was 47 deaths per 10,000 births. See Irvine

Loudon, *Death in Childbirth: An International Study of Maternal Care and Maternal Mortality, 1800–1950* (Oxford: Clarendon Press, 1992), table 1.1, p. 14.

3. These numbers are per white woman of childbearing age. See Jacqueline H. Wolf, *Deliver Me from Pain: Anesthesia and Birth in America* (Baltimore: Johns Hopkins University Press, 2009), p. 107.

4. R. I. Woods and C. W. Smith, "The Decline of Marital Fertility in the Late 19th Century: The Case of England and Wales," *Population Studies* 37 (1980), pp. 207–26.

5. Cited in Rosemarie Tong, *Feminist Approaches to Bioethics: Theoretical Reflections and Practical Applications* (Boulder, CO: Westview Press, 1997), p. 167.

6. Shulamith Firestone, *The Dialectic of Sex* (New York: Farrar, Straus and Giroux, 1970), pp. 175–216.

7. This section draws heavily on the author's early work, *The Baby Business: How Money, Science and Politics Drive the Commerce of Conception* (Boston: Harvard Business School Press, 2006), pp. 1–30.

8. The literature on ancient fertility rites is voluminous. See, for example, Cynthia Eller, *The Myth of Matriarchal Prehistory* (Boston: Beacon Press, 2000); Lotte Motz, *The Faces of the Goddess* (New York: Oxford University Press, 1997); Sir James George Frazer, *The Golden Bough: A Study in Magic and Religion* (New York: Macmillan Company, 1922); and Raine Eisler, *The Chalice and the Blade: Our History, Our Future* (New York: HarperCollins, 1987).

9. Adherents to this school of thought were known as "animalculists." See Elizabeth B. Gasking, *Investigations into Generation 1651–1828* (Baltimore: Johns Hopkins University Press, 1967); Charles W. Bodemer, "Embryological Thought in Seventeenth Century England," in Charles W. Bodemer and Lester S. King, *Medical Investigations in Seventeenth Century England* (Los Angeles: University of California Press, 1968), pp. 1–25; Joseph Needham, *A History of Embryology* (Cambridge: Cambridge University Press, 1934), pp. 115–230; and Peter J. Bowler, "Preformation and Pre-existence in the Seventeenth Century," *Journal of the History of Biology* 4 (1971), pp. 96–157.

10. Samuel L. Siegler, *Fertility in Women: Causes, Diagnosis, and Treatment of Impaired Fertility* (Philadelphia: J. B. Lippincott, 1944), p. 5.

11. See Jacques Gelis, *History of Childbirth: Fertility, Pregnancy and Birth in Early Modern Europe*, translated by Rosemary Morris (Boston: Northeastern University Press, 1991), pp. 26–33; Louis Portnoy and Jules Saltman, *Fertility in Marriage: A Guide for the Childless* (New York: Farrar, Straus and Giroux, 1950), pp. 3–4; and Siegler, *Fertility in Women*, pp. 5–10, cited in Spar, *Baby Business*, p. 8.

12. James Graham, *A Lecture on Love: or, Private Advice to Married Ladies and Gentlemen* (London: privately printed, c. 1784), p. 71, quoted in Margaret S. Marsh and Wanda Ronner, *The Empty Cradle: Infertility in America from Colonial Times to the Present* (Baltimore: Johns Hopkins University Press, 1996), p. 21.

13. Adrienne Rich, *Of Women Born* (New York: W. W. Norton, 1976), p. 11.

14. This story was not revealed until several decades later, when the former medical student documented his experience for a medical journal. Although the husband

in question had apparently known of the doctor's experiment, his wife was never informed. See Marsh and Ronner, *The Empty Cradle,* p. 93, and Cynthia R. Daniels and Janet Golden, "Procreative Compounds: Popular Eugenics, Artificial Insemination, and the Rise of the American Sperm Banking Industry," *Journal of Social History,* vol. 38, no. 1 (2004), pp. 5–27.

15. See David Plotz, *The Genius Factory: The Curious History of the Nobel Prize Sperm Bank* (New York: Random House, 2005), p. 173, and Daniels and Golden, "Procreative Compounds."

16. Leslie Milk, "Looking for Mr. Good Genes," *Washingtonian,* May 1999, p. 65. From Spar, *Baby Business,* p. 37. For current prices, see www.fairfaxcryobank .com/fees2010.shtml.

17. See Spar, *Baby Business,* pp. 26–27.

18. See, for example, Firestone, *Dialectic of Sex;* Dion Farquhar, *The Other Machine: Discourse and Reproductive Technologies* (New York: Routledge, 1996); and Janice G. Raymond, *Women as Wombs: Reproductive Technologies and the Battle over Women's Freedom* (San Francisco: HarperSanFrancisco, 1993).

19. In the aggregate, female fertility peaks at around age twenty-seven and then declines dramatically after thirty-five. Although many individual women are capable of bearing children later in life, the statistical chances of doing so drop precipitously over time. An average twenty-eight-year-old woman, for example, has a 72 percent chance of conceiving after a year of trying (that is, regular unprotected intercourse). An average thirty-eight-year-old, by contrast, has only a 24 percent chance. For more detail on the egg-aging process, see Randi Hutter Epstein, *Get Me Out: A History of Childbirth from the Garden of Eden to the Sperm Bank* (New York: W. W. Norton, 2010), pp. 232–33, and Spar, *Baby Business,* p. 15.

20. In 2008, 5,894 babies in the United States were born from donated eggs, a 31 percent increase since 1997. See www.cdc.gov/art/ART2008/section4.htm#f48 and http://apps.nccd.cdc.gov/art/Apps/NationalSummaryReport.aspx#b.

21. See, for instance, Maggie Jones, "Looking for Their Children's Birth Mother," *New York Times Magazine,* October 28, 2007, pp. 47–51; Juan Forero, "U.S. Baptist Group Charged in Haiti: Lawyer for 10 Accused of Child Kidnapping Says They Wanted to Help," *Washington Post,* February 5, 2010, p. A6; and Damien Cave, "In Tennessee, Reminders of a Boy Returned to Russia," *New York Times,* April 11, 2010, p. A16.

22. Available at www.celebritybabyscoop.com/2012/01/26/celebrity-moms-who-had -natural-vs-c-section-births.

23. See the wonderful description in Epstein, *Get Me Out,* pp. 51–62; and Irvine Loudon, *Death in Childbirth* (Oxford: Clarendon Press, 1992), p. 79.

24. As Epstein notes, citing Loudon, as late as 1927, 65 women in the United States died for every 10,000 births, compared with only 48 in England and 29 in Denmark. See Epstein, *Get Me Out,* p. 60.

25. Loudon, *Death in Childbirth,* table 15.1, p. 256.

26. Ibid., table 18.8, p. 315. These figures are for white women. Black women in the

United States tragically faced, and still face, considerably higher rates of maternal mortality.

27. Marguerite Tracy and Mary Boyd, "Painless Childbirth," *McClure's Magazine*, vol. XLIII, no. 2, June 1914, p. 38.

28. Marguerite Tracy and Mary Boyd, *Painless Childbirth* (New York: Frederick A. Stokes Company, 1915), p. xxxi.

29. Charlotte Carmody, quoted in Epstein, *Get Me Out*, p. 82.

30. See Jacqueline H. Wolf, *Deliver Me from Pain* (Baltimore: Johns Hopkins University Press, 2009), p. 78.

31. The first book to spur this line of thinking was Grantly Dick-Read's *Childbirth Without Fear*. First published in 1942, it spawned a small movement of natural childbirth but didn't really get a significant following for another two decades.

32. *The New Our Bodies, Ourselves* (New York: Simon and Schuster, 1992), p. 454. Similar sentiments are expressed in the book's earlier edition, The Boston Women's Health Book Collective, *Our Bodies, Ourselves: A Book By and For Women* (New York: Simon and Schuster, 1976), p. 267.

33. Ruth Claire, "They Don't Call It a Peak Experience for Nothing," *Mothering*, Fall 1989, p. 58.

34. Heidi Murkoff, Arlene Eisenberg, and Sandee Hathaway, *What to Expect When You're Expecting*, 3rd ed. (New York: Workman, 2002), pp. 21 and 54.

35. Murkoff et al., *What to Expect*, pp. 84 and 113.

36. Ibid., p. 322.

37. In a lovely book, and one that grapples with her earlier and passionate defense of feminism, Naomi Wolf reflects similarly on her feelings about pregnancy in general and *What to Expect* in particular. See Naomi Wolf, *Misconceptions: Truth, Lies, and the Unexpected on the Journey to Motherhood* (New York: Doubleday, 2001).

38. *The Womanly Art of Breastfeeding* (Franklin Park, IL: La Leche League International, 1981), p. 5.

7. The Good Wife's Guide to Life and Love

1. As cited in Steven Erlanger and Maïa de la Baume, "In Defense of the Imperfect Mother," *New York Times*, June 6, 2010, Style section, p. 2.

2. See the description in Estelle Freedman, *No Turning Back: The History of Feminism and the Future of Women* (New York: Ballantine, 2002), pp. 25–27; Peggy Reeves Sanday, *Female Power and Male Dominance: On the Origins of Sexual Inequality* (Cambridge: Cambridge University Press, 1981), pp. 79–81.

3. As historians and anthropologists have noted, the shift to gender-based roles accelerated along with the shift to settled agriculture. See, for example, Freedman, *No Turning Back*, pp. 22–42. For more detailed histories of the traditional distribution of work within households, see Alice Kessler-Harris, *Out to Work: A History of Wage-Earning Women in the United States* (New York: Oxford

University Press, 2003); Nancy F. Cott, *The Bonds of Womanhood* (New Haven, CT: Yale University Press, 1977); and Julie A. Matthaei, *An Economic History of Women in America* (New York: Schocken, 1982).

4. Frederick [*sic*] Engels, *The Origin of the Family, Private Property and the State* (New York: International Publishers, 1972). For a critical feminist revision of Engels's view, see Gerda Lerner, *The Creation of Patriarchy* (New York: Oxford University Press, 1986).

5. Engels, *Origin of the Family*, p. 218.

6. Gary S. Becker, *A Treatise on the Family* (Cambridge, MA: Harvard University Press, 1981), p. 17. Becker claims that a large component of comparative advantage stems from biologically intrinsic characteristics. Because a woman invests more biological energy in reproduction than does a man, she has a greater interest in preserving her investment by caring for her children.

7. Betty Friedan, *The Feminine Mystique* (New York: Norton, 2001), p. 469.

8. Eduardo Porter, "Stretched to Limit, Women Stall March to Work," *New York Times*, March 2, 2006, pp. A1, C2.

9. See, for example, Karin L. Brewster and Irene Padavic, "Change in Gender-Ideology, 1977–1996: The Contributions of Intracohort Change and Population Turnover," *Journal of Marriage and Family*, vol. 62, no. 2 (May 2000), pp. 477–87; and Arland Thornton and Linda Young-DeMarco, "Four Decades of Trends in Attitudes Toward Family Issues in the United States: The 1960s Through the 1990s," *Journal of Marriage and Family*, vol. 63, no. 4 (November 2001), pp. 1009–37.

10. "The Good Wife's Guide," *Housekeeping Monthly*, May 13, 1955.

11. Tracee Stukes, *Maintain a Keeper: A Woman's Guide to Loving and Understanding Her Man* (Brooklyn, NY: Chocolate Ice Publishing, 2006), p. 47.

12. Arlie Russell Hochschild, *The Second Shift* (New York: Penguin, 2003), p. 3.

13. Ibid. Italics in original.

14. See Bobbie Mixon, "Chore Wars: Men, Women and Housework," National Science Foundation, reporting on research conducted by Frank Stafford at the University of Michigan. Similar data are reported in Suzanne M. Bianchi, John P. Robinson, and Melissa Milkie, *Changing Rhythms of American Family Life* (New York: Russell Sage Foundation, 2006). One recent study does show relatively equal declines in total work hours since 1965 for men and women. Yet as some commentators on that paper argue, men's hours "helping" around the house may not be equivalent to women's continued ownership of domestic responsibilities. See Mark Aguiar and Erik Hurst, "Measuring Trends in Leisure: The Allocation of Time over Five Decades," *Quarterly Journal of Economics*, vol. 122, no. 3 (2007), pp. 969–1006; and Betsey Stevenson and Justin Wolfers, "The Paradox of Declining Female Happiness," *American Economic Journal: Economic Policy*, vol. 1, no. 2 (August 2009), pp. 191–225.

15. Sylvia Ann Hewlett, "Executive Women and the Myth of Having It All," *Harvard Business Review*, April 2002, p. 70.

16. Chris A. Higgins, Linda E. Duxbury, and Sean T. Lyons, "Coping with Overload and Stress: Men and Women in Dual-Earner Families," *Journal of Marriage and Family*, vol. 72, no. 4 (August 2010), pp. 847–59.

17. Anne-Rigt Poortman and Tanja Van Der Lippe, "Attitudes Toward Housework and Child Care and Gendered Division of Labor," *Journal of Marriage and Family*, vol. 71, no. 3 (August 2009), pp. 526–41.

18. Suzanne M. Bianchi, "Family Change and Time Allocation in American Families" (Washington, DC: Alfred P. Sloan Foundation, November 29–30, 2010), pp. 7–8.

19. Ibid., p. 4; and Andrea Doucet, *Do Men Mother? Fathering, Care, and Domestic Responsibility* (Toronto: University of Toronto Press, 2006).

20. This 42 percent of working class fathers compares to only 20 percent of fathers in managerial or professional jobs. See Michael Kimmel, "Has a Man's World Become a Woman's Nation?" in *The Shriver Report: A Woman's Nation Changes Everything*, ed. Heather Boushey and Ann O'Leary (Washington, DC: Center for American Progress, 2009): p. 349.

21. Joan Williams, for instance, attributes women's reduced bargaining power within marriage to what she calls "choice rhetoric." Women, she argues, are actually being forced to curtail their paid labor, but they rationalize their decisions as choice. See Williams, *Unbending Gender* (New York: Oxford University Press, 2000). Also Daphne Spain and Suzanne M. Bianchi, *Balancing Act* (New York: Russell Sage Foundation, 1996) and Rosanna Hertz, *More Equal Than Others: Women and Men in Dual-Career Marriages* (Berkeley: University of California Press, 1986).

22. For a fascinating view of just how time-intensive and complicated washing was in earlier decades, see the description in Catharine E. Beecher, *A Treatise on Domestic Economy for the Use of Young Ladies at Home and at School* (New York: Harper, 1848), pp. 284–292. Also Harvey Green and Mary-Ellen Perry, *The Light of the Home: An Intimate View of the Lives of Women in Victorian America* (New York: Pantheon, 1983), pp. 73–74.

23. Friedan discusses this phenomenon in chapter 10, "Housewifery Expands to Fill the Time Available." Friedan, *Feminine Mystique*, pp. 233–57. For an intriguing and more in-depth analysis, see Ruth Schwartz Cowan, *More Work for Mother: The Ironies of Household Technology from the Open Hearth to the Microwave* (New York: Basic, 1983).

24. This figure (more precisely, 39.4 hours a week) had fallen over the period from 49.5 hours—a sizable decrease, yet still one that left women with a severe time constraint. See Bianchi, "Family Change and Time Allocation." Within the broad category of "family care," there has, slowly, been a movement away from pure housekeeping duties in favor of child care. See the analysis in Bianchi et al., *Changing Rhythms of American Family Life*, pp. 89–112.

25. Benjamin Spock, *The Common Sense Book of Baby and Child Care* (New York: Duell, Sloan and Pearce, 1946), p. 3. For a fascinating examination of shifting

American trends in child rearing, see also Rebecca Jo Plant, *Mom: The Transformation of Motherhood in Modern America* (Chicago: University of Chicago Press, 2010).

26. Spock, *Baby and Child Care*, p. 265.

27. Penelope Leach, *Children First: What Our Society Must Do—and Is Not Doing—for Our Children Today* (New York: Alfred A. Knopf, 1994), p. 87.

28. See www.askdrsears.com. Also William Sears and Martha Sears, *The Attachment Parenting Book: A Commonsense Guide to Understanding and Nurturing Your Baby* (Boston: Little, Brown, 2001) and William Sears, Martha Sears, and Elizabeth Pantley, *The Successful Child: What Parents Can Do to Help Kids Turn Out Well* (Boston: Little, Brown, 2002).

29. Barbara Rowley, "Toy Story: How to Choose the Best Playthings for Your Child, Age by Age," *Parenting*, May 1, 2002, p. 135.

30. For an excellent survey of how the media encourages and exhorts women to be "perfect" mothers, see Susan J. Douglas and Meredith W. Michaels, *The Mommy Myth: The Idealization of Motherhood and How It Has Undermined Women* (New York: Free Press, 2004).

31. Ibid., p. 292. Judith Warner similarly notes that "the icon of ideal motherhood at the dawn of the twenty-first century was a woman so bound up in her child, so tightly bonded and fused, that she herself—soul, mind, and body—all but disappeared." See Judith Warner, *Perfect Madness: Motherhood in the Age of Anxiety* (New York: Riverhead, 2005), p. 68.

32. The literature here is extensive. See, for instance, Warner, *Perfect Madness*; Douglas and Michaels, *Mommy Myth*; Sharon Hays, *The Cultural Contradictions of Motherhood* (New Haven, CT: Yale University Press, 1996); Anna Quindlen, "Playing God on No Sleep," *Newsweek*, July 2, 2001, p. 64; and Annette Lareau and Elliot B. Weininger, "Time, Work and Family Life: Reconceptualizing Gendered Time Patterns Through the Case of Children's Organized Activities," *Sociological Forum*, vol. 23, no. 3 (2008), pp. 419–54.

33. Calculated from data presented in Bianchi et al., *Changing Rhythms*, table 5.3, p. 97. Remarkably, though, in 2000, mothers were actually spending more time with their children than they were in 1965. See Bianchi et al., *Changing Rhythms*, p. 87.

34. Bianchi et al., *Changing Rhythms*, table 5.2, "Trends in Personal Care Activities of Parents, Hours per Week." The difference was even more acute for single mothers, who lost five hours a week.

35. For anecdotal evidence on sex, see Warner, *Perfect Madness*, pp. 239–57. For data on the percent of women who feel rushed, see Bianchi, "Family Change and Time Allocation," p. 12.

36. This finding holds regardless of race, income level, and employment status. See Betsey Stevenson and Justin Wolfers, "The Paradox of Declining Female Happiness," *American Economic Journal: Economic Policy*, vol. 1, no. 2 (August 2009), pp. 190–223. Men, by contrast, have generally become happier over this period.

For similar results, see Alan B. Krueger, "Are We Having More Fun Yet? Categorizing and Evaluating Changes in Time Allocation," *Brookings Papers on Economic Activity*, vol. 2007, no. 2 (2007), pp. 193–215.

37. In fact, the number of middle- and upper-middle-class kids getting into the United States' most selective colleges is actually declining, as these schools strive to increase their enrollments of lower-income and foreign-born students. This trend, to some extent, describes why parents are trying ever harder to boost their children's chances, and why some of the elite schools have been considering expanding their class size.

38. For the prevalence of attention deficit disorder and its treatment, see "Increasing Prevalence of Parent-Reported Attention-Deficit/Hyperactivity Disorder Among Children—United States, 2003 and 2007," Centers for Disease Control, *Morbidity and Mortality Weekly Report*, November 12, 2010, vol. 59, no. 44, pp. 1439–43; for data on the prevalence of autism, see Catherine Rice, "Prevalence of Autism Spectrum Disorders—Autism and Developmental Disabilities Monitoring Network, United States, 2006," *Morbidity and Mortality Weekly Report*, December 18, 2009, vol. 58, no. 10, pp. 1–20; for asthma, B. Bloom et al., "Summary Health Statistics for U.S. Children: National Health Interview Survey, 2009," *Vital and Health Statistics*, series 10, no. 247 (December 2010), pp. 5 and 9.

39. By contrast, only 3 percent of the graduating class of 1960 described themselves as drug users or former drug users, and 4 percent admitted to drinking too much. See "Seniors Then and Now," *New York*, June 27–July 4, 2011, p. 21.

40. In fact, most women feel that their husbands *should* be the primary providers in the family, even when they're not. See Williams, *Unbending Gender*, p. 27.

41. Laura Schlessinger, *The Proper Care and Feeding of Husbands* (New York: Harper, 2006), p. 102.

42. Ibid., p. 3.

43. Ibid., p. xxii. Schlessinger here is quoting one of her listeners, but similar views and advice are repeated throughout the book—along with the suggestion that essentially what men want is less nagging and more sex.

44. Laura Doyle, *The Surrendered Wife: A Practical Guide to Finding Intimacy, Passion, and Peace with a Man* (New York: Simon and Schuster, 2001).

45. And these are just the chapter titles.

46. Laura Schlessinger, *The Proper Care and Feeding of Husbands* (New York: Harper Perennial, 2006), p. 3.

47. Venker writes with her aunt, the well-known archconservative, Phyllis Schlafly. See Suzanne Venker and Phyllis Schlafly, *The Flipside of Feminism: What Conservative Women Know—and Men Can't Say* (Washington, DC: WND Books, 2011), p. 55. Doyle, meanwhile, is an interesting anomaly in this respect. Although her message is quite conservative, she makes clear that she draws a line between behavior in the home and at work. Or, as she writes, "In the workplace, I would never settle for anything less than equal pay, equal opportunity, and having an equal voice to my male counterparts. But at home, these qualities contribute

nothing to the romantic, intimate relationship I want. See Doyle, *Surrendered Wife*, p. 158.

48. Tracee Stukes, *Maintain a Keeper: A Woman's Guide to Loving and Understanding Her Man* (Brooklyn, NY: Chocolate Ice Publishing, 2006), p. 27.

49. Naomi Wolf, *Misconceptions: Truth, Lies, and the Unexpected on the Journey to Motherhood* (New York: Doubleday, 2001), p. 261.

50. Stephanie Staal, *Reading Women: How the Great Books of Feminism Changed My Life* (New York: Public Affairs, 2011), p. 78.

51. Sylvia Ann Hewlett, "Executive Women and the Myth of Having It All," *Harvard Business Review*, April 2002, pp. 66–73.

52. Lisa Belkin, "Judging Women," *New York Times Magazine*, May 23, 2010, p. 11; and Peter Beinart, "Put a Mom on the Court," *Daily Beast*, April 25, 2010. In a provocative book, Linda Hirshman also argues that professional women should never have more than one child. See Linda R. Hirshman, *Get to Work: A Manifesto for Women of the World* (New York: Viking, 2006).

53. In *Where the Girls Are*, Susan Douglas intriguingly attributes this trend to the ideology of the Reagan years, arguing that "for women in the age of Reagan, elitism and narcissism merged in a perfect appeal to forget the political already, and get back to the personal, which you might be able to do something about." Susan J. Douglas, *Where the Girls Are: Growing Up Female with the Mass Media* (New York: Times Books, 1994), p. 247.

8. Crashing into Ceilings: A Report from the Nine-to-Five Shift

1. For a detailed description of the phases of this migration, see Claudia Goldin, "The Quiet Revolution that Transformed Women's Employment, Education, and Family," *AEA Papers and Proceedings*, vol. 96, no. 2 (May 2006), pp. 1–21.

2. To repeat: the literature here is vast. Some representative titles include Joan Williams, *Unbending Gender: Why Family and Work Conflict and What to Do About It* (Oxford: Oxford University Press, 2000); Heather Boushey and Ann O'Leary, eds., *The Shriver Report: A Woman's Nation Changes Everything* (Washington, DC: Center for American Progress, 2009); and Sylvia Ann Hewlett and Ripa Rashid, *Winning the War for Talent: Why Women Are the Solution* (Boston: Harvard Business Press, 2011).

3. Under the Family and Medical Leave Act of 1993, all qualified employees have the right to take up to twelve weeks each year of unpaid leave for the birth or care of their child. Because the law applies only to qualified employees, not all workers are necessarily eligible for its benefits. For a description and analysis of how the law has worked in practice, see Ann O'Leary, "How Family Leave Laws Left Out Low-Wage Workers," *Berkeley Journal of Employment and Labor Law*, vol. 28, no. 1 (2007), pp. 1–62.

4. Catalyst Inc., "Women CEOs of the Fortune 1000" (2013), available at www.cata lyst.org/knowledge/women-ceos-fortune-1000.

5. Catalyst Inc., "2012 Catalyst Census: Fortune 500 Women Board Directors," available at www.catalyst.org/knowledge/2012-catalyst-census-fortune-500-women -board-directors.

6. U.S. Census Bureau, 2009, "Income, Poverty and Health Insurance in the United States: 2009," Current Population Reports, fig. 2, p. 11. Available at www.census .gov/prod/2010pubs/p60-238.pdf (accessed September 4, 2010).

7. Data are for cities with populations above thirty thousand. See *National Directory of Women Elected Officials*, National Women's Political Caucus, 1983, and Center for American Women and Politics, "Women in Elective Office 2013," available at www.cawp.rutgers.edu/fast_facts/levels_of_office/Current_Numbers.php.

8. Judith S. Kaye and Anne C. Reddy, "The Progress of Women Lawyers at Big Firms: Steadied or Simply Studied?" *Fordham Law Review*, vol. 76, no. 4 (March 2008), p. 1944, n6.

9. Ibid., pp. 1945–46.

10. Ibid., p. 1954.

11. See www.catalyst.org/publication/504/women-in-us-finance.

12. Bureau of Labor Statistics, "Quick Stats on Women Workers, 2008" (2009), available at www.dol.gov/wb/stats/main.htm.

13. See Boushey and O'Leary, eds., *The Shriver Report*, pp. 6 and 32; Ellen Galinsky, Kerstin Aumann, and James T. Bond, *Times Are Changing: Gender and Generation at Work and at Home* (New York: Family Work Institute, 2008), p. 8; and Institute for Women's Policy Research, "Unemployment Among Single Mother Families," IWPR Publication #C369 (2009).

14. This is the median wage in 2009 for all women earners in the United States. See U.S. Census Bureau, September 10, 2009, www.census.gov/Press-Release /www/releases/archives/income_wealth/014227.html.

15. Center for Women's Business Research, "Key Facts About Women-Owned Businesses" (2009), available at www.womensbusinessresearchcenter.org/research /keyfacts; and Darrene Hackler, Ellen Harpel, and Heike Mayer, "Human Capital and Women's Business Ownership" (Washington, DC: Small Business Administration, 2008).

16. See www.census.gov/econ/sbo/get07sof.html?12.

17. Felice N. Schwartz, "Management Women and the New Facts of Life," *Harvard Business Review*, January–February 1989, pp. 65–76.

18. Ibid., p. 69.

19. Ibid., pp. 69–71.

20. It also brought Schwartz far more criticism than was almost certainly warranted. A lifelong feminist, she was pilloried for having advanced what many saw as an antifeminist argument. See Tony Schwartz, "Life/Work–Issue 30, December 19, 2007," at www.fastcompany.com.

21. Schwartz, "Management Women," p. 72.

22. Personal conversation, August 2011.

23. "Part-Time Work Among Lawyers Declined for the First Time in 17 Years—Most

Working Part-Time Continue to Be Women," National Association for Legal Career Professionals (NALP), January 19, 2012, accessed at www.nalp.org/part-time_jan2012; and unpublished tabulation from the *Current Population Survey*, Bureau of Labor Statistics, 2011.

24. Personal communication, July 2011.

25. Brad Harrington and Jamie J. Ladge, "Got Talent? It Isn't Hard to Find," in Boushey and O'Leary, eds., *The Shriver Report*, p. 205. A major exception is the field of medicine, where nearly 40 percent of women between the ages of thirty-five and forty-four report working part time. See Karen S. Seibert, "Don't Quit This Day Job," *New York Times*, Week in Review, June 12, 2011, p. 9.

26. Sylvia Ann Hewlett and Carolyn Buck Luce, "Off-Ramps and On-Ramps: Keeping Talented Women on the Road to Success," *Harvard Business Review*, March 2005, p. 5.

27. Lisa Belkin, "The Opt-Out Revolution," *New York Times Magazine*, October 23, 2003, pp. 42–47, 58, 85–86.

28. Louise Story, "Many Women at Elite Colleges Set Career Path to Motherhood," *New York Times*, September 20, 2005, pp. A1, A18.

29. See Susan J. Douglas, "Where Have You Gone, Roseanne Barr?" in Boushey and O'Leary, eds., *The Shriver Report*, p. 295; also Letters to the Editor, *New York Times Magazine*, November 9, 2003, p. 14.

30. Letters to the Editor, *New York Times Magazine*, November 9, 2003, p. 14.

31. Katha Pollitt, "There They Go Again," *Nation*, October 30, 2003, available at www.thenation.com/article/there-they-go-again. For an extensive statistical inquiry that also finds no more than a blip in the data, see Heather Boushey, "'Opting Out?' The Effect of Children on Women's Employment in the United States," *Feminist Economics*, vol. 14, no. 1 (January 2008), pp. 1–36.

32. "A Revived Debate: Babies, Careers, 'Having It All,'" *New York Times*, September 22, 2005, p. A30.

33. As one economist notes, the population profiled in Belkin's piece—highly educated older mothers—is a tiny share of all women with children. See Boushey, "'Opting Out?'" p. 29.

34. Marianne Bertrand, Claudia Goldin, and Lawrence Katz, "Dynamics of the Gender Gap for Young Professionals in the Financial and Corporate Sector," *American Economic Journal: Applied Economics*, vol. 2 (July 2010), pp. 228–55. For similar results for women graduates of Harvard Business School, see Linda R. Hirshman, *Get to Work: A Manifesto for Women of the World* (New York: Viking, 2006), p. 8. A broader but earlier study likewise found that 12 percent of American women with MBA degrees were not working ten years after graduation; 72 percent of these women cited family responsibilities as the reason they left. See Joe G. Baker, "The Influx of Women into Legal Professions: An Economic Analysis," *Monthly Labor Review*, vol. 25 (2002), p. 17.

35. So severe was this outflow that the firm in question, Deloitte Touche, eventually took aggressive measures to retain their female employees. See Douglas M.

McCracken, "Winning the Talent War for Women: Sometimes It Takes a Revolution," *Harvard Business Review*, vol. 78, no. 6 (2000), pp. 159–67.

36. U.S. Census Bureau data, cited in Sylvia Ann Hewlett, "Executive Women and the Myth of Having it All," *Harvard Business Review*, April 2002, p. 71.

37. Joan Williams et al., "Opt Out or Pushed Out?" (San Francisco: Center for WorkLife Law, 2006); and Pamela Stone and Meg Lovejoy, "Fast-Track Women and the 'Choice' to Stay Home," *Annals of the American Academy of Political and Social Science*, vol. 596 (November 2004).

38. Stone and Lovejoy, "Fast-Track Women," pp. 62–83.

39. Ibid., p. 80.

40. Belinda Luscombe, "Who Needs Marriage? A Changing Institution," *Time*, November 18, 2010, pp. 48–56.

41. As Joan Williams notes, women whose husbands' incomes range from zero to the 95th percentile stay in the workforce at roughly the same rates (ranging from 71 to 78 percent). Women whose husbands' incomes put them in the top 5 percent of earners, though, are much less likely (54 percent) to be employed. See Williams et al., "Opt Out or Pushed Out?" p. 25. See also Bertrand et al., "Dynamics of the Gender Gap." Some recent data, though, suggest that, overall, women's decisions about whether to remain in the workforce are being driven less and less by the level of their husbands' income. See Francine D. Blau and Lawrence M. Kahn, "Changes in the Labor Supply Behavior of Married Women, 1980–2000," *Journal of Labor Economics*, vol. 25, no. 3 (July 2007), pp. 393–438.

42. Data cited in Karen S. Seibert, "Don't Quit This Day Job," *New York Times*, Week in Review, June 12, 2011, p. 9.

43. Indeed, fully four out of every ten female doctors between the ages of thirty-five and forty-four reported in 2010 that they worked part time. See Seibert, "Don't Quit This Day Job."

44. Sheryl Sandberg, Barnard commencement address, May 18, 2011, reprinted in *New York Times*, June 12, 2011, p. 25.

45. See Ruth Sunderland, "After the Crash, Iceland's Women Lead the Rescue," *Observer*, February 22, 2009.

46. See Michael Scherer, "The New Sheriffs of Wall Street," *Time*, May 13, 2010.

47. Anthony Faiola and Steven Mufson, "France's Lagarde Bids for Top IMF Job," *Washington Post*, May 25, 2011.

48. *Bradwell v. Illinois*, 83 U.S. 130, 141 (1872), quoted in Christine Sgarlata Chung, "From Lily Bart to the Boom-Boom Room: How Wall Street's Social and Cultural Response to Women has Shaped Securities Regulation," *Harvard Journal of Law and Gender*, vol. 33 (2010), n57, p. 186. See also Frances E. Olsen, "The Family and the Market: A Study of Ideology and Legal Reform," *Harvard Law Review*, vol. 96 (1983), pp. 1499–1501.

49. Mary Wollstonecraft, *The Vindication of the Rights of Woman* (New York: Penguin, 2004), p. 12. The book was originally published in 1792.

50. Simone de Beauvoir, *The Second Sex* (New York: Vintage, 1989), p. 143.

51. For a description of this law and the debate that surrounded it, see Ann O'Leary, "How Family Leave Laws Left Out Low-Wage Workers," *Berkeley Journal of Employment and Labor Law*, vol. 28, no. 1 (2007), pp. 16–22.

52. Or, more precisely: "women affected by pregnancy, childbirth, or related medical conditions shall be treated the same for all employment-related purposes . . . as other persons not so affected but similar in their ability or inability to work." 42 U.S.C. § 2000-e(k) (2006), cited in Ann O'Leary, "How Family Leave Laws Left Out Low-Wage Workers," *Berkeley Journal of Employment and Labor Law*, vol. 28, no. 1 (2007), p. 28.

53. For an extensive discussion of how these laws emerged, and how "equality feminists" triumphed over "accommodation feminists" in shaping their passage, see Alice Kessler-Harris, *Out to Work: A History of Wage-Earning Women in the United States* (Oxford: Oxford University Press, 2003); Theda Skocpol, *Protecting Soldiers and Mothers: The Political Origins of Social Policy in the United States* (Cambridge, MA: Harvard University Press, 1992); and Dorothy Sue Cobble, *The Other Women's Movement: Workplace Justice and Social Rights in Modern America* (Princeton: Princeton University Press, 2004).

54. This is not a new view, actually, so much as the reemergence of an older view, seen not only in historic treatments of women as different but also, and more sympathetically, in the views of "accommodation" or "difference" feminists. For a description of this school of thought, see Estelle Freedman, *No Turning Back: The History of Feminism and the Future of Women* (New York: Ballantine, 2002), pp. 64–72.

55. See Debora Spar, "One Gender's Crash," *Washington Post*, January 4, 2009, p. B7, and William D. Cohan, "Does Wall Street Need an Estrogen Injection?" *New York Times*, April 1, 2010.

56. See Deborah Tannen, *Talking from 9 to 5: How Women's and Men's Conversational Styles Affect Who Gets Heard, Who Gets Credit, and What Gets Done at Work* (London: Virago, 1994). Works in a similar vein include Deborah Kolb, Judith Williams, and Carol Frohlinger, *Her Place at the Table: A Woman's Guide to Negotiating Five Key Challenges to Leadership Success* (San Francisco: Jossey-Bass, 2004), and Judy Rosener, "Ways Women Lead," *Harvard Business Review* 68:6 (November–December 1990), pp. 119–25.

57. See Linda Babcock and others, "Nice Girls Don't Ask," *Harvard Business Review*, vol. 81, no. 10 (2003), pp. 14–16, and Hannah Riley Bowles and Katherine L. McGinn, "Claiming Authority: Negotiating Challenges for Women Leaders," in David M. Messick and Roderick M. Kramer, eds., *The Psychology of Leadership: New Perspectives and Research* (Mahwah, NJ: Lawrence Erlbaum Associates, 2005), pp. 191–208.

58. See Rosener, "Ways Women Lead," and Babcock, "Nice Girls Don't Ask." For an argument against these views, see Alice Eagly and Linda Carli, *Through the Labyrinth: The Truth About How Women Become Leaders* (Boston: Harvard Business School Press, 2007).

59. Boris Groysberg, *Chasing Stars: The Myth of Talent and the Portability of Performance* (Princeton: Princeton University Press, 2010).

60. J. M. Coates and J. Herbert, "Endogenous Steroids and Financial Risk Taking on a London Trading Floor," *Proceedings of the National Academy of Sciences of the United States of America*, vol. 105, no. 16 (April 22, 2008), pp. 6167–72.

61. Muriel Niederle and Lise Vesterlund, "Do Women Shy Away from Competition? Do Men Compete Too Much?" *Quarterly Journal of Economics*, vol. 122, no. 3 (August 2007), pp. 1067–1101.

62. A major caveat is in order here: Harvard Business School is, of course, not only an organization dominated by men, but also one devoted to graduate education and blessed with a vast endowment. Barnard is a liberal arts college, devoted to undergraduate education and far less well endowed. Some of the differences I have experienced, therefore, may be attributable to these other factors.

63. For an excellent review that concludes, in part, that adding women to corporate boards has little or no effect on profits, see Frank Dobbin and Jiwook Jung, "Corporate Board Gender Diversity and Stock Performance: The Competence Gap or Institutional Investor Bias?" *North Carolina Law Review*, vol. 89 (2011), pp. 809–38.

64. For an argument along these lines, see "A Guide to Womenomics," *Economist*, April 16, 2006, p. 80.

65. Douglas M. McCracken, "Winning the Talent War for Women: Sometimes It Takes a Revolution," *Harvard Business Review*, vol. 78, no. 6 (2000), pp. 159–67.

66. See the description in Judith S. Kaye and Anne C. Reddy, "The Progress of Women Lawyers at Big Firms: Steadied or Simply Studied?" *Fordham Law Review*, vol. 76, no. 4 (March 2008), p. 1967, n135. For other examples, see Claudia Deutsch, "Behind the Exodus of Executive Women: Boredom," *New York Times*, May 1, 2005, section 3, p. 4.

9. Memories of My Waist

1. Simone de Beauvoir, *The Second Sex*, translated by H. M. Parshley (New York: Vintage, 1989), pp. 575–76.

2. Tina Fey, "Confessions of a Juggler," *New Yorker*, February 14 and 21, 2011, p. 65.

3. From Bob Dylan's "It's Alright, Ma (I'm Only Bleeding)," released on *Bringing It All Back Home* in 1965.

4. Among the Iroquois, older women were often the heads of their clans. In China, women generally assumed a position of authority over their grown sons and daughters-in-law. See Bella Vivante, ed., *Women's Roles in Ancient Civilization* (Westport, CT: Greenwood Press, 1999).

5. See Herbert Moller, "The Social Causation of the Courtly Love Complex," *Comparative Studies in Society and History*, vol. 1, no. 2 (January 1959), pp. 137–63.

6. One of Europe's earliest feminists, Christine de Pisan, advised aging widows in the fourteenth century to "be sensible in [their] actions, [their] clothing, facial

expression and speech . . . the elderly woman ought to see to it that she does nothing that looks foolish." See Christine de Pisan, *Treasure of the City of Ladies*, translated by Sarah Lawson (London: Penguin, 2003), p. 147.

7. William Matthews, "The Wife of Bath and All Her Sect," *Viator*, vol. 5 (1974), pp. 413–43. And as Matthews notes, this Wife is markedly more jolly in her old age than nearly any other female figure of her era. See also the discussion in Lois W. Banner, *In Full Flower: Aging Women, Power, and Sexuality* (New York: Alfred A. Knopf, 1992), pp. 131–54.

8. See Matthews, "Wife of Bath," pp. 418–19.

9. For an overview of the literature on witchcraft, see Alan Charles Kors and Edward Peters, eds., *Witchcraft in Europe, 400–1700: A Documentary History* (Philadelphia: University of Pennsylvania Press, 2001); Thomas Forbes, *The Midwife and the Witch* (New Haven, CT: Yale University Press, 1966); and Joseph Klaits, *Servants of Satan: The Age of the Witch Hunts* (Bloomington: Indiana University Press, 1985).

10. For key excerpts, see Heinrich Kramer and Jacob Sprenger, *Malleus Maleficarum*, reproduced in Kors and Peters, *Witchcraft in Europe*, pp. 180–229.

11. Quoted in Banner, *In Full Flower*, p. 191.

12. For more on the development of the grandmother figure, see Eckart Voland, Athanasios Chasiotis, and Wulf Schiefenhövel, eds., *Grandmotherhood: The Evolutionary Significance of the Second Half of Female Life* (New Brunswick, NJ: Rutgers University Press, 2005), and Kay Heath, *Aging by the Book: The Emergence of Midlife in Victorian Britain* (Albany: State University of New York Press, 2009).

13. Zelda Popkin, "Widows and the Perilous Years," *Harper's Magazine*, September 1949, p. 70.

14. See, for example, "80-Year-Old Rock Stars," www.thedailybeast.com/articles/2010 /03/16/80-is-the-new-30.html, and Shira Springer, "For Some, Marathon a Lifelong Love," *Boston Globe*, April 19, 2010, p. A1.

15. Lisa Miller, "Parents of a Certain Age," *New York*, October 3, 2011, pp. 44–48, 102–3.

16. www.msnbc.msn.com/id/21644753/ns/business-personal_finance/t/forget-bingo -new/#.TyGndRwmofk.

17. Richard Corliss and Michael D. Lemonick, "How to Live to Be 100," *Time*, August 30, 2004, pp. 41–48.

18. See www.levitra.com and www.drugs.com/viagra.html.

19. Even today, a statistically large percentage of children die in infancy, and another rather large number of men die from violence in their teens and early twenties. Accordingly, life expectancy rises considerably once people have reached middle age. See U.S. National Center for Health Statistics, National Vital Statistics Report, *Deaths: Preliminary Data for 2010*, vol. 60, no. 4, January 11, 2012.

20. See, for instance, Joel D. Wallach, *Dead Doctors Don't Lie* (Franklin, TN: Legacy Communications Group, 1999); Marvin J. Cetron and Owen Davies, *Cheating Death: The Promise and the Future Impact of Trying to Live Forever* (New York: St. Martin's Press, 1998); and Aubrey DeGrey and Michael Rae, *Ending Age: The*

Rejuvenation Breakthroughs That Could Reverse Human Aging in Our Lifetime (New York: St. Martin's Press, 2007).

21. This was the title of an address Pollitt delivered at a 2008 conference titled "Gender, Creativity, and the New Longevity." Cited in Margaret Morganroth Gullette, *Agewise: Fighting the New Ageism in America* (Chicago: University of Chicago Press, 2011), p. 23.

22. Nora Ephron, *I Feel Bad About My Neck* (New York: Alfred A. Knopf, 2006), p. 5.

23. For a fascinating argument that it is, and that the medicalization of menopause has come largely at the hands of the pharmaceutical industry, see Gullette, *Agewise*, pp. 85–102.

24. Mead used this phrase frequently. See, for instance, the description in Nancy C. Lutkehaus, *Margaret Mead: The Making of an American Icon* (Princeton: Princeton University Press, 2008), p. 73.

25. Lois W. Banner, *Elizabeth Cady Stanton: A Radical for Woman's Rights* (Boston: Little, Brown, 1979), pp. 109–10.

26. For a discussion, see Janette Perz and Jane M. Ussher, "The Horror of This Living Decay: Women's Negotiation and Resistance of Medical Discourse Around Menopause and Midlife," *Women's Studies International Forum*, vol. 31, no. 4 (2008), pp. 293–99.

27. See Carroll Smith-Rosenberg, "Puberty to Menopause: The Cycle of Femininity in Nineteenth-Century America," in Smith-Rosenberg, *Disorderly Conduct: Visions of Gender in Victorian America* (New York: Alfred A. Knopf, 1985), pp. 182–96; and Judith Houck, *Hot and Bothered: Women, Medicine, and Menopause in Modern America* (Cambridge, MA: Harvard University Press, 2006).

28. See Houck, *Hot and Bothered*, p. 40, and John M. Upshur, "Menopause and Climacteric," *Virginia Medical Monthly*, vol. 51 (January 1925), pp. 620–24.

29. This view was argued most vehemently by Helen Deutsch, in her 1945 text, *The Psychology of Women*. See Deutsch, *The Psychology of Women*, vol. 2 (New York: Grune and Stratton, 1945), pp. 456–87. See also Beka Doherty and Lena Levine, *The Menopause* (New York: Random House, 1952); Laci Fessler, "The Psychopathology of Climacteric Depression," *Journal of the American Psychoanalytic Association*, vol. 19 (1950), pp. 28–42; and Susan E. Bell, "Changing Ideas: The Medicalization of Menopause," *Social Science and Medicine*, vol. 24, no. 6 (1987), pp. 535–42.

30. The antiageist activist Margaret Morganroth Gullette suggests replacing the word "postmenopausal" with "postmaternal." See Gullette, *Agewise*, p. 92.

31. See Christa Grössinger, *Picturing Women in Late Medieval and Renaissance Art* (New York: Manchester University Press, 1997); and Edelgard E. DuBruck, *New Images of Medieval Women: Essays Toward a Cultural Anthropology* (Lewiston, NY: Edwin Mellen, 1989).

32. Yes, there are some alternative methods, but very few adoption agencies will place a child with a mother over forty-five, and assisted reproduction, using another woman's eggs and perhaps womb, is very problematic and hugely expensive.

33. In this beautiful essay, the author, Bob Shacochis, also reflects on the biological inequities that can hit a marriage: "For a man, history's answer . . . had been brutally simple: choose between the barren woman and your unborn children." Shacochis, "Missing Children," in Jill Bialosky and Helen Schulman, *Wanting a Child* (New York: Farrar, Straus and Giroux, 1998), p. 54.

34. Simone de Beauvoir, *The Second Sex*, translated by H. M. Parshley (New York: Vintage, 1989), p. 575.

35. Ibid., p. 37.

36. Ibid., p. 576.

37. For a discussion of this absence, plus a review of the feminist work that does consider aging, see Laura Hurd Clarke, *Facing Age: Women Growing Older in Anti-Aging Culture* (New York: Rowman and Littlefield, 2011), esp. pp. 2–3. Some notable exceptions include Toni M. Casalanti and Kathleen F. Slevin, eds., *Age Matters: Realigning Feminist Thinking* (New York: Routledge, 2006); Frida Kerner Furman, *Facing the Mirror: Older Women and Beauty Shop Culture* (New York: Routledge, 1997); and Barbara MacDonald, *Look Me in the Eye: Old Women, Aging and Ageism* (San Francisco: Spinsters, Inc., 1983).

38. At a 2011 gathering of women at the State Department, Gloria Steinem wryly remarked upon the ironies of her own life. "For the first half of my career," she recalled, "I was always the youngest person in the room. Now, in the second half, I am consistently the oldest."

39. Betty Friedan, *The Fountain of Age* (New York: Simon and Schuster, 1993).

40. For example: J. Lorber and L. J. Moore, *Gendered Bodies: Feminist Perspectives* (Los Angeles: Roxbury Publishing, 2007) and Julia Twigg, "The Body, Gender, and Age: Feminist Insights in Social Gerontology," *Journal of Aging Studies*, vol. 18, no. 1 (2004), pp. 59–73.

41. As one recent study showed, even magazines that cater to women over 50 rarely include images of women over 40. See Denise C. Lewis, Katalin Medvedev, and Desiree M. Seponski, "Awakening to the Desires of Older Women: Deconstructing Ageism within Fashion Magazines," *Journal of Aging Studies*, vol. 25, no. 2 (April 2011), pp. 101–9. For a broader, and fascinating, survey of the homogenization of global beauty standards, see Geoffrey Jones, *Beauty Imagined: A History of the Global Beauty Industry* (Oxford: Oxford University Press, 2010).

42. There is a small but intriguing feminist literature that sees cosmetic surgery as potentially empowering to women. See, for instance, Kathy Davis, "My Body Is My Art: Cosmetic Surgery as Feminist Utopia?" *European Journal of Women's Studies*, vol. 4. no. 1 (1997), pp. 23–37; Debra Gimlin, "Cosmetic Surgery: Beauty as Commodity," *Qualitative Sociology*, vol. 23, no. 1 (2000), pp. 77–98; and Llewellyn Negrin, "Cosmetic Surgery and the Eclipse of Identity," *Body and Society*, vol. 8, no. 4 (2002), pp. 21–42.

43. In one study of women's magazines, 78 percent of all the advertisements made reference to antiaging products; 86 percent of these were specifically targeting the face and facial wrinkles. See Clarke, *Facing Age*, p. 106.

44. Quoted in Elizabeth Haiken, *Venus Envy: A History of Cosmetic Surgery* (Baltimore: Johns Hopkins University Press, 1997), p. 139.

45. See Stephanie Rosenbloom, "Beauty by the Bite," *New York Times*, December 15, 2011, pp. E1, E3.

46. See Joann Fletcher, *Cleopatra the Great: The Woman Behind the Legend* (New York: Harper, 2011), p. 236.

47. Cited in Kay Heath, *Aging by the Book* (Albany: State University of New York Press, 2009), p. 184. See also Geoffrey Jones, *Beauty Imagined: A History of the Global Beauty Industry* (Oxford: Oxford University Press, 2010), pp. 81–88.

48. All figures are national averages, compiled from American Society for Aesthetic Plastic Surgery, *Cosmetic Surgery National Data Bank Statistics, 2010*, p. 11.

49. In her fascinating discussion of cosmetic surgery, the feminist and antiageism activist Margaret Morganroth Gullette argues that the tide is actually turning, and that the rate of women choosing to undergo cosmetic surgery has declined since 2000. The data, though, reveal more subtle trends. If you take 2000 as the base year, then yes, the total number of cosmetic surgical procedures has dipped slightly (by 10 percent), while the total number of minimally invasive procedures has surged by a remarkable 109 percent. If, however, you use 1997 as the base year, the total number of surgical procedures has actually risen by more than 71 percent. See Margaret Morganroth Gullette, *Agewise: Fighting the New Ageism in America* (Chicago: University of Chicago Press, 2011), p. 104; American Society for Aesthetic Plastic Surgery, *Cosmetic Surgery National Data Bank Statistics, 2010*; and American Society for Aesthetic Plastic Surgery, *Report of the 2010 Plastic Surgery Statistics*.

50. For data, see Rose M. Kreider and Renee Ellis, "Number, Timing, and Duration of Marriages and Divorces: 2009," *Current Population Reports*, P70-125 (Washington, DC: U.S. Census Bureau, 2011), p. 16, www.census.gov/prod/2011pubs/p70-125.pdf.

51. Anna Quindlen, "Memoirs: Aging Gracefully," *More*, May 2012, pp. 152 and 154. For fascinating data along these lines, see Paul Taylor et al., "Growing Old in America: Expectations vs. Reality," Pew Research Center Report, June 29, 2009.

52. Kreider and Ellis, "Number, Timing, and Duration of Marriages and Divorces: 2009," p. 16.

53. Ibid., p. 6. For similar, albeit slightly older, data, see Paul R. Amato and Shelley Irvin, "Historical Trends in Divorce in the United States," in Mark A. Fine and John H. Harvey, eds., *Handbook of Divorce and Relationship Dissolution* (Mahwah, NJ: Lawrence Erlbaum, 2006), pp. 47–48.

54. See, for example, Karen Holden and Pamela J. Smock, "The Economic Costs of Marital Dissolution: Why Do Women Bear a Disproportionate Cost?" *Annual Review of Sociology*, vol. 17 (1991), pp. 51–78, and Leslie Morgan, *After Marriage Ends: Economic Consequences for Midlife Women* (New York: Russell Sage, 1991).

55. See Diana B. Elliott and Tavia Simmons, "Marital Events of Americans: 2009,"

American Community Survey Reports, ACS-13 (Washington, DC: U.S. Census Bureau, 2011).

56. Stephen P. Jenkins, "Marital Splits and Income Changes Over the Longer Term," Institute for Social and Economic Research, University of Essex, no. 2008-07, February 2008. For a broader but older survey of U.S. data, see Pamela J. Smock, Wendy D. Manning, and Sanjiv Gupta, "The Effect of Marriage and Divorce on Women's Economic Well-Being," *American Sociological Review*, vol. 64 (December 1999), pp. 794–812. For a fascinating study that attempts to separate the effects of divorce on already-poor or already-rich women, see Elizabeth O. Ananat and Guy Michaels, "The Effect of Marital Breakup on the Income Distribution of Women with Children," *Journal of Human Resources*, vol. 43, no. 3 (Summer 2008), pp. 611–29.

57. Margaret M. Mahoney, "The Law of Divorce and Relationship Dissolution," in Mark A. Fine and John H. Harvey, eds., *Handbook of Divorce and Relationship Dissolution* (Mahwah, NJ: Lawrence Erlbaum, 2006), p. 536; and Constance L. Sheldon, Felix M. Berardo, Erica Owens, and Donna H. Berardo, "Alimony: An Anomaly in Family Social Science," *Family Relations*, vol. 51, no. 4 (October 2002), pp. 308–16.

58. Terry Martin Hekker, "Paradise Lost (Domestic Division)," *New York Times*, January 1, 2006, p. ST9. What made this writer's case particularly poignant was that she had earlier achieved a fair measure of renown by publishing an op-ed article in the *Times* celebrating the satisfaction of being a "full-time housewife in the new age of the liberated woman." See Hekker, "The Satisfactions of Housewifery and Motherhood in an Age of Do-Your-Own-Thing," *New York Times*, December 20, 1977, p. 35.

59. See David M. Buss, *The Evolution of Desire: Strategies of Human Mating* (New York: Basic, 1994); and Donald Symons, *The Evolution of Human Sexuality* (New York: Oxford University Press, 1979).

60. U.S. Census Bureau, *Statistical Abstract of the United States: 2012*, table 34, "Persons 65 Years Old and Over—Characteristics by Sex: 1990 to 2010," Population, p. 39. This figure was calculated as the sum of women never married, married with absent spouses, widowed, and divorced.

61. The Baby Boom generation accounts for roughly one-quarter of the entire U.S. population. As the Boomers age, their health care and pension costs will likely exacerbate budget deficits in the United States and lower savings rates. Matters are likely to be even more precarious in Europe and parts of Asia, where the demographic balance is further askew. See Diana Farrell et al., "The Coming Demographic Deficit: How Aging Populations Will Reduce Global Savings," McKinsey Global Institute, January 2005. Also Joshua M. Wiener and Jane Tilly, "Population Ageing in the United States of America: Implications for Public Programmes," *International Journal of Epidemiology*, vol. 31 (2002), pp. 776–81.

62. Written and illustrated by Barbara Cooney, *Miss Rumphius* (published first in 1982) won the American Book Award in 1983.

63. An intriguing reference, it seems, to the Land of the Lotus-Eaters described in *The Odyssey*, a seductive place that lures its visitors never to leave.

10. Kissing Charlie Goodbye

1. Gloria Steinem, "I Was a Playboy Bunny," in *Outrageous Acts and Everyday Rebellions* (New York: Henry Holt, 1995), pp. 33–75.

2. Andrea Dworkin, *Woman Hating* (New York: E. P. Dutton, 1974); Naomi Wolf, *The Beauty Myth* (New York: Harper Perennial, 2002).

3. In *Murphy Brown*, Candice Bergen plays a talented reporter who works full time while raising her child as a single mother. In *The Cosby Show*, Phylicia Rashad plays Clair Huxtable, a lawyer and mother of five.

4. See, for example, Judith Duffett, "WLM vs. Miss America," *Voice of the Women's Liberation Movement*, October 1968, p. 4; Dworkin, *Woman Hating*; and Shulamith Firestone, *The Dialectic of Sex* (New York: William Morrow, 1970).

5. Recently, more than 84,000 teenage girls signed an online petition asking *Seventeen* magazine to include at least one unaltered photograph in each edition. "I know that most of these girls . . . are photoshopped, airbrushed and edited," acknowledged one young signatory, "but yet, when you're looking at those photographs physically, you can't help but think, 'Wow. I wish I looked like that.'" Quoted in Christine Haughney, "*Seventeen* Magazine Vows to Show Girls 'As They Really Are,'" *New York Times*, July 4, 2012, pp. B1–B2. Meanwhile, a front-page story in the Middlebury College newspaper reported in May 2012 that a record number of young men were seeking medical treatment for erectile dysfunction, an increase that the college's physician attributed to the increased reliance on online pornography. "For many," he stated, "real sex does not always live up to the expectations pornography provides. Therefore [men] might experience difficulty when they are faced with the real thing." See Saadiah Schmidt, "Parton Sees Rise in Erectile Dysfunction," *Middlebury Campus*, May 3, 2012, p. 1.

6. The press reaction to Mayer's announcement was quite stunning, with many observers swiftly condemning her for somehow letting down women and families by stating that she would be taking only a brief maternity leave. See, for example, Janice D'Arcy, "Is Marissa Mayer doing parents any favors?" On Parenting, at www.washingtonpost.com/blogs/on-parenting/post/is-marissa-mayer-doing-parents-any-favors/2012/07/19/gJQAc7ouvW_blog.html.

7. All titles are taken from the July 2012 issues of *O*, *Allure*, *Prevention*, and *Good Housekeeping*.

8. Port Huron Statement, June 15, 1962, available at www.h-net.org/~hst306/documents/huron.html.

9. Kurt Anderson, "The Downside of Liberty," *New York Times*, July 4, 2012, p. A19. A similar point was made more broadly (and earlier) by Tom Wolfe in his famous article "The 'Me' Decade and the Third Great Awakening," *New York*, August 23, 1976, pp. 26–40.

10. In 1950, women comprised 29.6 percent of the U.S. civilian workforce; by 2000, their representation had increased to 46.9 percent. See Mitra Toosi, "A Century of Change: The U.S. Labor Force, 1950–2050," *Monthly Labor Review*, vol. 124, no. 5 (May 2002), pp. 15–28; and *Current Population Survey*, "2011 Employment and Earnings Online," Annual Average Household Data, table 9 (Bureau of Labor Statistics, Washington, DC, March 1, 2012), available at www.bls.gov/cps/tables .htm#empstat.

11. See, for instance, www.plannedparenthoodaction.org/positions/facts-on-birth -control-coverage-for-women-1117.htm.

12. "The Harried Life of the Working Mother," Pew Social and Demographic Trends, October 1, 2009, www.pewsocialtrends.org/2009/10/01/the-harried-life-of -the-working-mother.

13. Dworkin, *Woman Hating*, p. 17.

14. There is a burgeoning and fascinating literature that examines the physical differences between men and women, suggesting that the two sexes are not absolutes but rather points on a continuum. See, for example, Rebecca Jordan-Young, *Brain Storm: The Flaws in the Science of Sex Differences* (Cambridge, MA: Harvard University Press, 2010), and Katrina Karkazis, *Fixing Sex: Intersex, Medical Authority, and Lived Experience* (Durham, NC: Duke University Press, 2008). This argument has taken on particular importance with regard to the treatment of female Olympic athletes who demonstrate some typically male attributes. See Rebecca Jordan-Young and Katrina Karkazis, "You Say You're a Woman? That Should Be Enough," *New York Times*, June 18, 2012, p. D8.

15. See, for example, Beauvoir, *Second Sex*, and Millett, *Sexual Politics*. For a wonderful, if somewhat dismissive, discussion of how feminism tried to ignore women's "dark involvement with blood and birth and death," see Joan Didion, "The Women's Movement," *New York Times*, July 30, 1972, section 7, pp. 1–2 and 14.

16. See, for example, Christine L. Williams, Patti A. Giuffre, and Kirsten Dellinger, "Sexuality in the Workplace: Organizational Control, Sexual Harassment, and the Pursuit of Pleasure," *Annual Review of Sociology*, vol. 25, no. 1 (1999), pp. 73–93.

17. See http://newemployee.usbank.com/Assets/PDFs/Employee_Handbook.pdf.

18. In Sweden, for example, parents receive 390 days of paid leave, which they may use at any point, or distribute as they choose, until the child's eighth birthday. The law also reserves at least two months of the total thirteen-month parental leave exclusively for fathers. See Katrin Bennhold, "Paternity Leave Law Helps Redefine Masculinity in Sweden," *New York Times*, June 15, 2010, pp. A6 and A8.

19. O'Connor had her first child at age twenty-seven and her third at thirty-two.

Pelosi had her first at twenty-four and her fifth at thirty. Clinton had her first and only child at age thirty-three.

20. Anne-Marie Slaughter, "Why Women Still Can't Have It All," *Atlantic*, July–August 2012, p. 93.

21. For a similar and excellent argument, see Judith Warner, *Perfect Madness: Motherhood in the Age of Anxiety* (New York: Riverhead, 2005).

Acknowledgments

I wasn't supposed to write this book. I meant, six years ago, to write a book about the global water market, focusing on the economic quirks that inevitably adhere to a product that is truly priceless. But then I took a new job, and moved to a new city, and was told in no uncertain terms by a person I admire, "Don't write the water book."

So I scrambled to write about something else instead; something that was close enough to my own life and experience that I could squeeze its construction into the confines of already-busy weeks.

As would have to be the case under these circumstances, I relied more than ever on the kindness of others to bring this project into being. My greatest debts, perhaps, are to those long-standing feminist authors and scholars who not only accepted an interloper in their midst but graciously offered their wisdom, counsel, and reading suggestions. Estelle Freedman, Janet Jakobsen, and Anna Quindlen all took precious time away from their own work to pore over mine, offering hugely valuable insights and corrections. Robin Morgan was a committed critic and steadfast source of writerly inspiration. Through her deeds and words, she embodies what sisterhood really means. Gloria Steinem graciously took time to meet with me as I was first launching this project; Kitty Kolbert and Rosabeth Moss Kanter were sources of knowledge and advice throughout.

Because this book is in part a personal tale, it benefited greatly from the many friends who both listened to my stories and let me borrow pieces of theirs. One of the things I've learned in tracing through the stages of a woman's life is that none of us goes through it alone. I am grateful to have had the company of Stephen Barden, Sarah Doebler, Kit Haggard, Noreena Hertz, Kelly Jackson, Allegra Jordan, Hannah Lauber, Claire Newman, Kalypso Nicolaidis, Kimberley Patton, Richard Tedlow, David Welsh, and Madelyne Yucht. Special thanks go to Alison Stanger, who, as always, provided words of encouragement and wise counsel in equal measure.

I am also grateful to a particularly talented group of research assistants, who stayed with the project as they began to navigate their own paths forward and embraced the book as their own: Maya Popa, a talented writer who helped explore the world of girls; Mary Billington, who is tough and smart and always made me laugh;

Ashley Walker Bush, who greeted every assignment with enthusiasm and verve; and Aryanna Garber, who devoted perhaps even more hours to it than I did, and whose voice is reflected in its pages. In the office, meanwhile, I am thankful for the continued good cheer and great work of DiAnn Pierce, Jane Holmes, Jackie Hockersmith, and, especially, Jamie Coffey. On the home front, I couldn't have done much of anything over the years without the loving help of Irene Saavedra, Maria Araujo, and Zaida Sagastume.

My agent, Will Lippincott, was magnificent throughout. My editor, Sarah Crichton, was a joy to work with and for. I appreciate all that they—and the fine staffs at both Lippincott Massie and McQuilkin and Farrar, Straus and Giroux—did to support the book's progression. I am also deeply and forever grateful to the two great institutions that I have served during the course of my career: Barnard College and Harvard Business School. In very different ways, they have each provided resources, comfort, and a phenomenal environment in which to grow and learn.

In a book about women and families and love, it is only appropriate for me to conclude with what matters most. I couldn't have written *Wonder Women* if my parents, Judith and Martin Spar, hadn't propelled me long ago on the path they did, and if they hadn't been there to support me along the way. I couldn't have written it if my three amazing, gorgeous, and generous children, Daniel, Andrew, and Kristina Catomeris, hadn't been willing to put up with a mother who works too much, abandons the laundry, and has missed more dinners at home than she cares to recall. And I certainly couldn't have done it without the extraordinary love and support of my husband, Miltos Catomeris. I can't, and won't, try to speak for all women here. But this wonder woman wouldn't be anything without the devotion and kindness of a wonderful, wonderful man.

InDEX

Page numbers in *italics* refer to illustrations.

Permissions Acknowledgments and Illustration Credits

Grateful acknowledgment is made for permission to reprint the following material:

Excerpt from *Little Shop of Horrors*: "Somewhere That's Green," lyrics by Howard Ashman, music by Alan Menken. 1982 Trunksong Music, Ltd., Menken Music, and Universal-Geffen Music (c/o Universal Music Publishing Group). Used by permission of Alfred Music Publishing and Hal Leonard Corporation.

Excerpts from *Free to Be . . . You and Me*: "Free to Be . . . You and Me" and "Parents Are People," written by Carol Hall, copyright © 1972 by Free to Be Foundation, Inc. Permission granted. www.freetobefoundation.org.

Image of a toddler beauty pageant winner: Copyright © Chad Merrell.

Excerpt from Meat Loaf's "Paradise by the Dashboard Light": Written by Jim Steinman. Used by permission of Edward B. Marks Music Company.

Excerpt from Rihanna's "Rude Boy": Written by Fenty, Riddick, Hermansen, Eriksen, and Thom. Used by permission of Hal Leonard.

Excerpt from Dolly Parton's "9 to 5": Copyright © 1980 by Velvet Apple Music. All rights reserved. Used by permission.

Image of Cindy Joseph, a sixty-one-year-old supermodel: Copyright © Heather Weston, 2009.

Image of Miss Rumphius: From *Miss Rumphius* by Barbara Cooney, copyright © 1982 by Barbara Cooney Porter. Used by permission of Viking Children's Books, a division of Penguin Group (USA) Inc.

Excerpt from Helen Reddy's "I Am Woman": Written by Helen Reddy and Ray Burton. Used by permission of Hal Leonard.

Excerpt from Jordin Sparks's "I Am Woman": Written by Ryan Tedder, Dean Josiah, and Ali Pierre Gaschani. Published by Write 2 Live Publishing & Patriot Entertainment, LLC. Administration by Kobalt Music Publishing America, Inc.

A Note About the Author

Debora Spar is the president of Barnard of College, a position she has held since 2008. Previously, she served as the Spangler Family Professor of Business Administration and as senior associate dean, director of research, at Harvard Business School. Dr. Spar's earlier books include *Ruling the Waves: Cycles of Discovery, Chaos, and Wealth from the Compass to the Internet* and *The Baby Business: How Money, Science, and Politics Drive the Commerce of Conception.* She lives in Manhattan with her husband and three children.